RAISING
THE BAR

RAISING
THE BAR

A BOTTLE-BY-BOTTLE GUIDE TO MIXING
MASTERFUL COCKTAILS AT HOME

BRETT ADAMS & JACOB GRIER

ILLUSTRATIONS BY WOODY HARRINGTON

CHRONICLE BOOKS

SAN FRANCISCO

Library of Congress Cataloging-in-
Publication Data available.

ISBN 978-1-7972- 1032-2

Manufactured in China.

MIX
Paper | Supporting
responsible forestry
FSC™ C008047
www.fsc.org

Art Direction by Lizzie Vaughan.
Design by Woody Harrington.

10 9 8 7 6 5 4 3 2

Chronicle books and gifts are
available at special quantity discounts
to corporations, professional
associations, literacy programs,
and other organizations. For details
and discount information, please
contact our premiums department at
corporatesales@chroniclebooks.com or
at 1-800-759-0190.

CHRONICLE BOOKS LLC
680 Second Street
San Francisco, California 94107
www.chroniclebooks.com

TO ELIZABETH,
FOR A LIFETIME OF TOASTS
AND TINNED FISH —BA

TO MARIE GERWIN,
FOR TEACHING THE IMPORTANCE
OF COCKTAIL HOUR —JG

INTRODUCTION 9

PART I

THE CLASSIC BAR 41

INTRODUCTION

MAKING COCKTAILS AT HOME IS EASY; THE HARD PART IS FIGURING OUT WHERE TO BEGIN. WITH THOUSANDS OF SPIRITS ON THE MARKET AND A NEARLY INFINITE VARIETY OF COCKTAIL RECIPES PUBLISHED IN BOOKS AND ONLINE, JUST GETTING STARTED CAN BE A DIZZYING PROSPECT. MOST COCKTAIL GUIDES AREN'T WRITTEN WITH THE HOME BARTENDER IN MIND, ESPECIALLY SOMEONE WHO HASN'T YET BUILT UP AN EXTENSIVE COLLECTION OF BOTTLES. AS PROFESSIONAL BARTENDERS, WE ARE ASKED ALL THE TIME FOR ADVICE ON THE BEST AND MOST USEFUL SPIRITS TO STOCK AT HOME. THOSE CONVERSATIONS ARE WHAT INSPIRED *RAISING THE BAR.* ALTHOUGH BETWEEN US WE NOW HAVE DECADES OF EXPERIENCE WORKING IN BARS AND RESTAURANTS, WE BOTH BEGAN OUR EXPLORATION OF COCKTAILS BY MAKING THEM AT HOME FOR OURSELVES, FRIENDS, AND FAMILIES, PICKING UP ONE BOTTLE AT A TIME AND FIGURING OUT WHAT TO DO WITH IT. THIS, IN SHORT, IS THE BOOK WE WISH WE'D HAD IN THOSE EARLY DAYS OF MIXING.

In some respects, making cocktails at home isn't any different than making them in a bar. You shake and stir the same way, and if you do things right, the Old-Fashioned or margarita you mix up in your kitchen should taste just like the ones you get when you're going out. The differences come into play when you decide *which* drinks to make, because more elaborate cocktails require more elaborate ingredients, many of which you may not have on hand in a typical home bar. A professional bar might stock dozens or hundreds of bottles; the place where we worked together, the Multnomah Whiskey Library in Portland, Oregon, boasts a collection of about two thousand. In a bar like that, there's almost no cocktail too obscure for us to make. At home is a different story. Unless you have a mega budget and a massive amount of storage space, you'll probably want to limit your personal collection to a more reasonable size.

The same logic applies to ingredients used to accent and modify cocktails. An inventive cocktail bar might incorporate all kinds of house-made syrups, esoteric bitters, special infusions, and uncommon fruits, herbs, and spices into its drinks. That makes sense in a professional setting where a cocktail on a seasonal menu might be ordered by thousands of guests. We love drinks like these and have made our careers combining unexpected ingredients in our cocktails. But that's when we're at work. When we're at home, we tend to rely on a simpler arsenal. If we asked you to make lemongrass-coriander syrup or celery-habanero bitters for a cocktail, that would demand a lot of effort. And then you'd be stuck with a bottle of lemongrass-coriander syrup and only one cocktail to use it in. Even if it's a great drink, that's a lot to ask.

Don't get us wrong, there are amazing cocktail books that are full of wonderful recipes that use advanced ingredients like these. We own stacks of them and enjoy perusing creative ideas from our fellow bartenders. Sometimes we even make the drinks. However, we also know the frustration of flipping through a recipe book and not finding anything we can readily make with what we have on hand. When we set out to write this book, that's precisely the experience we wanted to avoid.

So how do you mix creative cocktails at home that rival those of professional bars while drawing from a limited selection of ingredients? By building a smart, stream-lined home bar where every bottle you buy builds on the one before. To achieve this, we've organized this book quite a bit differently than your typical cocktail recipe book. First, we're limiting our syrups, citrus, bitters, and other pantry items to a very attainable list. We're going to ask you to keep lemons and limes on hand, for example, but we're not going to surprise you with yuzu or dragon fruit. With this reasonable pantry, you'll be able to make every drink in the book.

Second, instead of expecting you to have every bottle of spirits available at once, we're going to take things one bottle at a time. That means you can expand your home bar at your own pace. In our first chapter, we'll walk you through nine dif-ferent cocktails you can mix with just one bottle of bourbon and the ingredients in your pantry. In each subsequent chapter, we'll add another bottle and show you how it expands the possibilities of what you can make, combining it with the pantry items as well as with the bottles that came before. As your selection grows and you gain experience making cocktails, the complexity of the drinks you can make will increase as well. And if you follow along in order, you'll never encounter a cocktail that you don't have the skills and the ingredients to mix.

Third, we won't ask you to buy anything that isn't versatile. Food writer and TV host Alton Brown is famous for railing against "unitaskers," those gimmicky kitchen tools that are designed to do one thing and that are absolutely useless for anything else. A lot of modern cocktail ingredients are the equivalent of a

unitasker: a specialized bottle that you might use in one specific recipe but that otherwise gathers dust. We didn't allow any of those in this book. When we ask you to buy or make an ingredient, it's because we're giving you multiple cocktails in which to use it.

The book is split into two sections—the Classic Bar (page 41) and the Advanced Bar (page 199)—so that no matter what your experience level is with home bartending, there's a place for you to continue building on your cocktail repertoire. If you're a beginner, we'll provide you with the knowledge you need to start making fantastic cocktails in no time, then walk you through stocking your home bar with bottles that you'll reach for time and again. If you're already a skilled home bartender with an extensive collection of spirits, we're confident you'll find new recipes to try in the pages to follow. We dove deep into vintage bar books, sourced recipes from contemporary bartenders, and included some of our own creations to ensure there's something for everyone.

Our aim in *Raising the Bar* is to provide you with a solid foundation. By the end you'll have an extremely versatile collection of bottles and, more importantly, the knowledge of how to use them. But this is just the beginning. We hope that our book will help you better appreciate the drinks found in the books and bars that have inspired us over the years, and perhaps even create some cocktails of your own. There is no end to what you can learn. Sometimes you just need to find the right place to start.

GETTING STARTED

AS YOU BEGIN LEARNING ABOUT COCKTAILS AND HOW TO MAKE THEM, IT'S EASY TO FEEL OVERWHELMED BY THE NEARLY ENDLESS VARIETY OF SPIRITS AND RECIPES. With so many esoteric bottles on store shelves and infinite ways to combine them, orienting oneself in that confusing array of options can seem a near-impossible task. But the truth is that learning how to make truly great drinks is actually rather simple. With the right tools, a few fundamental techniques, and an understanding of how cocktails work, you can make drinks at home that are every bit as good as those served by professional bartenders in the world's best bars.

That's because the vast majority of cocktails, no matter how complex they seem on paper, build off a few basic principles and ways of combining essential elements. The art of mixology is the art of balance: mixing ingredients that are strong, sweet, sour, or bitter and bringing them into harmony. Once you get the hang of putting those elements together, the daunting variety of cocktails becomes a lot more approachable. You'll be able to make exceptional cocktails with all kinds of ingredients.

Great cocktails are made by balancing spirit, sweetness, and acidity and/or bitterness. Combining these elements in the proper proportions, and then chilling and diluting them with ice, are the keys to making an excellent drink. These elements are at the heart of almost every cocktail. It's a tug-of-war between the burn of alcohol, the rounding qualities of sugars and syrups, and the distinguishing sharpness of acidity and bitterness. If any one of these dominates the others, a drink will taste too strong, too sweet, too sour, or too bitter. When we talk about balance, we mean blending diverse flavors to make a cocktail that's greater than the sum of its parts.

A FORMULA FOR SUCCESS

SPIRIT

+

SWEETNESS

+

ACIDITY AND/OR BITTERNESS

=

AN AMAZING COCKTAIL

INGREDIENTS THAT PROVIDE SWEETNESS	INGREDIENTS THAT PROVIDE BITTERNESS	INGREDIENTS THAT PROVIDE ACIDITY
Sugar, Honey, Syrups Such As Grenadine and Orgeat, Liqueurs	Bitters, Amari, Coffee	Lime Juice, Lemon Juice, Other Citrus Fruits, Vinegar, Wine

SPIRIT

Distilled spirits are the foundation of cocktails. Whether whiskey, gin, vodka, rum, or any of the other bottles discussed in this book, nearly every drink begins with one or more spirits as its primary ingredient. These generally have a high alcohol content, often 40 percent alcohol by volume or more. (The term proof is also used to reference the strength of a spirit. In the United States, proof is expressed as twice the alcohol by volume (ABV), so 50 percent ABV is 100 proof. Other countries use different scales, however, so to keep things clear, we use the ABV measure throughout the book.) Alcohol affects the way we perceive a drink, determining which molecules evaporate and which interfere with our taste receptors. Adding booze to a cocktail is like adding jalapeños to a salsa; it makes things brighter and more vibrant, and enlivens otherwise bland mixtures. But how to mix with spirits? That's where the other elements come in.

SWEETNESS

Many spirits were at one time believed to be medicinal, and as Mary Poppins famously observed, a spoonful of sugar helps the medicine go down. She knew of what she spoke. Cocktail drinkers are often wary of sugar, especially if they have prior experience drinking excessively saccharine concoctions, like those found in nightclubs and chain restaurants. "Something not too sweet" is an order we hear often when working behind the bar. But sugar is vital for mixology. Just as cocktails take the edge off you, sweetness takes the edge off spirits. It helps keep a cocktail on an even keel, preventing it from leaning too far toward sour, boozy, or bitter. Not all drinks require a lot of sugar, but the stronger the ingredients, the more you'll appreciate the role of sweetness as an equalizer. When deployed correctly, it works to make everything else more delicious.

ACIDITY

Sweetness makes spirits more approachable by rounding them out, but it takes more than that to make an interesting drink. We need a couple of other elements to prevent cocktails from tasting dull and flabby. To use a music analogy, spirits and sugar provide the bass notes of mixology: They fill the room, establish movement and tone, and often drive the music. But bass needs treble, a sharp tone to give it distinction and keep the song from sounding muddy and muffled. The same is true for drinks. Think of acidity—typically provided by citrus fruit juices—as one form of treble. It provides lift and contrast so that the liveliness of a cocktail will not be smothered by the richness of sugar. Take the classic three-ingredient daiquiri, for example. Rum and sugar? Kind of boring. Rum, sugar, and freshly squeezed lime juice? Divine.

BITTERNESS

Bitter is a potentially off-putting word. But don't be afraid of bitter! Of all the elements that make up a cocktail, bitterness is the most difficult to appreciate, but learning to use it and love it opens up a whole new world of flavors. It's often used in subtle ways to bring depth, complexity, and vibrancy to cocktails. A little bit of bitter can go a long way, even if the finished cocktail doesn't taste bitter itself. Just a dash or two of bitter ingredients can take a drab drink and make it shine. The little bottles of bitters one finds arrayed in any cocktail bar are used much like salt and pepper in the kitchen: You may not taste them explicitly in the final dish, but you'd certainly notice their absence. A great example of this is the Old-Fashioned. A glass of bourbon and sugar would taste flat, but the addition of a couple dashes of bitters transforms it into one of the world's greatest drinks. (Some drinks are intensely bitter, and many cocktail drinkers come to crave bitter flavors. We'll have plenty of recipes for them too.)

Although these four elements are the building blocks of great cocktails, there is one incredibly important ingredient we omitted from our formula: ice. Whether we stir it, shake it, or simply build it in a glass, nearly every cocktail in this book comes into contact with ice at some point in its preparation. Ice makes drinks cold, obviously, but it also provides the crucial element of dilution.

The word *dilution* is often used in a pejorative sense as something that weakens or diminishes. But in the world of cocktails, dilution is the great unifier. That's because the elements of cocktails tend to be extremely dense in flavor. A spoonful of sugar is tooth-achingly sweet. A sip of pure lemon juice pulls painfully at your cheeks. Blend both together and the result isn't much better. But add ice-cold water to the mix and now you have lemonade, a drink so universally enjoyable as to be the reward offered in a platitude about life treating you unfairly. What turns lemons into lemonade isn't just sugar—it's also dilution with ice and water. Dilution takes bold flavors and stretches them out, softens their harsh edges, and makes them more enjoyable.

Most of the time, this dilution is accomplished by melting ice cubes. When you stir or shake a cocktail, you are simultaneously chilling and diluting it. It's all part of the same process, and both of these contributions are essential for achieving a perfect cocktail.

SO, TO SLIGHTLY TWEAK OUR FORMULA:

SPIRIT + SWEETNESS
(+)
ACIDITY AND/OR BITTERNESS
(+)
CHILLING AND DILUTION
(=)
AN AMAZING COCKTAIL

THIS PROBABLY SOUNDS A BIT ABSTRACT RIGHT NOW, SO LET'S LOOK AT A FEW CLASSIC COCKTAILS TO SEE HOW THIS WORKS OUT IN PRACTICE.

CLASSIC COCKTAIL STRUCTURES

**THE WORLD OF COCKTAILS IS VAST AND VARIABLE, AND WRITERS OF COCK-
TAIL BOOKS HAVE COME UP WITH DIFFERENT TAXONOMIES TO CLASSIFY
THEM.** Although there are always a few oddball outliers, thinking about cocktails in
terms of a few broadly defined styles is helpful for getting the lay of the land. The
Old-Fashioned, the Manhattan, and the Sour provide three useful templates for
thinking about almost all the drinks to follow. Old-Fashioneds and Manhattans are
both "spirit forward," while sours are tart and refreshing. Old-Fashioneds are made
up of a spirit balanced with a relatively small amount of bitters and sugar. Manhattans are balanced with vermouth or other fortified wines. Sours are balanced with
sugar and acidity, typically in the form of lemon or lime.

Once you view a cocktail through the lens of the style that it belongs to, you'll gain
a better understanding of that drink, and you'll also have the knowledge to come
up with delicious variations or successful ingredient substitutions. Great musi-
cians are able to improvise because they understand what key they're playing in;
artists and designers rely on color theory to guide them toward tones that appealingly complement and contrast each other. In the same way, mixing up cocktails
becomes a whole lot easier and much more fun when you realize that there are
guidelines you can follow to make the endeavor more manageable. Understanding
the three basic formats that follow will help you achieve that. Before long, balancing a cocktail will become second nature.

While not every cocktail in the world fits into these three stylistic categories, you'll
be amazed at how much mileage you can get out of them. By thinking about the
basic elements of cocktails and how they combine in these three broad templates,
you're well on your way to understanding every drink from the basic martini you
might mix yourself up after a long day of work to the elaborate seven-ingredient
concoction you might find on a professional cocktail menu. But theory is nothing
without practice, and when it comes to making cocktails, practice is definitely the
fun part. In the next section we'll look at the basic techniques you'll need to get
started making drinks at home.

THE OLD-FASHIONED

A drink made the "Old-Fashioned" way is one that showcases the spirit while using a small amount of sugar, bitters, and dilution to make it more enjoyable. The classic example is a mix of bourbon, sugar, and a couple dashes of bitters. An Old-Fashioned is a lot like late-era Destiny's Child. The sugar and bitters are Kelly and Michelle, essential elements that provide structure. But the spirit, both in the drink and, let's be honest, in the group, is Beyoncé. It's why we're here. It's what makes it truly great.

THE STRUCTURE OF AN OLD-FASHIONED-STYLE
COCKTAIL IS SOMETHING LIKE THE FOLLOWING:

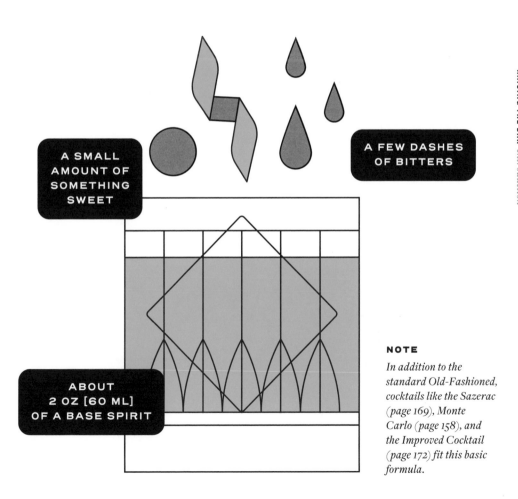

A SMALL
AMOUNT OF
SOMETHING
SWEET

A FEW DASHES
OF BITTERS

ABOUT
2 OZ [60 ML]
OF A BASE SPIRIT

NOTE

In addition to the standard Old-Fashioned, cocktails like the Sazerac (page 169), Monte Carlo (page 158), and the Improved Cocktail (page 172) fit this basic formula.

THE SOUR

Sour refers to an extremely broad category of cocktails likely familiar to anyone who's ever had a drink in a bar. The margarita, probably the most popular cocktail in America, is a sour. The Whiskey Sour is, you guessed it, a sour. Gimlets, daiquiris, cosmopolitans, and even that 1980s standby the kamikaze are all sours. The amaretto sour? That's a sour too. What all these different drinks have in common is a very basic formula balancing the strength of their primary spirit with a healthy dose of acidity and sugar. (*Sour* can also be used to mean a specific category of drinks shaken with egg whites, but we use it here in a more general sense.) Compared to Old-Fashioneds, sours are much more of a team effort. The main spirit is still the strongest voice, but it's blending into the choir much more than singing the solo.

A BASIC SOUR LOOKS LIKE THIS:

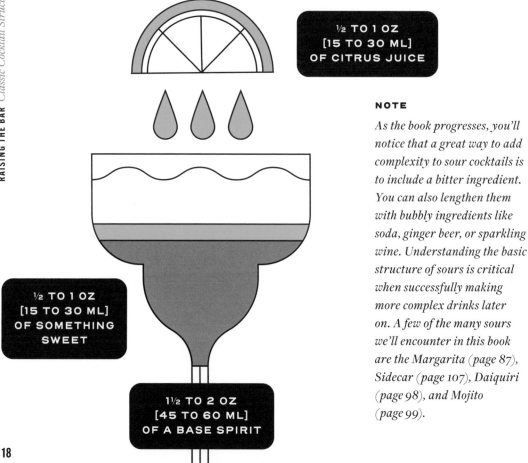

½ TO 1 OZ
[15 TO 30 ML]
OF CITRUS JUICE

½ TO 1 OZ
[15 TO 30 ML]
OF SOMETHING
SWEET

1½ TO 2 OZ
[45 TO 60 ML]
OF A BASE SPIRIT

NOTE

As the book progresses, you'll notice that a great way to add complexity to sour cocktails is to include a bitter ingredient. You can also lengthen them with bubbly ingredients like soda, ginger beer, or sparkling wine. Understanding the basic structure of sours is critical when successfully making more complex drinks later on. A few of the many sours we'll encounter in this book are the Margarita (page 87), Sidecar (page 107), Daiquiri (page 98), and Mojito (page 99).

THE MANHATTAN

The Manhattan exemplifies a third way of balancing cocktails, which is by mixing them with vermouth or other fortified wines. A classic Manhattan combines whiskey and bitters with sweet vermouth. Wine itself has a small amount of acidity—not the sharp acidity of lemon or lime juice, but a subtle brightness—so when you add vermouth to a cocktail, you're adding restrained acidity, bitterness, and sweetness all at once. These cocktails are still spirit forward but less assertively so than the almost entirely spirit-based Old-Fashioned. Drinks in the Manhattan format are capable of incredible diversity, ranging from light, delicate aperitifs to boozy cocktails bursting with bitterness. What unites them is a sophisticated complexity achieved by using spirits and fortified wines together.

A BASIC MANHATTAN-STYLE COCKTAIL WOULD BE MADE LIKE THIS:

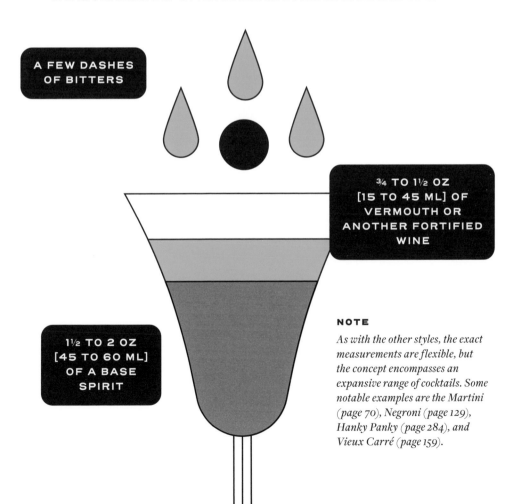

A FEW DASHES OF BITTERS

¾ TO 1½ OZ [15 TO 45 ML] OF VERMOUTH OR ANOTHER FORTIFIED WINE

1½ TO 2 OZ [45 TO 60 ML] OF A BASE SPIRIT

NOTE

As with the other styles, the exact measurements are flexible, but the concept encompasses an expansive range of cocktails. Some notable examples are the Martini (page 70), Negroni (page 129), Hanky Panky (page 284), and Vieux Carré (page 159).

BUILDING A DRINK

THERE ARE THREE PHASES TO BUILDING A COCKTAIL. First, you carefully measure and combine each ingredient. Next, you chill and dilute them with ice, typically by shaking or stirring. Lastly, you pour the drink into a glass and add any necessary garnishes. Sound easy? Good, because it is! Still, it's important to get the details right, so let's go over each of these in turn.

Cocktails are all about balance, and some of the ingredients we're working with are extremely potent. That means that if you use just a little too much or too little of them, the resulting drink is going to fall short of the ideal you're aiming for. The key to making a good drink every time is precision. By making exact measurements, your cocktails will be consistent and taste the way you want them to taste.

We'll talk about the jiggers and other tools you'll need for this in the next section, but for now let's talk about how to build a drink. Occasionally you'll pour the ingredients directly into the glass you're serving it in; more often you'll start with a shaker or mixing glass. This is a simple process—you're just pouring stuff!—but we do have a few pieces of advice for you to keep in mind.

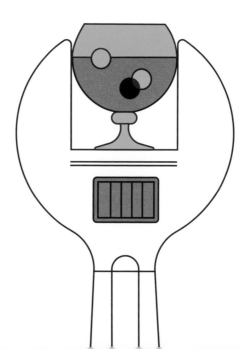

1

A JIGGER IS ONLY AS PRECISE AS THE PERSON USING IT.

Hold the jigger straight up and down and measure precisely to the lines. If you're off by a little bit, the cocktail will be off too.

2

MEASURE SYRUPS FIRST.

The remaining ingredients will rinse the jigger of the syrup, ensuring it all makes it into the drink.

3

ADD JUICES AND OTHER MODIFIERS BEFORE YOUR MAIN SPIRITS.

Why? They typically cost less, so if you make a mistake and have to start over, you haven't lost much.

4

IN DRINKS THAT CALL FOR EGG WHITES, ADD THEM AFTER THE OTHER INGREDIENTS.

Alcohol can denature the proteins in egg whites and prevent them from becoming foamy when shaken. For the frothiest egg white cocktails, minimize the time the egg whites are in contact with undiluted alcohol.

5

ADD ICE LAST. IF YOU START WITH ICE IN YOUR MIXING GLASS OR SHAKER, THE DRINK WILL START TO DILUTE TOO SOON.

And if you have to step away for a minute—say, to answer the doorbell or find a missing ingredient—melting ice could throw off the whole drink. Add your ice right before stirring or shaking.

6

IF POSSIBLE, USE ICE STRAIGHT FROM THE FREEZER.

Ice that has been sitting out in an ice bucket is already starting to melt, meaning that it will be covered in a thin layer of water. This wet ice tends to result in an excessively diluted cocktail.

SHAKING AND STIRRING

THE RECIPES IN THIS BOOK WILL SPECIFY WHETHER THEY SHOULD BE SHAKEN OR STIRRED. It's not an arbitrary distinction. While both processes mix the ingredients, the decision of whether to shake or to stir is all about controlling the final temperature and texture of the cocktail. Let's look at how each of these processes works.

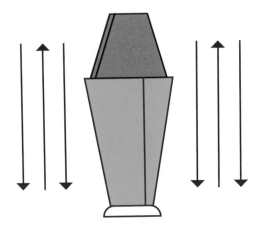

HOW TO SHAKE A COCKTAIL

Build your cocktail in the smaller shaking tin, adding ice last. Place the larger tin on top and give it a light tap to seal the two pieces together. Flip it over so the small tin is closest to your body and, holding it together, give it a firm shake for 10 to 12 seconds. The exact technique you use for shaking isn't important; what matters is that you shake with enough force to fully aerate the drink, as this has a direct impact on the final flavor of the cocktail. When finished, separate the containers by squeezing the larger one to pop the small tin free, or hit the heel of your palm just to the side of where the lips of both tins come together.

SHAKING: Shaking is a vigorous action that breaks up the ice, rapidly diluting and chilling the drink. It also whips air into the cocktail, which gets trapped in viscous ingredients like juices and syrups. When should you shake a cocktail? Pretty much anytime a drink contains citrus juices, dairy, or eggs. Sours are almost always shaken. In drinks that call for eggs or egg whites, we'll typically suggest that you shake first without ice to aerate the egg white before shaking again with ice. Bartenders call this a "dry shake." (See the instructions in the Whiskey Sour on page 47 for details.)

HOW TO STIR A COCKTAIL

Stirring is simply moving ice through a liquid; any tool that accomplishes this is sufficient for stirring. We typically use a barspoon, but we find that a chopstick works just as well. Hold the spoon or chopstick between your middle and ring finger. Pull the spoon toward you with your top two fingers then push it away with the bottom ones, all while keeping your wrist relatively steady. It may help to envision keeping the bowl of the spoon moving along the inside of the mixing glass while you stir. This takes time to master, but once you get the hang of it you'll look very suave. You may want to practice with just ice and water. Sexy technique or not, your drinks will turn out correctly as long as you stir them for the correct amount of time.

Whereas shaking is a fairly forgiving process, technique matters a bit more for stirring. Stir for too short a time, and you'll end up with a drink that's too strong and insufficiently chilled. Stir for too long, and you'll end up with a drink that's too weak and thrown off balance. There's no substitute for practice, and you'll figure out what works for you as you build experience mixing drinks. As a general rule, a drink should be stirred for 20 to 30 seconds, but this is a moving target and depends on speed, serving style, and personal preference.

STIRRING: Shaking is all about achieving full chilling and dilution very quickly. Stirring is slower and focused on precision. Stirred drinks are almost always what are referred to as "spirit forward," which is to say they are meant to highlight the flavor of the spirits in them. In these drinks, the chilling and diluting effects of ice work to round off the alcohol's rough edges, soften the sugars, and give each ingredient a little bit of space to be enjoyed more fully. The faster and more vigorously you stir, the faster the ice will melt. When should you stir a cocktail? Pretty much anytime it doesn't contain citrus or dairy. Old-Fashioned- and Manhattan-style cocktails are almost always stirred.

SERVING AND GARNISHING

YOU'VE MEASURED YOUR INGREDIENTS. YOU'VE SHAKEN OR STIRRED THEM WITH ICE. NOW IT'S TIME TO SERVE THE COCKTAIL. This is when you'll strain it out of your shaker or mixing glass and into the glass you'll serve it in, as well as add any necessary garnishes. This is all pretty easy, but let's talk about each step.

PREPARING YOUR GLASS: You've gotta pour your cocktail into something. We'll go into glassware in more detail on page 36, but first let's talk about how to prepare the glass. If your cocktail is served on the rocks, meaning over ice, you can just pour the drink in the glass. If your drink is served chilled but without ice—"up" in cocktail parlance—your drink will last longer and taste better if you can chill the glass before serving. One way to do this is to fill it with ice and water while you prepare the cocktail. An even better option is to pull the glass directly from the freezer. We always keep a few coupe glasses in our freezers so that we'll have ice-cold glassware on hand when we want to make a drink like a Manhattan or martini, and we recommend that you do the same if you have the space for it. One last consideration: If a recipe calls for a glass to be garnished with a rim of salt or sugar, you should prepare that before making your cocktail.

STRAINING YOUR COCKTAIL: Aside from a few unusual exceptions, you'll almost always want to strain your cocktail off of the ice that you used to chill it. This is where a cocktail strainer comes in. It fits over the shaker or mixing glass so that you can pour the cocktail into your serving glass. If it's a stirred cocktail, a single strainer is all you need. If it's a shaken cocktail, we recommend double-straining through a second fine strainer to take out ice chips or any fragments of mint or other items that might be in the drink.

UP OR ON THE ROCKS?

A drink that is served on the rocks will continue to be diluted as it sits, while a drink that is served up (chilled, but not over ice) will get warmer. Typically, it's more important to fully stir a cocktail that will be served up, whereas it's OK to under-stir a cocktail that will be served over ice.

In a bar the bartender will make these decisions for you, but at home you have more say in the matter. Some people love an Old-Fashioned or Negroni that starts bracingly strong and then dilutes on ice over time. Other people want a drink that starts out a bit colder and more diluted.

GARNISHING: Some drinks don't require any garnish at all. In others, a garnish is nice but optional. Sometimes, particularly in the cases of citrus garnishes, they provide an essential finishing touch. Let's look at four ways we'll use garnishes throughout the book.

CITRUS GARNISH: Citrus is the most common, and often the most essential, of the garnishes we'll use in cocktails. Occasionally we'll call for a wedge or wheel of citrus, which you can simply slice and perch on the edge of the glass or on top of the drink. Most of the time, however, we'll be using just a strip of peel. When we call for a strip of citrus peel as a garnish, it's not just because it looks pretty. The oils in the peel are intensely flavorful and aromatic. By squeezing the peel over the surface of the cocktail, you can dramatically change the way you perceive it when you drink. Even before you take the first sip, you'll pick up the fresh aroma of the citrus. After you've expressed the citrus, it's up to you whether to discard the peel or to drop it into the drink. At home we'll typically drop it in for cocktails served on the rocks and discard it for drinks that are served up, but this is a matter of personal preference.

RIM GARNISH: A few cocktails are served with salt or sugar along the rim of the glass, providing a little extra sweetness or saltiness as you drink. To prepare glasses for this, you moisten the rim with a wedge of citrus and then drag it through a plate of the salt or sugar so that it sticks. We'll usually cover only half the rim so that the drinker has the choice of whether or not to sip from the garnished part of the glass.

SNACK GARNISH: Olives and cherries are the two most popular garnishes that fall into this category. The brine of the olive or syrup on the cherry might contribute a small amount of flavor to the cocktail, but the garnish is also a tasty treat to go along with it. You can simply drop these into the cocktail or, if you're feeling fancy, skewer them on a pick.

SPICE AND HERB GARNISHES: Much like a citrus peel, spices and fresh herbs are all about the aromatics. We're keeping things simple in this book, but cinnamon, nutmeg, and fresh mint are worth keeping on hand. A bouquet of fresh mint or a grating of cinnamon or nutmeg can take a drink from good to great.

After the garnish is on your cocktail, it's time for the best and final step: drinking and enjoying it. If you put care into all the aforementioned steps, the cocktail you make for yourself will be every bit as good as what you'd be served in a professional bar.

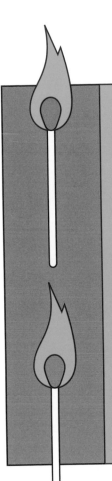

HOW TO FLAME AN ORANGE PEEL

If you'd like to add a bit of flare to your garnish game, you can "flame" an orange peel over your cocktail. It's just like the normal process of expressing an orange peel, but with a flame in between the peel and the drink to ignite the oils. With a fresh orange and in a dimly lit setting, the resulting flash of fire is a real attention-grabber. It also adds a subtly smoky aroma to cocktails. To do it, light a match and hold it a few inches below a strip of orange peel for a few seconds to warm it up. Then, squeeze the peel so that the oils pass through the flame and onto the surface of the drink. If everything works correctly, you'll get a bright burst of fire.

It takes a little practice and the results are highly dependent on the quality of the orange, but it's a fun skill worth developing for when you want to impress your guests. That said, we suggest deploying this move with restraint. Not every drink benefits from the hint of smoke. Save it for cocktails with richer, bolder flavors, like the Ritz (page 153) and the Latin Trifecta (page 252). And this should go without saying, but take care when combining alcohol and fire! We wrote this book to help you stock your home bar, not burn it down.

BAR TOOLS

AS IN SO MANY OTHER PURSUITS, HAVING THE RIGHT TOOLS IN YOUR HOME BAR WILL MAKE ALL THE DIFFERENCE FOR YOUR HOME BARTENDING. The good news is that you don't really need that much, and the tools you buy will last pretty much forever. Our advice is to buy good-quality tools right from the start. Chances are you'll never have to replace them, and it's cheaper and less of a hassle than buying low-quality now and upgrading later.

A few pieces of equipment are crucial to your home bar, while others are just nice to have. We've divided this list in two sections so that you can get started right away with the important ones and take your time with the others.

THE ESSENTIALS

BOTTLES: You'll need something to keep your homemade syrups in. Aesthetically, we like glass bottles with flip-top lids. For practical purposes, you may prefer plastic squeeze bottles. (You can trim the tops to make them a bit wider for more viscous syrups.) You may also want to save your bitters bottles after you empty them—or purchase a dasher bottle from a specialty cocktail-gear shop—to store potent ingredients like absinthe that you can add to cocktails a dash at a time.

CITRUS JUICER: Unless you have much stronger hands than we do, you'll probably want a tool to help you extract the juice from your citrus fruits. You don't need anything fancy here, just a simple handheld squeezer. These are perfect for lemons and limes, quick to use, and easy to clean. Oranges and grapefruits are a bit too large for these, so you'll want a juicer/reamer for those. Get something with the least amount of moving parts to keep things easy for yourself.

HAWTHORNE STRAINER: This is the kind of strainer that has a spring around the edge to catch ice shards, and it's necessary for straining shaken drinks. The denser and tighter the spring, the better.

JIGGER: This is the little device used to measure out small amounts of liquid for drinks. The jigger matters more than just about anything else because it's what you'll depend on to ensure your drinks are accurately measured. For cocktail purposes, it's useful to have measurements ranging from as small as ¼ oz [7.5 ml] all the way up to 2 oz [60 ml]. We typically work with slim, two-sided jiggers in two sizes, but you can also use a mini shot glass–size measuring cup as long as it has clearly visible markings

PARING KNIFE: You need something to cut your citrus fruit, and a good knife is also useful if you decide to get into making fancy garnishes. It doesn't have to be expensive, but it does need to be sharp. Almost nothing is more dangerous in a bar than a dull blade trying to slice through a thick piece of citrus.

PEELER: You could cut your citrus peels with a paring knife, but don't be a hero: Just get a Y-shaped vegetable peeler. They're easy to use, cheap to buy, and produce attractive strips of peel in no time.

SHAKER TINS: There are numerous vessels you that you could shake a cocktail in, but nothing beats a good set of tins. They're easy to use and easy to clean, and, with no moving parts, there's pretty much nothing to break. There are a lot of different styles of shakers out there, but there's a reason basically every bartender uses tins. Standard sizing is 18 oz [532 ml] and 28 oz [828 ml]. We like cheaper tins made of thin metal, which makes

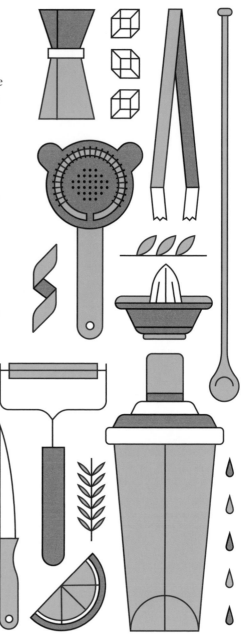

them easier to seal and separate. (Other styles of shaker are the Boston shaker, which uses metal and glass, and the cobbler shaker, which comes in three pieces with a removable cap. Do these options work? Sure, but we stand by the speed and ease of using two metal tins.)

THE NICE-TO-HAVES

ATOMIZER: An atomizer is useful for spritzing aromatic spirits onto cocktails or into glasses. (Pro tip: You may want to pick one up when you get to the absinthe chapter. In addition to its use in cocktails, an atomizer filled with absinthe is a pretty killer breath freshener.) As your bar grows, you may also want to have an atomizer for smoky scotch or a favorite liqueur.

BARSPOON: A well-designed barspoon is tall, slender, and easy to turn in your fingers while stirring a cocktail. The bowl of the spoon can also be used for measuring small amounts of syrups or extracting olives and cherries from the jar. If you don't have a barspoon, a chopstick makes a fine substitute for stirring.

DIGITAL SCALE: We recommend making syrups by weight rather than volume. It's easier and more accurate, and you don't have to wash your measuring cups. Following an exact syrup recipe results in better drinks. A scale doesn't cost much and you can also use it for coffee and cooking, so we think it's a worthwhile investment.

FINE STRAINER: Also known as a tea strainer, this is the fine-mesh strainer that can be used in addition to a Hawthorne strainer when serving a shaken drink. While not strictly necessary, it helps remove smaller shards of ice as well as any bits of fruit or herbs that might get through the coils of the Hawthorne strainer, resulting in a cleaner cocktail.

ICE MOLDS: If your freezer produces good-tasting, all-purpose ice, then lucky you! Regardless, you may still want some specialty ice molds. Standard 1 in [2.5 cm] cubes are useful for drinks on the rocks, and many stirred cocktails like the Old-Fashioned benefit from being served on a single, large 2 in [5 cm] cube. Silicone molds for both sizes are readily available. If you like, you can also invest in even fancier molds that will produce perfectly clear ice, but this is purely a matter of personal preference.

JULEP STRAINER: If you already have a Hawthorne strainer, you don't strictly need a julep strainer too. This is more of a stylistic luxury. Julep strainers are meant for straining stirred cocktails. They're elegant to use yet they don't do the job any better than a Hawthorne.

LEWIS BAG AND HAMMER: A Lewis bag is a cloth bag that you fill with ice and smash with a hammer, producing perfectly crushed ice for drinks like juleps and mojitos. It probably sounds decadent to have a dedicated bag and hammer just for ice. Sure, you could smash your ice some other way, wrapped in a clean towel perhaps, but if you pick up a Lewis bag you may find yourself using it more often than you imagined. Plus, think of how much your guests will appreciate you smashing ice by hand just for them—that's what we call hospitality.

MIXING GLASS: This is something we recommend that anyone serious about making cocktails add to their collection, and of the nice-to-haves in this list, it's probably the first one you should invest in. A good stirring glass will have a wide base and straight sides. The idea is that you want maximum contact between ice and liquid, and a wider base accomplishes this. This design also makes it much easier to stir a drink and prevents the glass from tipping over while doing so. Can you stir a cocktail successfully in just about any container? Sure. But once you get a good glass, you'll never want to go back.

MUDDLER: A muddler is a blunt tool similar to a pestle that you use to smash fresh fruit and herbs while mixing a cocktail. It's not something you'll need for the majority of drinks in this book, and you probably have something else in your kitchen that will get the job done, such as a big wooden spoon. If you get into making cocktails like the Mint Julep (page 52), Mojito (page 99), or Caipirinha (page 276), however, it's absolutely worth picking up the right tool for the job.

SPICE GRATER: When you garnish a cocktail with cinnamon or nutmeg, the aromatics will be much fresher if you grate them on the spot rather than pour them from a jar. Yes, this is a niche item, but you'll probably find all sorts of other uses for it in your kitchen.

A PERFECT PANTRY

THE LIST OF POTENTIAL INGREDIENTS THAT YOU COULD PUT INTO A COCKTAIL IS ENDLESS. Trust us, we've put some weird stuff into drinks in the bars where we've worked. At home, though, we tend to keep things simple. The concept of this book is to focus on essential ingredients that are easy to keep around and that you can use time and again. These are the pantry workhorses of the home bar.

BITTERS

Bitters are the tiny bottles arrayed on any decent cocktail bar that are used a dash or two at a time to add depth and complexity. There's an endless variety of bitters to choose from, but we limit our recipes to the classic trinity that bartenders rely on more than any others. The bottles last a long time and we'll be using them throughout the book. You don't have to get all three right away, but we recommend doing so sooner rather than later. These are high in alcohol, but because they are classified as nonpotable, you can often find them in ordinary grocery stores.

ANGOSTURA BITTERS: This is a famous brand of bitters and the most ubiquitous. Based on a secret recipe dating back to 1824, it boasts intensely aromatic spice notes. There are other brands that can play the role of aromatic bitters, but we recommend starting with the classic. A few dashes of Angostura bitters are also an excellent addition to sparkling water when you want complex taste without the boozy hit of a cocktail.

ORANGE BITTERS: As the name implies, these are flavored with bittering ingredients, orange peels, and other spices. They have numerous uses and a particular affinity for gin. No single brand of orange bitters dominates the market, and you likely won't go wrong with whichever one you happen to pick up. (Angostura also makes an orange bitters, and theirs is a fine example.)

PEYCHAUD'S BITTERS: Created around 1830 by Antoine Amédée Peychaud, a New Orleans pharmacist, Peychaud's bitters are strongly associated with New Orleans cocktails to this day. Bright red, bitter, and with a subtle anise note, they'll come into play most often once we make it to the rye and absinthe chapters of the book.

SYRUPS ADD BOTH SWEETNESS AND FLAVOR TO COCKTAILS, AND THERE'S A WHOLE WORLD OF SYRUP OPTIONS OUT THERE. For the purposes of this book, we limited our selection to just five of the most useful, for which we've included recipes opposite.

RICH SIMPLE SYRUP: Made from nothing more than plain white sugar and water, this is the go-to syrup for when you want to add sweetness without other characterizing flavors. Typical "simple syrup" is made from equal parts sugar and water. We prefer to use two parts sugar to one part water, hence "rich simple syrup." You can buy simple syrup in stores, but it's so easy to make at home.

RICH DEMERARA SYRUP: Demerara is a sugar that's less refined than white sugar, retaining a small amount of molasses. With a darker color and richer character, it works particularly well with dark spirits, and adds a little more heft to a cocktail.

HONEY SYRUP: Honey is another great way to add sweetness and flavor. The problem with honey is that it's too thick to mix or pour easily. How to fix that? Make a solution—literally. Dissolving the honey in hot water will make it just runny enough for ease of use when mixing. Honey can be remarkably variable. For everyday use, try a simple honey that plays well with others, such as one from wildflowers or clover.

GRENADINE: As a kid, you might have enjoyed grenadine in a Shirley Temple. At the risk of ruining the magic, that was probably made with corn syrup dyed red. Real grenadine as used in cocktail bars today is another thing entirely—a syrup flavored with actual pomegranate juice. It's bright and fruity, and plays a major role in classic cocktails. When buying a commercial grenadine, always check the label to make sure it's made with real pomegranate juice. We like the grenadines from Small Hand Foods and B. G. Reynolds, but you can also make your own.

ORGEAT: Orgeat (pronounced "or-zhaat") is made from almonds and adds a creamy, marzipan note to cocktails. Traditionally made orgeat starts with making almond milk from scratch, which is why we almost always buy it commercially. Our favorites are from Small Hand Foods and Liber & Co., both of which have great depth and aren't as saccharine as other brands. If you do want to make your own, our recipe accents commercially available almond milk with toasted almonds. It's a great hack for making delicious orgeat without laborious processes or specialized tools.

SYRUP RECIPES

RICH SIMPLE SYRUP

1½ cups [300 g] white sugar

¾ cup [150 g] water

YIELDS ABOUT 1½ CUPS [360 ML]. *Add sugar and water to a small pot over medium-high heat. Bring to a simmer, stirring constantly to prevent the sugar from burning. Once sugar is dissolved, remove from heat and let cool. Will last 3 to 4 weeks refrigerated in a sealed container.*

RICH DEMERARA SYRUP

1½ cups [300 g] demerara sugar, or if unavailable, substitute another flavorful sugar, such as turbinado

¾ cup [150 g] water

YIELDS ABOUT 1½ CUPS [360 ML]. *Add sugar and water to a small pot over medium-high heat. Bring to a simmer, stirring constantly to prevent the sugar from burning. Once sugar is dissolved, remove from heat and let cool. Will last 3 to 4 weeks refrigerated in a sealed container.*

HONEY SYRUP

1 cup [350 g] honey

⅞ cup [175 g] water

YIELDS SCANT 2 CUPS [475 ML]. *Add honey and water to a small pot over medium-high heat. Heat and stir until the honey is fully dissolved. Remove from heat and let cool. Will last 3 to 4 weeks refrigerated in a sealed container.*

GRENADINE

1¼ cups [300 g] pomegranate juice

1½ cups [300 g] white sugar

½ tsp [2 g] orange flower water

YIELDS ABOUT 2 CUPS [475 ML]. *Combine half of the pomegranate juice and all of the sugar in a small pot over medium-high heat. Bring to a simmer, stirring constantly until sugar is dissolved. Remove from heat and let cool. Add remaining pomegranate juice and orange flower water. Will last 3 to 4 weeks refrigerated in a sealed container.*

ORGEAT

1 cup [100 g] blanched, slivered almonds

1¼ cups [300 g] unsweetened almond milk

1½ cups [300 g] white sugar

½ tsp [2 g] orange flower water

YIELDS SCANT 2 CUPS [475 ML]. *Add almonds to a pan on medium heat. Toast them, tossing constantly to prevent burning. Remove from heat when lightly brown and aromatic. In a small pot, combine the almonds, almond milk, and sugar. Bring to a simmer and stir to dissolve the sugar; attend the pot to ensure it does not boil over. Remove from heat and cover. Allow it to cool (1 to 2 hours). When cool, strain the almond milk, pressing on the solids to get as much liquid out as possible. Stir in the orange flower water. Will last 3 to 4 weeks refrigerated in a sealed container.*

Sparkling and carbonated ingredients are used when you want to lengthen and lighten a cocktail. There are as many options here as there are sodas in your grocery store, but in this book we'll focus on just three. Keep these on hand and keep them chilled in your refrigerator; the colder they are, the better they retain their bubbles.

SODA WATER: Nothing fancy here, just regular, unflavored club soda, seltzer, or sparkling water. As long as it has tight bubbles and no characterizing flavor, it should be fine for cocktails.

GINGER BEER: Slightly spicier than ginger ale, ginger beer has a spicy kick that plays well with citrus and strong spirits.

SPARKLING WINE: Sparkling wine has a long history in cocktails and makes elegant drinks. Some classic recipes call specifically for champagne, but realistically, we're usually mixing with something that's more within our budget. A bottle that's crisp, dry, and not too expensive, such as a brut cava, will do nicely.

OLIVES AND PRESERVED CHERRIES ARE GREAT TO KEEP ON HAND FOR COCKTAIL GARNISHES. Since you or your guests will be consuming them, it's important to find ones that you enjoy. We suggest choosing pitted, unstuffed olives. Our preferred olive is the green, firm, and buttery Castelvetrano from Sicily. It adds a clean salinity to martinis, doesn't fall apart in the drink, and is a wonderful snack. For cherries, steer clear of the candy-red maraschino variety; we believe the only cocktail these belong in is the canned fruit kind. Look for high-quality, naturally colored cherries preserved in sweetened cherry juice. Luxardo, Toschi, and Fabbri all make excellent examples. If you find yourself in peak cherry season with a penchant for preservation, you can also make your own brandied sour cherries. The process is quite simple and if you'd like to learn more, we suggest consulting your favorite internet search engine.

Citrus fruits are vital for cocktails for both their peels and their juices. Most cocktails in the sour family are made with lemon or lime juice, and the aromatics of lemon and orange peels are used to garnish all kinds of drinks. Grapefruit appears less frequently, but we do call for it occasionally. There's no substitute at all for fresh lime and lemon juice, so we highly recommend juicing them yourself and using it the same day you squeeze it. We also recommend juicing your own orange and grapefruit juice, but we acknowledge that quality bottled versions can be acceptable. When buying citrus, look for fruits that are firm but supple and that have healthy-looking, bright skin.

There's a good chance you keep these items in your kitchen anyway, but we'll occasionally call for them in cocktail recipes: white sugar, cream, eggs, fresh mint, cinnamon, and nutmeg.

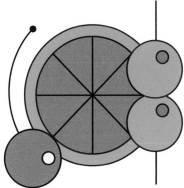

NOTE FOR VEGETARIANS, VEGANS OR ANYONE ELSE WHO'D PREFER TO AVOID EGGS

Aquafaba, the liquid you'll find in cans of chickpeas, offers an alternative for creating a foamy texture in cocktails. Simply use about ¾ of an ounce as a substitute for egg white in the drinks that call for it.

GLASSWARE

SO YOU HAVE A FORMULA FOR YOUR COCKTAIL, you have your ingredients and supplies, and now it's time to find a glass to put it in. This could be anything: a beer pint glass, a coffee mug, a giant glass boot. If it holds liquid, you could serve a cocktail in it. That said, your enjoyment will be enhanced with some proper glassware.

You don't have to get carried away, but it is nice to have a few different styles of glassware from which to choose. And much like stocking the bottles in your home bar, you don't have to buy it all at once. Start with a few very functional glasses and build out from there. The main consideration is that you'll need some glasses for drinks that are served with ice ("on the rocks") and some for drinks served without it ("up"). Here are our recommendations for how to begin.

These are our workhorse glasses, the ones that we use over and over again when making drinks both at home and in professional bars. Get these three and you'll be set up to serve 99 percent of the world's cocktails.

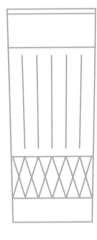

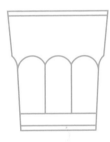

COUPE

The coupe is our go-to for drinks served up. It's a stemmed glass with a round bowl, usually in the range of 5 to 8 oz [150 to 240 ml] in volume. We like to keep a few of these on hand in a range of sizes, with smaller glasses for stirred, spirit-forward cocktails and a few larger ones for lighter shaken drinks.

HIGHBALL

These are tall, narrow glasses, the kind you'll often use to serve drinks topped with soda or over crushed ice. You might also see these named collins glasses, which tend to be on the higher side in volume. Look for a highball or collins in the 10 to 12 oz [300 to 360 ml] range. In truth, most drinks served in a highball would be just fine in a rocks glass, but sometimes the tall glass is aesthetically pleasing.

ROCKS GLASS

This is a short, stout glass designed for serving drinks on the rocks. The volume should be somewhere around 8 to 10 oz [240 to 300 ml], enough to hold your ice, a cocktail, and perhaps a bit of soda. It's an extremely versatile glass, perfect for Old-Fashioneds and whiskey sours and good enough for just about any cocktail that's served over ice.

These are glasses that, while not strictly necessary, are nice to have. Whether they're worth adding to your collection depends on your personal style and the specific drinks you like to make.

COPPER MUG OR JULEP CUP

Do you need a cup made of metal instead of glass? Not necessarily, but they frost up very appealingly when filled with ice-cold drinks. If you find yourself making Moscow mules or mint juleps on the regular, by all means, invest in a cup designed specifically for that purpose. Otherwise, a rocks glass will serve well.

MUG

We don't focus much on hot drinks in this book, but we do include a couple of them. If you drink coffee or tea, you likely already have a mug that will work. Look for one that's not too large and is made of ceramic or tempered glass.

SAZERAC GLASS

This isn't really a proper name for a glass, but there are a few drinks—notably the Sazerac—that are traditionally served in a rocks glass without any ice. A full-size rocks glass is a bit large for this, but one in the range of 5 to 7 oz [150 to 210 ml] works perfectly.

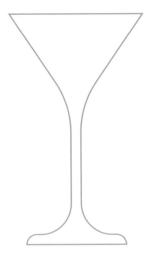

MARTINI GLASS

The V-shaped martini glass is the most iconic cocktail glass there is. Even so, we confess we hardly ever use it; a martini served in a coupe is every bit as delicious. If the style appeals to you, however, don't let us talk you out of it. Just make sure you get one that's on the smaller side. If you get an oversize glass, either your martini will end up looking ridiculously small or you'll have to make martinis that are way too large. (The latter may not sound like a problem, but keep in mind that cocktails do warm up as you drink. Two small, ice-cold martinis are better than one big warm one.)

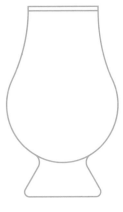

FIZZ GLASS

Like a highball or collins glass, the idea behind a fizz glass is to accentuate the height of a cocktail. These are smaller and lower volume, however, so that they can be used without ice. In drinks with a foamy texture, such as the Cream Puff (page 226), you may even get the foam to stand up over the rim of the glass. The glass can be tall and narrow like a highball or footed and a bit wider, as long as it's a suitable size.

SPIRITS GLASS

This book is more about making cocktails than it is about sipping individual spirits, but sometimes you'll be in the mood to simply enjoy some whiskey, cognac, or other liquor in your collection "neat," without ice or any other additions. A small glass, perhaps with a tulip shape to concentrate aromas, is an excellent choice for this, but follow your personal style.

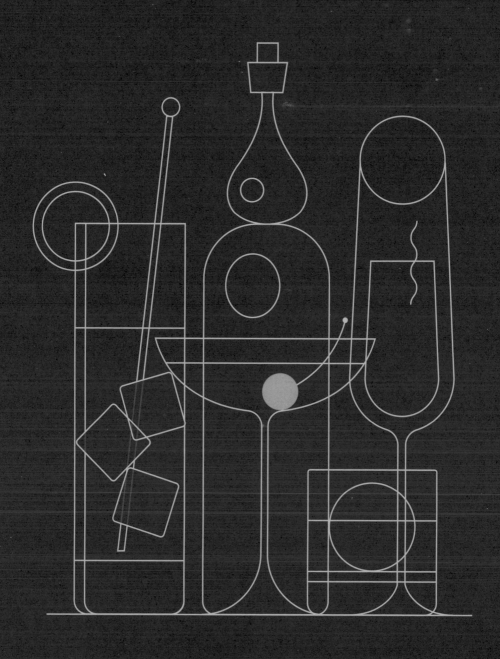

THE CLASSIC BAR

IN THIS FIRST HALF OF THE BOOK, we're going to focus on building up your home bar with the essential bottles for mixing classic cocktails. Some of these, like bourbon and gin, you're likely already familiar with. Others, like Benedictine and Chartreuse, may be new to you. What they all have in common is a long history and a strong presence in the cocktail canon; they're the bottles we reach for over and over again when making drinks. They are also, above all, versatile. We selected every bottle so that it builds on the ones before it and sets you up to make some of the world's most popular cocktails, such as the Old-Fashioned, Whiskey Sour, martini, Manhattan, and margarita. With every spirit you add to your collection, you'll be unlocking new potential avenues for mixing drinks. By the end of the first few chapters, you'll have a grounding in every major style of cocktail. Let's grab a bottle of bourbon and get started.

CHAPTER 1

BOURBON

IF YOUR HOME BAR IS MADE UP OF EXACTLY ONE BOTTLE, YOU CAN'T DO MUCH BETTER THAN BOURBON. Bourbon is versatile in cocktails, a good bottle won't break the bank, and on those nights when you want a drink but don't want to work for it, it's great all on its own. It's the perfect spirit to begin your venture into making cocktails at home.

Entire books have been written about the history of bourbon and the nuances of its production, but since we are focused on cocktails, we'll cover the three most important things to know about the spirit before moving on to advice about how to pick a bottle. First, bourbon must be made in the United States. Second, it's a whiskey, and all whiskeys are made from grain. The combination of grains used to make a specific whiskey is called its mashbill. For bourbon, the mashbill must be at least 51 percent corn. The remaining portion is typically composed of rye and barley, though occasionally wheat or other grains are used.

Finally, and perhaps most important, bourbon must be aged in brand-new, charred oak barrels. This is part of what makes bourbon unique. Most of the world ages its whiskey in barrels that have already been used for some other spirit or wine, which affects how the wood impacts the spirit. The charred oak of a bourbon barrel naturally sweetens the whiskey, contributing vanilla notes and giving bourbon its distinctive rich, round flavor.

THE BOURBON SECTION IN A LIQUOR STORE CAN BE DAUNTING, BUT THERE ARE A FEW THINGS THAT WILL CLEAR THE CONFUSION AND GET YOU ON YOUR WAY. HERE'S WHAT TO LOOK FOR WHEN PICKING OUT A BOTTLE WELL SUITED FOR MIXING:

BUY A KENTUCKY BOURBON. You'll know it's a Kentucky bourbon because it will say so right on the label (easy enough!). Although bourbon can be made anywhere in the United States, its historic home is Kentucky, and that's where most of the established, classic brands distill today. There are wonderful bourbons being made by both large and small distilleries all across the country, and we think that you should absolutely carve out space for these bottles in your home bar . . . eventually. But when it comes to your first bottle, you should be thinking about maximum reliability and versatility. You want classic bourbon for classic cocktails. And Kentucky makes classic bourbon.

BUY A BOURBON THAT IS STRONG ENOUGH FOR COCKTAILS. All bourbon is at least 40 percent alcohol by volume (ABV), but we recommend somewhere around 45 to 50 percent. This strength is just right to hold up in spirit-forward drinks without overwhelming lighter, more refreshing cocktails.

BUY A BOTTLE LABELED STRAIGHT OR BOTTLED IN BOND. Although bourbon tends to age more quickly than many other types of whiskey, we recommend that you buy a bottle that is at least four years old. At that age, it will have likely picked up the vanilla and caramel notes that are the signatures of classic bourbon. Not every bottle will have an age statement on it, but to be labeled *straight* or *bottled in bond*, they will have met an age minimum. Straight whiskey must be at least two years old, but if it's over four, then the age isn't required on the label. Pick up a bottle of straight bourbon and inspect it for an age statement (sometimes they're tiny, so look closely), and if you don't see one, then the whiskey is at least four years old. Bottled-in-bond whiskey is less common because the rules governing it are stricter (and worth reading about if you like history), but what you need to know is that any bottled-in-bond whiskey must be at least four years old and bottled at 50 percent ABV.

FORGET ABOUT MARKETING LINGO. There's no need to stress about terms like *small batch* or *single barrel. Small batch* is a marketing term and doesn't really mean anything. *Single barrel* refers to a whiskey that comes from only one barrel. That can be fun because each barrel has a subtly unique character, but it's not particularly relevant for making cocktails.

AGE IS JUST A NUMBER. Bourbon is typically aged in large, multistory, non-temperature regulated warehouses, so the location of a barrel has a tremendous impact on the whiskey. Think of the difference between a basement and an attic. A barrel on the sunny side of the top floor of a warehouse may come to maturity in a few years, while one located in the depths of the bottom floor could rest comfortably for a decade. Older doesn't necessarily mean better. Pay more attention to what your taste buds say and less to the number on the label.

If you follow these guidelines, you'll more than likely end up with a bottle of bourbon that you'll enjoy sipping neat in a glass or with a few ice cubes, as well as in the cocktail recipes to follow. And fortunately, you won't have to spend too much money on it. Delicious, high-quality bourbon that fulfills the above requirements can be had at a very moderate price. If you fall in love with bourbon, you'll eventually want to expand your collection to include more exclusive bottles, but there's no need to splurge on an expensive bourbon starting out. Just get a good bottle following the advice above and make some great drinks!

BOURBON 101

In the United States, the requirements for bourbon are defined by detailed regulations:

- It must be produced within the United States.
- Its mashbill (grain mix) must be comprised of at least 51 percent corn.
- It must be aged in new, charred oak containers (typically barrels).
- It must be distilled to no more than 80 percent ABV.
- It must enter its aging container at no more than 62.5 percent ABV.
- It must be bottled at 40 percent ABV or higher.

If all of those requirements are met, whiskey can be labeled as bourbon! Bourbon does not have a minimum age, but any bourbon under four years old will have an age statement on the bottle declaring the age of the youngest whiskey used to make it. Here are the two options:

STRAIGHT BOURBON: Straight bourbon must be aged at least two years.

BOTTLED-IN-BOND: Bottled-in-bond bourbon is aged for at least four years in a government bonded warehouse, distilled in one season by one distiller, and bottled at 50 percent ABV.

BOTTLES WE REACH FOR

RUSSELL'S RESERVE 10

Made at the Wild Turkey Distillery, Russell's Reserve 10 has a depth and complexity of bourbons that is usually found at a much higher price point. It works wonderfully in cocktails, with a spice note that plays well with other bold ingredients. On nights when we're feeling a bit more budget conscious, we also love the underrated Wild Turkey 101 in drinks or on its own in a glass.

FOUR ROSES SMALL BATCH

With a high rye content in its mashbill, Four Roses Small Batch is among the boldest of the bourbons we reach for. If you find yourself drawn more to Manhattans than sours, this is a great go-to.

EAGLE RARE

At 10 years old and priced reasonably, Eagle Rare is one of the better values in bourbon. Made at the Buffalo Trace distillery, its soft cherry fruits are a great counterpoint to spicier whiskeys and make it a fantastic introduction to the category. We pick up a bottle when we find it, but the standard (and more reliably obtainable) Buffalo Trace is a solid stand-in.

KNOB CREEK

Made at Jim Beam, Knob Creek is a blend of barrels from multiple locations in the warehouse, all a minimum of nine years old. It possesses the earthy, nutty note that carries through Beam's whiskies, and we reach for it first when mixing with sherry, orgeat, and amaretto.

OLD-FASHIONED

WE'VE TALKED ABOUT THEORY AND WHEN TO SHAKE OR STIR A COCKTAIL. You've bought a bottle of bourbon, stocked a few pantry essentials, and are ready to get to mixing. Where better to begin than with the most classic of classic cocktails, the Old-Fashioned?

The Old-Fashioned is the foundation for spirit-forward cocktails. It is and should be a simple drink, but it's an essential one to master. It teaches you how to balance three of the four essential elements of making cocktails—spirit, sugar, and bitter—and highlights the effects of chilling and dilution. At the beginning of the nineteenth century, it was the essence of what defined a cocktail. In these earliest days, it didn't even call for ice; the whole thing was simply diluted with a bit of a water, and any spirit could be used. The drink evolved for the better with the addition of ice, and whiskey became the spirit of choice. In the twentieth century, particularly after Prohibition, American cocktails went in a lighter and fruitier direction, and the Old-Fashioned followed suit. Orange slices and candy-bright cherries were often muddled into the drink, and it was sometimes topped with soda, while whiskey fell into the background.

The modern cocktail revival that began in the early 2000s brought with it a reverence for vintage cocktails, and the Old-Fashioned has thankfully come back to its roots with whiskey at center stage. The recipe we recommend isn't quite so austere as those rustic versions made without ice, but it is certainly more 1880s than 1980s. Follow this recipe to make one for yourself.

INGREDIENTS

2 oz [60 ml] bourbon

1 barspoon (⅙ oz [5 ml]) Rich Demerara Syrup (page 33)

2 dashes Angostura bitters

Orange peel, for garnish

DIRECTIONS

To a mixing glass, add the bourbon, syrup, bitters, and ice. Stir and strain into a rocks glass filled with ice or—even better—a single large cube. Garnish with an orange peel and serve.

CONT'D

OLD-FASHIONED NOTES

ON TECHNIQUE: As you advance through the book, we'll keep the recipe instructions simple. Precisely how long to stir the cocktail can be learned only through practice and by feel, varying by the ice one uses and by personal taste. Light stirring will produce an initially very strong drink that gradually dilutes over time; longer stirring will make one that's perfect for sipping right from the start. When garnishing with the orange peel, remember to first express the oils over the surface of the drink. Refer back to page 23 for more details on stirring and garnishing.

ON BITTERS: To keep things simple, we've called for just the 2 dashes of Angostura bitters. You may enjoy seeing how adding a dash of Peychaud's or orange bitters adds even more complexity to the cocktail. We typically add one or the other along with the Angostura.

ON SUGAR: We like the depth that demerara sugar adds to this and many other cocktails you'll find in the book. As an experiment, try two Old-Fashioneds side by side, one with Rich Demerara Syrup (page 33) and one with Rich Simple Syrup (page 33), and taste how they differ. You may also come across some recipes calling for a sugar cube rather than syrup; this just creates more work for yourself without adding anything to the drink. Save yourself the effort and use syrup for a smoother cocktail.

WHISKEY SOUR

LEARNING HOW TO MAKE A PROPER "SOUR" COCKTAIL IS ONE OF THE MOST FUNDA-MENTAL SKILLS IN MIXOLOGY. The idea of mixing a strong spirit with a bracing dose of citrus juice and a sweet syrup or liqueur is infinitely versatile, providing the template for thousands of drinks. By mastering the Whiskey Sour, you'll get the feel for balancing these three elements—a skill you'll use again and again throughout the book.

The Whiskey Sour is a venerable cocktail with a long history, but like many classic drinks, it became a shadow of its former self in the decades following Prohibition. In many bars, artificial "sour mix" took the place of fresh juice. There's really no substitute for squeezing actual fruit; bottled mixes and juices simply don't compare in flavor to the real thing. If you've never had a Whiskey Sour made with freshly squeezed lemon juice, this recipe will be a revelation. Once you start making cocktails this way, you'll never go back.

There's one other ingredient that may come as a surprise here: egg white. In the traditional definition of a proper sour—as opposed to the more general sense of any cocktail balanced with citrus juice—an egg white is an integral component. While the drink can be made without it, shaking an egg white into the cocktail adds a soft texture and makes it delightfully silky. We suggest you start by making the cocktail with only the bourbon, lemon juice, and syrup to see how all these ingredients come together, then try making it again with the egg white to see how it changes the experience of sipping it.

INGREDIENTS

2 oz [60 ml] bourbon

¾ oz [22.5 ml] fresh lemon juice

½ oz [15 ml] Rich Demerara Syrup (page 33)

1 egg white (optional; see headnote)

Lemon peel, for garnish

Cocktail cherry, for garnish

TO MAKE WITHOUT EGG WHITE

To a shaker, add the bourbon, lemon juice, syrup, and ice. Shake and strain into a rocks glass filled with ice. Garnish with a lemon peel and cherry and serve.

TO MAKE WITH EGG WHITE

To a shaker without ice, add the bourbon, lemon juice, syrup, and egg white. Dry shake for a few seconds to aerate the egg white. Add ice and shake again, then strain into a rocks glass filled with ice. Garnish with a lemon peel and cherry and serve.

BUSTER BROWN

A SOMEWHAT OBSCURE COCKTAIL FROM A 1917 BOOK OF RECIPES CALLED *THE IDEAL BARTENDER,* THE BUSTER BROWN IS EASY TO OVERLOOK. It is, after all, simply a Whiskey Sour with a few dashes of orange bitters. But those dashes *change* the drink, making it a new thing worthy of a new name. All of our cocktails so far have used bitters or acidity separately; this cocktail shows how well they can work together. Adding bitterness to a tart cocktail is like adding a second guitar player to the three-piece rock band, bringing new dimension and depth. Consider the Buster Brown a simple beginning to what will be, as you progress through this book, an evolving and expanding study of the way bitters and citrus work with one another. It's also a wonderful example of how a light touch can bring about a big change.

INGREDIENTS

2 oz [60 ml] bourbon

¾ oz [22.5 ml] fresh lemon juice

½ oz [15 ml] Rich Demerara Syrup (page 33)

3 dashes orange bitters

Orange peel, for garnish

DIRECTIONS

To a shaker, add the bourbon, lemon juice, syrup, bitters, and ice. Shake and strain into a chilled coupe glass. Garnish with an orange peel and serve.

VARIATION

Though not traditional, this could be made with egg white as well, following the same method as in the Whiskey Sour (page 47).

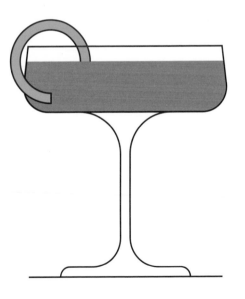

HOT TODDY

IF YOU'VE HAPPENED TO ACQUIRE THIS BOOK IN THE HEAT OF SUMMER, mark this page for when the weather turns cold. When you need to warm up after trekking through the snow or require a warming nightcap before bed on a winter's night, that's the time to pull out this old standby.

Recipes for the Hot Toddy are abundant and extremely variable, but they all follow the same formula: a spirit + something to sweeten it + hot water. Things diverge wildly from there, from austere early versions that call for nothing additional, save perhaps a strip of lemon peel, to contemporary recipes made with complex spice syrups. The two most important decisions are which spirit to use and whether to include citrus. Historical purists may insist that the use of lemon juice makes this a "hot punch" rather than a hot toddy, but we stand by the addition. In most bars today, ordering a Hot Toddy will get you a drink that looks something like this, while ordering a hot punch will get you only a look of confusion. This combination of ingredients works exceptionally well, which will come as no surprise if you enjoyed the Gold Rush (page 50) earlier in this chapter: This is essentially the same drink, served hot instead of cold.

INGREDIENTS

1½ oz [45 ml] bourbon

¾ oz [22.5 ml] Honey Syrup (page 33)

¼ oz [7.5 ml] fresh lemon juice

5 to 6 oz [150 to 180 ml] hot water, plus more for warming the mug

Cinnamon stick, for garnish

Lemon peel, for garnish

DIRECTIONS

In a kettle or small saucepan, heat water until just boiling. Add to a ceramic mug or tempered glass (see headnote) to warm the vessel, then discard. Add the bourbon, syrup, lemon juice, and hot water and stir gently to combine. If desired, grate a little cinnamon atop the drink (add the entire stick if you're feeling lavish), or simply garnish with a strip of lemon peel. Serve.

ONE IMPORTANT TIP

For this or any hot drink, heating the mug or glassware before adding the other ingredients is a vital step. Starting with a hot vessel keeps the drink warmer for longer.

GOLD RUSH

THE CLASSIC WHISKEY SOUR TEACHES THE BASICS OF HOW TO BALANCE A BASE SPIRIT WITH CITRUS AND SUGAR. In the next two cocktails, we look at how varying the citrus and sweetener takes the drink in different directions. In the Gold Rush, we substitute honey for sugar, bringing additional depth and complexity to the basic formula. A creation of bartender T. J. Siegal at Milk & Honey in New York City, it has earned a spot as a modern classic.

INGREDIENTS

2 oz [60 ml] bourbon

¾ oz [22.5 ml] fresh lemon juice

¾ oz [22.5 ml] Honey Syrup (page 33)

DIRECTIONS

To a shaker, add the bourbon, lemon juice, syrup, and ice. Shake, strain into a rocks glass filled with ice or a single large ice cube, and serve.

DE RIGUEUR

LIKE THE GOLD RUSH, THIS RIFF ON THE WHISKEY SOUR CALLS FOR HONEY IN PLACE OF SUGAR. It also switches out the citrus, swapping grapefruit for lemon. Because grapefruit juice is less acidic than lemon juice, we adjust the proportions to use a bit more juice and a bit less honey. (This same drink often goes by the name Brown Derby, along with a story tying it to vintage Hollywood bars. Alas, it's not clear that there's any truth to the tale. The De Rigueur name precedes it with a more verifiable origin.)

INGREDIENTS

2 oz [60 ml] bourbon

1 oz [30 ml] fresh grapefruit juice

½ oz [15 ml] Honey Syrup (page 33)

Grapefruit peel, for garnish

DIRECTIONS

To a shaker, add the bourbon, grapefruit juice, syrup, and ice. Shake and strain into a chilled coupe glass. Garnish with a grapefruit peel and serve.

KENTUCKY MULE

WALK INTO ANY BUSY COCKTAIL BAR TODAY, AND THERE'S A GOOD CHANCE SOMEONE WILL BE ORDERING A MOSCOW MULE. We'll cover that drink more in depth in the vodka chapter (see page 134), but we bring it up here because its popularity and versatility has spawned many variations using other spirits, including the bourbon-based Kentucky Mule. The Kentucky Mule simply calls for whiskey instead of vodka, making for a richer cocktail.

The most important ingredient here is the ginger beer, so be sure to choose one with plenty of kick. The squeeze of lime provides just a touch of acidity to balance the sweet and spice of the ginger beer. As with the Mint Julep (page 52), frequent mule makers may want to acquire specialized copper mugs for the drink and serve it over crushed ice. Neither is strictly necessary; the drink is equally tasty in a rocks or highball glass with ordinary ice cubes.

INGREDIENTS
Crushed ice (optional)

1½ oz [45 ml] bourbon

4 to 5 oz [120 to 150 ml] ginger beer

Lime wedge

DIRECTIONS
In a copper mug (or highball or rocks glass) filled with crushed ice or ice cubes, add the bourbon and ginger beer. Squeeze the lime wedge over the drink and drop it in. Stir gently to combine and serve.

EXPAT

BARTENDERS LAUREN SCHELL AND VITO DIETERLE CREATED THE EXPAT FOR LITTLE BRANCH IN NEW YORK CITY. It's another great example of how the deft use of bitters can transform a drink. The pronounced spice notes of Angostura and the unusual combination of bourbon and lime create a deliciously tropical spin on a whiskey cocktail.

INGREDIENTS
2 oz [60 ml] bourbon

1 oz [30 ml] fresh lime juice

½ oz [15 ml] Rich Simple Syrup (page 33)

2 dashes Angostura bitters

Mint leaf, for garnish

DIRECTIONS
To a shaker, add the bourbon, lime juice, syrup, bitters, and ice. Shake and strain into a chilled coupe glass. Garnish with a mint leaf and enjoy.

MINT JULEP

MODERN MINT JULEPS ARE INDELIBLY ASSOCIATED WITH THE KENTUCKY DERBY,
and for many of us that occasion may be the only day of the year we drink them. (Or if
we happen to be tending bar, it's the day we spend all morning picking thousands of mint
leaves in preparation for making them by the dozen.) By relegating this cocktail to a single
day's drinking, we deny ourselves the pleasure of a wonderful drink we could be enjoying
throughout the summer.

On paper, the Mint Julep is a simple three-ingredient cocktail of bourbon, mint, and sugar.
The transformative magic is created by the fourth ingredient: ice. Almost all the cocktails
in this book are stirred or shaken with ordinary ice cubes. Making a proper julep requires
smashing those cubes into crushed ice (see page 30 for the tools to do this). Your effort will
be rewarded with a wonderfully cooling summer beverage.

If you find yourself making juleps often, you may want to spring for julep cups made of copper, silver, or other metals, which frost up beautifully when filled with crushed ice. Don't let
the lack of these deter you from making the drink, however. An ordinary rocks glass works
just fine.

INGREDIENTS

Approximately 10 mint leaves

¼ oz [7.5 ml] Rich Demerara Syrup (page 33)

2 ½ oz [75 ml] bourbon

Crushed ice

Mint sprigs, for garnish

DIRECTIONS

*In the bottom of a julep cup or rocks glass,
gently muddle the mint leaves and syrup,
lightly pressing the leaves to extract their
flavor. Add the bourbon, rinsing the muddler
with it as you pour. Add crushed ice to nearly
fill the glass. Stir gently to combine, then top
off with more crushed ice. Garnish with a
substantial bouquet of mint and serve with a
straw.*

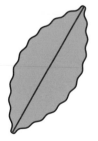

CHAPTER 2

GIN

GIN IS ONE OF THE MOST UBIQUITOUS SPIRITS IN THE CANON OF CLASSIC COCKTAILS, but it's not just for historical reasons that we call for it so early in the book. Gin is a supremely versatile ingredient, equally deft playing a supporting or leading role in cocktails and marrying marvelously with citrus. Despite this, we've noticed through interactions with guests at our bars that their opinions of gin are, pardon the pun, rather mixed. While the spirit certainly has its advocates, it seems that one bad experience with gin can turn people off for a lifetime. If that describes your own view, we urge you to join us in giving it a fresh look. Get to know gin and you'll see why the bottle deserves a prominent position in your home bar.

Gin is all about what distillers call "botanicals": the spices, herbs, roots, seeds, and other flavorful or aromatic ingredients that go into the recipe. That makes it different from whiskey, which derives its flavors from the grains used to ferment it and from the wood of the barrels in which it ages. Gin, in contrast, starts with alcohol that has been distilled to such a high degree of purity that it's essentially neutral in taste. This neutral spirit provides a clean slate on which distillers express the flavor of botanicals.

There's no limit to the botanicals that can be used in gin, but the one that *must* be used is juniper. In fact, the name *gin* derives from the Dutch word for juniper, *jenever*. Juniper berries are the main flavoring component of gin, offering a

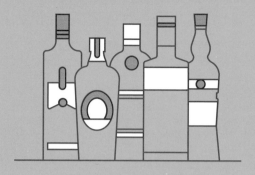

distinctly piney taste and aroma. The berries are actually seeds of a plant distantly related to pine trees. Grown in select regions throughout the northern hemisphere, each area of cultivation yields a seed with a distinct profile, and distillers are very particular about the source of their juniper.

While it's possible to make gin with only juniper, most brands include an array of other botanical elements. Coriander seeds, angelica, orris root, and lemon and orange peels are among the most common additions, and the selection and balancing of these other flavors is part of what gives each gin its unique character. Botanical blends range from the four ingredients in Tanqueray to the forty-seven in the aptly named Monkey 47 and can include unexpected additions such as galangal, seaweed, or even ants. Making gin is a bit like making perfume: Both rely on a delicate blending of potent ingredients that, when done well, results in something profound and unforgettable.

With so many gins on the market and an endless variety of botanicals to choose from, how do you choose a gin to begin with? Just as we recommended starting with a Kentucky bourbon before branching out into other whiskies, we suggest starting out with a London dry gin before expanding your bar with more unusual options. "London dry" doesn't have to be made in London—it can be made anywhere—but most of the classic brands do hail from England. These gins tend to be juniper-driven, bracingly crisp, and accented with a handful of other botanicals, which is just what you want for the drinks in this book.

That brings up one other thing worth noting about gin: Unlike many other spirits, it's rarely consumed neat. When we reach for a bottle of gin at home, it's almost always to make a cocktail, not to pour a dram. We encourage you to taste your gin neat to get to know it, but then move on to mixing. A classic way to ease into gin is with a simple gin and tonic: 1½ oz [45 ml] of gin, a squeeze of lime, and a pour of high-quality tonic water over ice. For more assertively gin-forward cocktails, read on.

GIN 101

THE CATEGORY OF GIN IS DIVERSE, AND RULES VARY COUNTRY BY COUNTRY, SO
IT'S EASIEST TO THINK ABOUT GIN IN TERMS OF A FEW DIFFERENT STYLES.
What they all have in common, of course, is flavoring with juniper.

A FEW STYLES TO KNOW

LONDON DRY

A classic style of gin for cocktails, boasting assertive juniper notes. As the name suggests, it is crisp and dry, but it doesn't necessarily have to be made in or anywhere near London.

CONTEMPORARY

As craft distilling and appreciation of gin has risen in recent years, the category has been diversified by brands introducing unusual botanicals to round out the traditional flavor profiles. "Contemporary" is not a defined style so much as it as a recognition of this innovation.

OLD TOM

A style of gin that is typically a little sweeter than London dry, often sweetened with a touch of sugar and sometimes aged in barrels.

GENEVER

An historic predecessor to gin that's really more of a distinct spirit of its own, genever is a Dutch and Belgian spirit that combines malty, grain-forward distillates with juniper and other botanicals.

BOTTLES WE REACH FOR

BEEFEATER

There's a lot to love about Beefeater. It has a higher proof and lower price than most gins of its quality, and it's hard to name a gin cocktail that it doesn't play well in. Both at work and at home, Beefeater is the gin we reach for most often.

PLYMOUTH

Gins from Plymouth, England, used to possess a protected geographic origin. That's no longer the case, but Plymouth is still an exemplar of what we look for in a gin. Hard to beat in a martini and a touch softer than a typical London dry, it's a mainstay in our home bars.

TANQUERAY

Intensely juniper-forward with the proof to stand up in cocktails, Tanqueray is justifiably a top-seller and a gin we particularly enjoy in citrusy drinks.

THE BOTANIST

Proving that Islay isn't just about scotch, The Botanist marries traditional gin botanicals with unique plants harvested around the island. It walks the line between classic London dry and unusual contemporary gin, earning a spot for its deliciousness and versatility.

FORDS

A relatively new player in the London dry category, Fords is distinguished by having the world's most bartender friendly bottle, which also happens to hold some seriously good gin. Its rich texture and balanced botanical profile are right at home in more classic cocktails.

GIMLET

NO ONE KNOWS PRECISELY WHEN THE GIMLET WAS INVENTED, BUT WE CAN MAKE A GOOD GUESS AS TO WHY IT WAS INVENTED. Credit goes to the master mixologists of the Royal British Navy for this one. The navy required sailors to consume a daily portion of citrus juice to prevent scurvy. Because the British had established trading routes with lime-producing regions and were often at war with countries that grew lemons, lime was the most common one on board (hence the slang term Limeys for the British) and it was often shipped in a preserved form. Sailors were also given a daily ration of alcohol: rum for the enlisted men, while higher-ranking officers received an allotment of gin. You can see where this is going. Preserved lime juice isn't very appealing on its own, so it wasn't long before it became standard practice to mix the gin and lime together. Thus, the Gimlet was born.

Back on land, we don't have to rely on preserved citrus cordials, and cocktail aficionados debate whether a genuine gimlet must be made with lime cordial or if fresh lime juice and simple syrup are equally true to the spirit of the drink. The former is immortalized in Raymond Chandler's *The Long Goodbye*, but the latter is what you'll be served in most cocktail bars today. Though it can be fun to make your own lime cordial, we recommend starting with a Gimlet made with fresh lime juice and simple syrup. While you're at it, you should also indulge in a luxury rarely afforded to nineteenth-century sailors: ice.

INGREDIENTS
2 oz [60 ml] gin
¾ oz [22.5 ml] fresh lime juice
½ oz [15 ml] Rich Simple Syrup (page 33)

DIRECTIONS
To a shaker, add the gin, lime juice, syrup, and ice. Shake, strain into a chilled coupe glass, and serve.

TOM COLLINS

THE TOM COLLINS IS A DRINK WITH A BIT OF A SILLY HISTORY. The very abridged version relates back to a drink known as a John Collins, which originated in England and was made with genever, the predecessor to modern gins. When the drink made its way to the United States, John became Tom and genever became gin. As explained by cocktail historian David Wondrich, one likely reason for this was a prank played in American bars that involved telling someone that a fellow named Tom Collins had been badmouthing him at a different drinking establishment, sending the person on a wild goose chase trying to find Mr. Collins. Silliness aside, the Tom Collins is an excellent drink for warm weather imbibing, and its influence is seen in the fact that the tall, narrow glasses used to serve it are called collins glasses to this day.

INGREDIENTS

1½ oz [45 ml] gin

¾ oz [22.5 ml] fresh lemon juice

½ oz [15 ml] Rich Simple Syrup (page 33)

4 to 5 oz [120 to 150 ml] soda water

Lemon peel, for garnish

THE SIMPLEST WAY TO MAKE THIS COCKTAIL

In a highball or collins glass, combine the gin, lemon juice, syrup, soda, and ice. Give it a brief stir, garnish with a lemon peel, and serve.

FOR A SLIGHTLY MORE INVOLVED PREPARATION

To a shaker, add the gin, lemon juice, syrup, and ice. Shake and strain into a highball or collins glass filled with ice. Top with the soda, stir gently to combine, garnish with a lemon peel, and serve.

VARIATIONS

The Tom Collins is perfectly delicious with dry gin, but if you happen to acquire a bottle of Old Tom–style gin, give that a try too. Collinses made with genever, bourbon, and rye all have their charms and are made the same way.

FRENCH 75

THE FRENCH 75 IS WHAT YOU GET WHEN YOU REPLACE THE SODA IN A TOM COLLINS WITH SPARKLING WINE. Aside from the source of the bubbles, the two recipes are essentially the same. Yet the French 75 is often served in a champagne flute, which is the way we were taught to make them in our early days of tending bar. We owe a debt of gratitude to our fellow Portland bartender Jeffrey Morgenthaler for pointing out that the drink is better served on the rocks, and that's how we make them now too.

INGREDIENTS

1½ oz [45 ml] gin

1 oz [30 ml] fresh lemon juice

½ oz [15 ml] Rich Simple Syrup (page 33)

2 to 3 oz [60 to 90 ml] sparkling wine

Lemon twist, for garnish

DIRECTIONS

To a shaker, add the gin, lemon juice, syrup, and ice. Strain into a rocks glass filled with ice, top with sparkling wine, and stir gently to combine. Garnish with a lemon twist and serve.

BENNETT

MUCH LIKE THE BUSTER BROWN IN THE PREVIOUS CHAPTER (PAGE 48), THE BENNETT SHOWCASES THE TRANSFORMATIVE POWER OF BITTERS. This is simply a Gimlet with a few dashes of bitters added, but oh, what a difference they make! The spice notes of Angostura play wonderfully with the botanicals of the gin and fresh lime juice.

INGREDIENTS

1½ oz [45 ml] gin

¾ oz [22.5 ml] fresh lime juice

½ oz [15 ml] Rich Simple Syrup (page 33)

2 dashes Angostura bitters

DIRECTIONS

To a shaker, add the gin, lime juice, syrup, bitters, and ice. Shake, strain into a chilled coupe glass, and serve.

GIN SOUR

THE GIN SOUR SITS TOO OFTEN IN THE SHADOW OF THE WHISKEY SOUR, which is a shame because the Gin Sour deserves a spotlight of its own. In a Whiskey Sour, the caramel and oak flavors contrast with the lemon, softening the citrus and leading to a rounder drink. It's a delicious cocktail, but one where the two main ingredients are in a sort of tug-of-war. In a Gin Sour, the bright botanicals of gin work alongside the lemon to produce a vibrantly cohesive cocktail. It's a fantastically refreshing drink that we highly recommend. Like a Whiskey Sour, a Gin Sour can be made with or without egg white. Both versions are great, but here we're a little more inclined to leave it out.

INGREDIENTS

2 oz [60 ml] gin

¾ oz [22.5 ml] fresh lemon juice

½ oz [15 ml] Rich Simple Syrup (page 33)

1 egg white (optional)

Lemon peel, for garnish

TO MAKE WITHOUT EGG WHITE

To a shaker, add the gin, lemon juice, syrup, and ice. Shake and strain into a chilled coupe glass. Garnish with a lemon peel and serve.

TO MAKE WITH EGG WHITE

To a shaker without ice, add the gin, lemon juice, syrup, and egg white. Dry shake for a few seconds to aerate the egg white. Add ice and shake again, then strain into a rocks glass filled with ice. Garnish with a lemon peel and serve.

SOUTHSIDE

THERE ARE TWO THINGS BARTENDERS AGREE ON ABOUT THE SOUTHSIDE. ONE IS THAT THE DRINK CONTAINS GIN, CITRUS, SUGAR, AND MINT. THE OTHER IS THAT IT'S DELICIOUS. The rest of the details are up for debate. Some recipes call for lemon, others for lime, still others for a mix of both. Some serve it straight up, others add a splash of soda, and some serve it tall like a minty collins. We like the specs below, but the other versions all have their merits. Experiment and find your bliss.

INGREDIENTS

2 oz [60 g] gin

¾ oz [22.5 ml] fresh lemon or lime juice

½ oz [15 ml] Rich Simple Syrup (page 33)

6 to 8 mint leaves

DIRECTIONS

To a shaker, add the gin, lemon or lime juice, syrup, mint leaves, and ice. Shake hard; you want to both chill the drink and extract flavor from the mint. Fine-strain into a chilled coupe glass, being sure to remove bits of mint leaf, and serve.

VARIATIONS

Some bartenders like to muddle the mint and syrup before adding the other ingredients and shaking, but we don't feel this step is necessary. To serve this as a tall drink, strain into an ice-filled glass, top with soda, and stir to combine. This cocktail also invites variation with other green herbs. Lime and basil make a refreshing combination, and dill and lemon work well too.

BEE'S KNEES

IF YOU ENJOYED THE GOLD RUSH FROM CHAPTER 1 (PAGE 50), YOU HAVE THE BEE'S KNEES TO THANK. The original honey sour, the Bee's Knees is a Prohibition-era drink invented to make do with the often less-than-delicious gins available at the time. Luckily for you, it tastes even better with modern, high-quality gins that don't come from a bathtub. The botanicals in gin and the floral flavors of honey work together so perfectly that it almost makes us want to utter the word *synergy*.

INGREDIENTS

2 oz [60 ml] gin

¾ oz [22.5 ml] fresh lemon juice

¾ oz [22.5 ml] Honey Syrup (page 33)

DIRECTIONS

To a shaker, add the gin, lemon juice, syrup, and ice. Shake, strain into a chilled coupe glass, and serve.

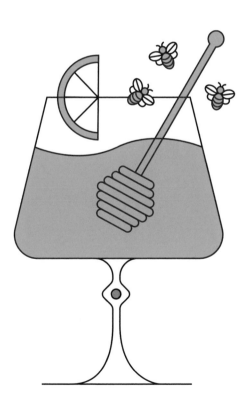

GIN RICKEY

ONE RULE OF MIXOLOGY IS THAT YOU NEED SWEETNESS TO BALANCE ACIDITY. The Rickey throws that rule out the window. Joe Rickey, a Democratic lobbyist who was imbibing his namesake beverage in Washington, DC, in the 1880s, believed that sugar warms the blood, and he intended this to be a cooling cocktail. Never mind the accuracy of the science: The drink works. The soda stretches the tartness of the lime, making it a pleasantly bright sipper in hot weather. Joe Rickey liked his cocktail made with whiskey, but the gin version is the one that came into popular favor. In 2011, the city council of Washington declared the Rickey the official drink of DC, which makes perfect sense if you've ever spent a sweltering summer in the capital.

INGREDIENTS

1½ oz [45 ml] gin

Juice of ½ lime, about ½ oz [15 ml]

Soda water, for topping

Squeezed lime shell, for garnish

DIRECTIONS

In a rocks glass filled with ice, pour the gin and lime juice. Top with the soda and gently stir to combine. Garnish with the squeezed shell of the lime and serve.

VARIATION

To make this Joe Rickey's way, simply replace the gin with bourbon.

ARMY AND NAVY

CONTINUING OUR THEME OF PLAYING WITH THE CITRUSY GIN COCKTAIL FORMAT, the Army and Navy brings in almondy orgeat as the sweetener in place of sugar or honey. This underrated vintage cocktail hails from David Embury's midcentury classic cocktail book *The Fine Art of Mixing Drinks* and is worthy of revival.

INGREDIENTS

1½ oz [45 ml] gin

¾ oz [22.5 ml] fresh lemon juice

½ oz [15 ml] orgeat

DIRECTIONS

To a shaker, add the gin, lemon juice, orgeat, and ice. Shake, strain into a chilled coupe glass, and serve.

SUFFERING BASTARD

THERE AREN'T MANY DRINKS THAT MIX GIN AND BOURBON IN THE SAME GLASS, and if you're thinking that some degree of desperation must have led to the creation of this cocktail, you wouldn't be far off the mark. The drink is credited to Joe Scialom of the Shepheard's Hotel in Cairo in 1947, intended as an improvised hangover cure. Beyond that the details get murky: Sometimes it's called the Suffering Bar Steward, sometimes it calls for brandy or rum, and sometimes it resembles a turbocharged mai tai. We enjoy this version, though we make no guarantee as to its curative properties.

INGREDIENTS

1 oz [30 ml] gin

1 oz [30 ml] bourbon

½ oz [15 ml] fresh lime juice

1 barspoon (⅙ oz [5 ml]) Rich Demerara Syrup (page 33)

3 dashes Angostura bitters

3 to 4 oz [90 to 120 ml] ginger beer

DIRECTIONS

To a shaker, add the gin, bourbon, lime juice, syrup, bitters, and ice. Shake, strain into a highball or rocks glass filled with ice, and top with the ginger beer. Give it a gentle stir to combine and serve. Alternately, if you're resorting to the Suffering Bastard as a hangover cure, feel free to make it the lazy way and just mix everything together in an ice-filled glass.

CHAPTER 3

VERMOUTH

SO FAR, WE'VE MADE COCKTAILS WITH A COUPLE BASIC SPIRITS AND STRAIGHT-FORWARD MODIFIERS. Citrus juices, syrups, and bitters are all bold ingredients that balance drinks by pushing or pulling in one direction: sour, sweet, or bitter, respectively. Vermouth is a subtle combination of all those things in one bottle. It's an ingredient that adds newfound depth and dimension to your cocktails, and it unlocks the Manhattan, the martini, and the entire world of amazing drinks that live in their shadow.

Before we start mixing those drinks, we should talk about what exactly vermouth is. Vermouth is a *fortified, aromatized wine*. Let's break down what each one of those words means. First, vermouth is made from wine (at least 75 percent wine, to be specific). Most often it's made from lighter white wine grapes such as ugni blanc or trebbiano. These varietals provide a pleasant acidity and a relatively blank slate upon which vermouth producers build more complex flavors. Muscat is another grape some producers use for a more flavorful foundation.

Since vermouth is mostly wine, what makes up the other portion? The answer is distilled spirits, which brings us to the word *fortified*. Producers raise the strength of vermouth by adding spirits to the wine. Sweet vermouths typically end up around 18 percent ABV, and dry vermouths a little higher.

This brings us to the final term, *aromatized*. Aromatizing wine is the process of infusing it with botanicals. That's right, botanicals aren't just for gin! They are infused into the wine via various techniques. Because higher alcohol concentrations extract flavors more quickly, many vermouth producers infuse their fortifying spirit with botanicals and then dose that spirit into the wine. A less common approach is to add the spirit to the wine first, then infuse the entire mixture with a botanical blend.

Once the infusion is complete, the vermouth will be sweetened, typically with sugar or caramel. The two main styles of vermouth, dry and sweet, are defined by how much sugar is added. Typically—but not always—sweet vermouths contain higher levels of both bitterness and sweetness, as well as bolder botanical blends. In contrast, dry vermouths tend to be a bit more restrained. Despite the difference in color, both are made from white wines, with sweet vermouth achieving its darker hue through the addition of caramel coloring.

While the United States does not mandate that vermouth be made with any specific botanical, traditional French and Italian vermouths feature wormwood, an extremely bitter root that has a very long history of (allegedly) medicinal uses. Much like gin, vermouth is also named after its primary botanical: *Wermut* is German for wormwood. Beyond wormwood, vermouth is infused with a wide array of bright, bitter, earthy, and sweet botanicals that each producer uses to make what they deem a delicious, balanced product, often in accordance with distinct regional traditions.

Though wormwood was infused into wine for thousands of years, it wasn't until the late eighteenth and early nineteenth centuries that vermouth was solidified as a distinct category and properly named. Antonio Benedetto Carpano released the first commercial vermouth in Torino, Italy, a city perfectly located to be the epicenter of commercial vermouth production thanks to Piedmontese wines and botanicals sourced from adjacent mountains or the port at Genoa. Torino was also relatively wealthy, and so the population had enough money to spend on non-essentials like bittersweet fortified wines.

The vermouth coming from Torino was of the sweeter variety, and it proved a natural match with spirits in cocktails such as the Manhattan and its many relatives. Lighter, drier styles emerged from southeastern France. Once this drier style made its way to cocktail bars, it was immediately embraced and had a substantial impact, forever changing the martini and leading to the creation of many new cocktails. Older cocktail manuals often refer to the styles as simply Italian or French, although today sweet and dry vermouths are made in both countries and in many others besides. (There is also a "blanc" or "bianco" style, which is essentially a sweeter white vermouth; while this is also excellent in cocktails, it's not an ingredient we call for in this book.)

Because the cocktail world is dependent on both dry and sweet vermouth, we are asking you to stock your bar with one bottle of each. Luckily fantastic examples of each style cost under or around twenty dollars. The category as a whole is wildly diverse, so remember that if you don't love a particular bottle, it doesn't mean you don't love any vermouth. There's a bottle out there for you, and we highly recommend you try as many as you can. Many vermouths are available in half-size (375 ml) bottles that are great for sampling, or you can get a few friends to each buy a different bottle and have a group tasting. You'll be amazed at the breadth of flavors available.

To get started, though, you can't go wrong with the sweet or dry offerings from the producers listed in the sidebar, and picking up a bottle of each will have you on your way to mixing the cocktails in this chapter and throughout the book. And a final but very important tip: refrigerate your vermouth after you open it! It's not as sensitive to air as the kind of wine you might drink with dinner, but it is still a wine. Many a cocktail has been ruined by use of an old, oxidized bottle of vermouth. Keeping it chilled will help preserve its freshness and ensure your cocktails taste they way they should.

VERMOUTH 101

VERMOUTH IS A FORTIFIED, AROMATIZED WINE. *Fortified* means that spirits have been added to the wine to raise its alcoholic strength. *Aromatized* means that botanicals have been used to contribute flavors. These botanicals can come from a variety of sources, but in the European Union, wormwood will always be among them. The two broad styles of vermouth we call for in this book are:

- **DRY VERMOUTH:** As the name suggests, these vermouths have a very low sugar content, and they will typically have a pale straw hue.
- **SWEET VERMOUTH:** This style contains more sugar, but this sweetness will usually be balanced by assertive botanicals for a bigger overall taste profile. These tend toward being deep red in color.

PERHAPS THE MOST IMPORTANT LESSON TO REMEMBER ABOUT VERMOUTH

HOW TO STORE IT: Once a bottle is opened, be sure to keep it refrigerated and use it within a few weeks for dry or a few months for sweet. The wine will oxidize and the flavor deaden over time. Off-peak vermouth won't hurt you, but it will hurt your drink!

DRY	BOTTLES WE REACH FOR	SWEET

DOLIN DRY

Chambery is a town in southeast France that is home to the country's only protected origin for vermouth. It's where Dolin dry is made, and Dolin has earned its role as a bartenders' favorite. It's bright and aromatic with the addition of alpine herbs, and it's superb in a martini or simply enjoyed fresh from the bottle.

NOILLY PRAT EXTRA DRY

With crisp acidity and minerality with a bit of a savory note, this is a go-to all-purpose dry vermouth for cocktails. Its clarity makes it ideal for cocktails, and it retains its character well too.

LO-FI DRY

Lo-Fi makes vermouths with a distinct anise note that adds an extra layer of richness and complexity to cocktails. A great contrast to bone-dry vermouths, Lo-Fi makes its presence known a bit more distinctly, but is still remarkably versatile.

LUSTAU ROJO

We've tried different vermouths, but Lustau stands out for its ability to provide a complex structure without hogging the spotlight. Perhaps the reason we like it so much is its use of sherry wines (see chapter 20) as a foundation. It's wonderfully versatile. Be it in a Manhattan, Negroni, or on the rocks with an olive, Lustau Rojo worked wonders.

COCCHI VERMOUTH DI TORINO

Cocchi Torino adds a distinctive cacao note to drinks, but does so with a deft hand. Its richness announces its presence, while leaving space for the other ingredients. We love it in bittersweet drinks like the Little Italy (page 211) or the Hanky Panky (page 284).

CARPANO ANTICA

Carpano Antica will change your perception of vermouth if you've sampled only bottom-shelf, oxidized bottles that have been open a few months too long. Fantastic on its own, it shines in cocktails that demand a vanilla-forward, heavy-bodied vermouth, but in lighter drinks it can seem like the loud talker in the library. Pour it when you want the word *velvet* to describe your cocktail.

MANHATTAN

The drinking world has evolved since the Manhattan's recipe was published in 1884, but it has managed to thrive through every cultural shift.

Early recipes for the Manhattan simply called for whiskey, the implication being American whiskey. The drink itself was more popular in the northern states where the go-to American whiskey was rye, and in recent years it's become associated more with rye than bourbon. We'll get to rye in a few chapters, but for now, we highly encourage you to make Manhattans with the bourbon you already have. Bourbon's higher corn content leads to a rounder Manhattan. If you find that your particular combination of bourbon and vermouth is a bit too sweet, you can always dial back the vermouth a bit or add an extra dash of bitters.

A successful Manhattan depends on maintaining tension between the whiskey and vermouth, and that unravels in the presence of too much water. With that in mind, we advise you to serve it up in a chilled glass rather than on the rocks.

INGREDIENTS

2 oz [60 ml] bourbon

1 oz [30 ml] sweet vermouth

2 dashes Angostura bitters

Cocktail cherry and/or orange twist, for garnish

DIRECTIONS

To a mixing glass, add the bourbon, vermouth, bitters, and ice. Stir and strain into a chilled coupe glass. Garnish with a cocktail cherry, orange twist, or both, and serve.

VARIATIONS

When you make a drink with an equal split between dry and sweet vermouth, it's referred to as "perfect." The most common perfect cocktail is the Perfect Manhattan. This switch leads to a dramatically different cocktail. Crisper than the standard Manhattan, the Perfect Manhattan is wonderful as an aperitif or as a summertime drink. Make it as above, splitting the vermouth portion equally between sweet and dry. Try revisiting the Manhattan once we get to the rye chapter (page 154)—swapping rye for bourbon for a spicier flavor profile.

LOS ANGELES

THE LOS ANGELES COCKTAIL ORIGINALLY APPEARED IN *THE SAVOY COCKTAIL BOOK*, published in 1930, so you can forgive the author for giving it a name that is all but impossible to Google. Perhaps that's why it's still obscure today; you'll most likely get perplexed looks from bartenders if you try ordering this by name. The good news is you're the bartender now.

The Los Angeles is a Whiskey Sour with sweet vermouth; the added herbal and bitter notes make this cocktail named for a warm city ironically well-suited for colder nights. We think this drink works particularly well with extra bitter vermouths like Punt e Mes. If your sweet vermouth is on the richer end of the spectrum, you may want to use a touch less sugar.

INGREDIENTS

2 oz [50 ml] bourbon

¾ oz [22.5 ml] fresh lemon juice

½ oz [15 ml] Rich Demerara Syrup (page 33)

¼ oz [7.5 ml] sweet vermouth

1 egg white

Orange peel, for garnish

DIRECTIONS

To a shaker without ice, add the bourbon, lemon juice, syrup, vermouth, and egg white. Dry shake for a few seconds to aerate the egg white. Add ice and shake again, then strain into a chilled coupe glass. Garnish with an orange peel and serve.

GIN AND IT

AS THE MARTINI DRIED OUT OVER THE YEARS, THE GIN AND IT KEPT IT REAL. The name is descriptive, the *It* reflecting some pre-Prohibition imbibers' overzealous abbreviation of "Italian" vermouth. Don't be misled by the drink's disarming simplicity; it was a favorite of bar legend Sasha Petraske of New York's Milk & Honey, which is all the endorsement we need to take it seriously. The next time you find yourself torn between a Manhattan and a martini, split the difference with a Gin and It. It's a joy to drink.

INGREDIENTS

2 oz [60 ml] gin

1 oz [30 ml] sweet vermouth

Lemon twist, for garnish

DIRECTIONS

To a mixing glass, add the gin, vermouth, and ice. Stir and strain into a chilled coupe glass. Garnish with a lemon twist and serve.

MARTINI

THE MARTINI SOMEHOW MANAGES THE TRICK OF BEING POSSIBLY THE WORLD'S MOST ICONIC COCKTAIL AND YET POSSESSING NO SINGLE STANDARD RECIPE. Ask ten people what their favorite Martini is, and you'll likely get ten different answers ranging from gin with dry vermouth, just ice-cold vodka, or even a chocolate martini. How in the world can these all describe one drink?

It helps to go back to earliest Martini recipes from the late 1800s, which were in essence gin-based riffs on the Manhattan format, enriched with sweet vermouth and orange liqueur. As the Martini evolved, it stepped out of the Manhattan's shadow to become a great cocktail in its own right. It did this by drying out. Old Tom gin was switched for London dry, sweet vermouth was replaced by dry vermouth, and the liqueur disappeared altogether.

The Martini continued to change in the middle of the century. Trends started to favor increasingly dry martinis made with less and less vermouth. As decades passed, vodka often replaced gin, and the vermouth sometimes disappeared entirely. By the dark ages of the 1990s, the martini had spawned countless 'tinis of various sorts, generally very sweet drinks whose only link to their classic namesake was the V-shaped glass they were served in.

Given that the Martini has worn so many guises throughout its history, it makes sense that it means different things to different people today. It also means that despite what we fancy bartender types may insist, there is no one "right" Martini. That said, we definitely do have a preferred recipe. We argue for a Martini made with gin and dry vermouth; two-to-one is a good starting point, and you can adjust from there. Orange bitters are desirable, though optional. The garnish is up to you. The preparation? Always stirred, never shaken.

INGREDIENTS

2 oz [60 ml] gin

1 oz [30 ml] dry vermouth

1 dash orange bitters (optional)

Lemon peel or olive, for garnish

DIRECTIONS

To a mixing glass, add the gin, vermouth, bitters, and ice. Stir and strain into a chilled coupe glass (or a V-shaped martini glass, if you happen to have one). Garnish with a lemon peel or olive and serve.

VARIATION

Olives or lemon peels are the most common garnishes for the martini, though you might also enjoy a Gibson, which is simply a Martini garnished with a cocktail onion instead.

DUPLEX

THE DUPLEX IS A FORGOTTEN, CHARMING LOW-ABV SIPPER FROM THE 1935 OLD
WALDORF-ASTORIA BAR BOOK. A simple combo of sweet and dry vermouth with a few
dashes of bitters, it's perfect for when you want another Manhattan but don't want the
hangover that would come with it. You know those parachutes that shoot out the back of
drag racers to slow them down? Consider the Duplex your late-night parachute.

INGREDIENTS
1½ oz [45 ml] sweet vermouth
1½ oz [45 ml] dry vermouth
2 dashes orange bitters
Orange peel, for garnish

DIRECTIONS
*To a mixing glass, add the sweet and dry
vermouths, bitters, and ice. Stir and strain into
a chilled coupe glass. Garnish with an orange
peel and serve.*

VERMOUTH PANACHÉ

THOUGH SIMILAR TO THE DUPLEX, THE VERMOUTH PANACHÉ IS NOTEWORTHY FOR
BEING A RARE COCKTAIL POPULARIZED BY ERNEST HEMINGWAY THAT DOESN'T CON-
TAIN A MASSIVE AMOUNT OF ALCOHOL. When a few too many stiff drinks leave you
writing only the simplest of sentences, take a cue from Hemingway himself and make a
Vermouth Panaché, sit back, relax, and contemplate the uselessness of the semicolon.

INGREDIENTS
2 oz [60 ml] dry vermouth
1 oz [30 ml] sweet vermouth
1 dash Angostura bitters
Lemon peel, for garnish

DIRECTIONS
*In a rocks glass filled with ice, pour the dry and
sweet vermouths and bitters. Give it a few stirs,
garnish with a lemon peel, and serve.*

DRY VERMOUTH SOUR

WHILE WE'RE SURE THAT THIS DRINK HAS EXISTED AT SOME POINT IN THE HISTORY OF COCKTAILS, WE COULDN'T FIND A SPECIFIC REFERENCE TO IT. Rather than give it a silly or creative name, we figured we should give it to you straight. This is a sour made with dry vermouth and you should absolutely add it to your repertoire. Low on alcohol but high on refreshment, this is the perfect drink for a hot afternoon.

INGREDIENTS

2 oz [60 ml] dry vermouth

¾ oz [22.5 ml] fresh lemon juice

½ oz [15 ml] Rich Simple Syrup (page 33)

1 egg white

DIRECTIONS

To a shaker without ice, add the vermouth, lemon juice, syrup, and egg white. Dry shake for a few seconds to aerate the egg white. Add ice and shake again. Strain into a chilled coupe glass and serve.

CHAPTER 4

ORANGE LIQUEUR

ORANGE LIQUEUR, REALLY? BEFORE BASIC SPIRITS LIKE TEQUILA OR COGNAC? WELL, YES, AND THERE'S A GOOD REASON FOR THAT. While foundational spirits are important, they don't often mix together very well. There aren't many cocktails that combine gin and cognac or bourbon and tequila. Orange liqueur mixes with just about everything, appearing in some of the world's most famous cocktails. You could buy a bottle of tequila, but you'll need orange liqueur before you can make a margarita. You could buy a bottle of cognac, but you'll need orange liqueur to make a sidecar. Orange liqueur is easy to overlook, but it's one of the workhorses of a thoughtfully stocked bar.

Making cocktails with orange liqueur also adds a new technique to your mixology arsenal. The first two chapters focused on balancing base spirits with bitters, sugar, and citrus. The third chapter introduced the subtle interplay of vermouth. In this chapter we explore how to balance a cocktail with liqueur. A liqueur is simply a flavorful spirit that has been sweetened. Using liqueurs in cocktails is a way of adding complexity and combining sweetness, flavor, and potency in one ingredient. It's an approach we'll be coming back to again and again throughout the book, and by the end of this chapter you'll have mastered most of the fundamental techniques of making cocktails.

The case for stocking orange liqueur in your bar is straightforward, but choosing which orange liqueur to buy is a little more complicated. It helps to start with some history. The origins of the spirit go back to the introduction of Seville orange trees to the Caribbean island Curaçao in the sixteenth century. The oranges grew poorly there, but they evolved into a citrus fruit now known as *laraha*. These are bitter oranges with scant flesh that's no good for eating, but they have wonderfully aromatic peels. Dutch traders brought the dried peels back to Holland and began using them to flavor spirits. These became popular in Europe first under the name *curaçao*, then in the 1800s under the French name *triple sec*. (*Sec* means dry, but the relevance of the word *triple* in this context is a matter of speculation. Despite the name, triple sec is indeed sweet!)

Orange liqueurs are made in a variety of ways, but they all combine the flavor and aroma of orange peels with an alcohol base and some kind of sugar. The selection of oranges, alcohol, and sweetener all affect the final taste, as does the addition of other botanicals that may be used to accent the liqueur. At the risk of oversimplifying, the main factor to consider is whether the liqueur is made with a neutral spirit or with something that contributes a character of its own. A neutral spirit base allows the essence of the orange peel to stand out cleanly. A more flavorful base, such as brandy or cognac, will have more richness and complexity. In modern usage of the terms, triple sec tends to be clean and clear, while liqueurs using a richer spirit base may use the description *curaçao* or simply a brand name, such as Grand Marnier.

Neither style is inherently better than the other. The difference is analogous to that between a syrup made with white sugar and a syrup made with demerara; the former allows the other ingredients in a cocktail to shine through, while the latter adds weight and depth of its own. For both styles, it's worth spending a little extra for a premium bottle; the cheapest options tend to taste cloying, artificial, and one-note.

So, which to get for your home bar? In the recipes that follow, we call for "orange liqueur" and leave the decision up to you. We suggest starting with a high-quality triple sec, which will play wonderfully in the citrusy cocktails that we expect you'll be making most often, and all of our recipes are designed with that style of liqueurs in mind. If you'd like to also branch out into other styles, we'll mention in the cocktail notes when a drink might benefit from a richer orange liqueur, should you happen to have one on hand.

ORANGE LIQUEUR 101

AT THE MOST BASIC LEVEL, ORANGE LIQUEUR IS PRETTY EASY TO UNDERSTAND. It's a liqueur, meaning it's sweet, and it tastes like oranges. Of course, it does get more complicated; variables, including the types of oranges, base spirits, and accenting botanicals used, all affect the quality of what's in the bottle. Liqueurs made with neutral spirits allow the flavor and aroma of orange peel to shine brightly; those blended with spirits such as brandy, cognac, or rum will offer a more multilayered profile. Terms you'll often see on labels are "triple sec" and "orange curaçao," but since neither is rigidly defined, we opt for the directly descriptive "orange liqueur" for recipes in this book and leave the selection up to you.

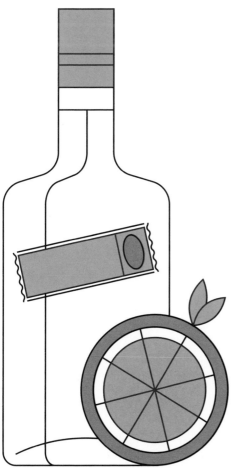

BOTTLES WE REACH FOR

COINTREAU
This is one of the most popular and well-known orange liqueurs, and for good reason. Cointreau is superbly balanced with a candied orange peel flavor and a subtly floral finish.

COMBIER LIQUEUR D'ORANGE
Redolent with bright orange peel aroma, clean flavor, and a sweetness balanced by a sharp edge, Combier makes a very versatile triple sec.

PIERRE FERRAND DRY CURAÇAO
If you'd like to try an orange liqueur with a more complex base, Ferrand Dry Curaçao is a great place to start. Blended with brandy and cognac, it layers oak and vanilla alongside orange peel and spices.

PEGU CLUB

WITH FIVE INGREDIENTS—GIN, ORANGE LIQUEUR, LIME JUICE, AND TWO DIFFERENT KINDS OF BITTERS—the Pegu Club may at first glance seem like a complicated recipe. But if you've followed along with drinks like the Gold Rush (page 50), the Gimlet (page 56), or the Bennett (page 58), the basic structure should be familiar. This is yet another variation on the sour, but with the balancing sweetness now provided by orange liqueur rather than a syrup. We'll use liqueurs this way throughout the book, and orange liqueur in particular shows up in myriad cocktails of the sour style.

This cocktail was the namesake drink of the actual Pegu Club, a gathering spot for colonial-era Brits in present day Yangon, Myanmar. By 1927, the formula had achieved sufficient popularity to appear in Harry MacElhone's *Barflies and Cocktails*, where he wrote that the Pegu Club "has travelled, and is asked for, around the world." It's come back into vogue in recent years, even lending its name to the Pegu Club in New York City, one of the pioneering bars of the contemporary cocktail renaissance. Give it a try and we're confident you'll see the appeal. It's bracingly tart and one of our favorite warm-weather cocktails.

INGREDIENTS

1¾ oz [52.5 ml] gin

¾ oz [22.5 ml] orange liqueur

½ oz [15 ml] fresh lime juice

1 dash Angostura bitters

1 dash orange bitters

DIRECTIONS

To a shaker, add the gin, orange liqueur, lime juice, both bitters, and ice. Shake, strain into a chilled coupe glass, and serve.

FANCY COCKTAIL

IF YOU WALK INTO A BAR TODAY AND ASK FOR A "FANCY COCKTAIL," THE BARTENDER WILL MOST LIKELY ASK YOU TO BE A LITTLE MORE SPECIFIC ABOUT WHAT YOU HAVE IN MIND. In the nineteenth century, however, the Fancy Cocktail had at least a loosely defined meaning. It was a cocktail—meaning a spirit, sugar, and bitters—made a bit fancier. The boundary between a cocktail and a Fancy Cocktail is admittedly a little vague, but one way of making it fancy was to add a touch of orange liqueur. It's a subtle distinction, but it does make a difference. (If you happen to have a richer variety of orange liqueur, this is a good cocktail in which to use it.)

INGREDIENTS

1½ oz [45 ml] bourbon

¼ oz [7.5 ml] orange liqueur

Scant barspoon (⅙ oz [5 ml]) Rich Demerara Syrup (page 33)

2 dashes Angostura bitters

Lemon peel, for garnish

DIRECTIONS

To a mixing glass, add the bourbon, orange liqueur, syrup, bitters, and ice. Stir and strain into a rocks glass filled with ice or a single large cube. Garnish with a lemon peel and serve.

VARIATIONS

We've described this as a whiskey cocktail, but you can of course use other spirits as you build up your home bar. Cognac is a prime candidate for fancifyin'.

WHISKEY DAISY

THE POPULARITY OF THE DAISY IN THE LATE 1800S AND EARLY 1900S IS EVIDENT FROM ITS MANY APPEARANCES IN COCKTAIL BOOKS OF THE TIME. Precisely what went into the Daisy, however, is a little harder to pin down. Sources converge on the cocktail following the basic formula of a sour topped with at least a splash of soda. Beyond that, things get blurry, as mixological history tends to do. Which spirit to use, whether to sweeten it with simple syrup or something a little more complex, how much soda to lengthen it with, and how to serve it all vary considerably. Here we include a bit of a throwback version, before the drink went in more elaborate directions.

INGREDIENTS

Crushed ice

2 oz [60 ml] bourbon

¾ oz [22.5 ml] fresh lemon juice

¼ oz [7.5 ml] orange liqueur

1 barspoon (⅙ oz [5 ml]) Rich Simple Syrup (page 33)

Approximately 1 oz [30 oz] soda water

DIRECTIONS

Fill a large coupe glass or a rocks glass with crushed ice. To a shaker, add the bourbon, lemon juice, orange liqueur, syrup, and ice cubes. Shake and strain over the crushed ice. Top with a splash of soda and serve.

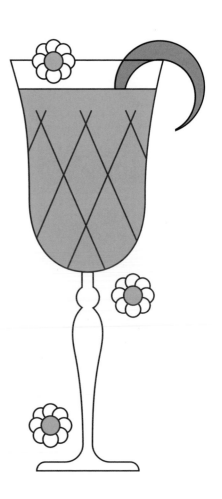

WHITE LADY

BY NOW YOU'RE FAMILIAR WITH THE BASIC ROUTINE OF MAKING COCKTAILS WITH EGG WHITES: Do a "dry shake" to aerate the foam, then shake again with ice to chill and dilute the drink. If you try that with this cocktail, however, you may run into a problem. The White Lady is sweetened less by sugar than it is by orange liqueur. That raises the alcohol content, especially if you're using a quality liqueur. That higher proof runs the risk of breaking down the egg, resulting in a gloopy texture instead of the light, airy foam that makes egg white cocktails so appealing. Fear not, we have solutions! In fact, we offer two of them—an easy way and a hard way. In both cases we advise adding the egg white last, immediately followed by the ice.

INGREDIENTS

1½ oz [45 ml] gin

¾ oz [22.5 ml] orange liqueur

¾ oz [22.5 ml] fresh lemon juice

1 barspoon (⅙ oz [5 ml]) Rich Simple Syrup (page 33)

1 egg white

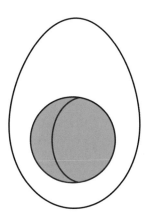

THE EASY WAY

To a shaker, add the gin, orange liqueur, lemon juice, syrup, egg white, and ice. Start shaking the cocktail right away, but shake it extra vigorously. You'll still get an acceptable level of foam, even without the dry shake. Strain into a chilled coupe glass and serve. (If you really want to build up the foam, you can strain the cocktail, discard the ice, and shake it a second time to aerate further. Bartenders call this the "reverse shake.")

THE HARD WAY

To a shaker, add the gin, orange liqueur, lemon juice, syrup, egg white, and just a few ice cubes. Shake the drink for a long time. By that we mean literally shake it until the ice has completely melted into the drink and you can no longer hear it clanking around in the shaker. This will give you great foam, and it will also give your arms a workout. When finished, pour directly into a chilled coupe glass and serve.

DRY ORANGE MARTINI

MANY COCKTAIL NAMES ARE EVOCATIVE, BUT THE DRY ORANGE MARTINI IS JUST PURE TRUTH IN ADVERTISING: It's a martini, it's dry, and it's accented with hints of orange from both bitters and liqueur. Created by influential English barman Wayne Collins, it's nuanced, spirit forward, and appealingly crisp.

INGREDIENTS

2 oz [60 ml] gin

¾ oz [22.5 ml] dry vermouth

¼ oz [7.5 ml] orange liqueur

2 dashes orange bitters

Grapefruit peel, for garnish

DIRECTIONS

To a mixing glass, add the gin, vermouth, orange liqueur, bitters, and ice. Stir and strain into a chilled coupe glass. Garnish with a grapefruit peel and serve.

MAN O' WAR

MAN O' WAR WAS ONE OF THE MOST STORIED THOROUGHBREDS IN RACING HISTORY, winning twenty of his twenty-one horse races before retiring to stud. The cocktail that bears his name is a more modest achievement but nonetheless worthy of your attention.

INGREDIENTS

2 oz [60 ml] bourbon

¾ oz [22.5 ml] orange liqueur

½ oz [15 ml] sweet vermouth

½ oz [15 ml] fresh lemon juice

Lemon peel, for garnish

DIRECTIONS

To a shaker, add the bourbon, orange liqueur, vermouth, lemon juice, and ice. Shake and strain into a chilled coupe glass. Garnish with a lemon peel and serve.

FINE AND DANDY

THIS IS A RATHER SIMPLE COCKTAIL ADAPTED FROM *THE SAVOY COCKTAIL BOOK*, **BUT DON'T OVERLOOK IT.** It's a nice recipe to keep in mind for when you just want to shake up a simple gin sour without too much fuss. Fine and Dandy, indeed.

INGREDIENTS

1½ oz [45 ml] gin

¾ oz [22.5 ml] orange liqueur

¾ oz [22.5 ml] fresh lemon juice

1 barspoon (⅙ oz [5 ml]) Rich Simple Syrup (page 33)

2 dashes Angostura bitters

DIRECTIONS

To a shaker, add the gin, orange liqueur, lemon juice, syrup, bitters, and ice. Shake, strain into a chilled coupe glass, and serve.

MAIDEN'S PRAYER

ORANGE JUICE DOESN'T GET AS MUCH IN PLAY IN COCKTAILS AS LEMON AND LIME, MOSTLY BECAUSE IT DOESN'T HAVE QUITE AS MUCH ZING AS THOSE MORE ACIDIC FRUIT JUICES. One way to make it work is to use it in conjunction with other citrus instead of expecting the orange to carry the drink on its own. In the Maiden's Prayer, the sweet orange juice nicely rounds out the sharp notes of gin while the splash of lemon provides just enough tartness to keep things interesting.

INGREDIENTS

1½ oz [45 ml] gin

¾ oz [22.5 ml] orange liqueur

1 oz [30 ml] fresh orange juice

½ oz [15 ml] fresh lemon juice

DIRECTIONS

To a shaker, add the gin, orange liqueur, orange and lemon juices, and ice. Shake, strain into a chilled coupe glass, and serve.

JOURNALIST

THIS COCKTAIL BRINGS TOGETHER A CLASSIC PAIRING: JOURNALISTS AND DRINKING.
From *The Savoy Cocktail Book*, it's a stirred cocktail made with citrus juice, which makes it
a bit unorthodox by modern standards. We give you two options for addressing this. One
is to embrace the anachronism, making it as originally intended. The other is to omit the
juice, placing a strip of lemon peel directly in the mixing glass to extract its essence as you
stir. The former method makes a light drink with a little acidity. The latter is more spirit
forward with only a hint of lemon. Both are eminently enjoyable.

INGREDIENTS

1½ oz [45 ml] gin

½ oz [15 ml] sweet vermouth

½ oz [15 ml] dry vermouth

¼ oz [7.5 ml] orange liqueur

¼ oz [7.5 ml] fresh lemon juice, or 1 strip lemon peel

1 dash Angostura bitters

Lemon peel, for garnish

DIRECTIONS

*To a mixing glass, add the gin, sweet and dry
vermouths, orange liqueur, lemon juice or peel,
bitters, and ice. Stir and strain into a chilled
coupe glass. Garnish with a lemon peel and
serve.*

DERBY

**MANY COCKTAILS HAVE WORN THE NAME *DERBY* OVER THE YEARS; THIS ONE COMES
FROM *TRADER VIC'S BARTENDER'S GUIDE*.** It's an unexpectedly excellent marriage of
bourbon, vermouth, citrus, and orange liqueur, with just a slight nod to the tropical liba-
tions Trader Vic was known for with the uncommon marriage of lime and whiskey.

INGREDIENTS

2 oz [60 ml] bourbon

¾ oz [22.5 ml] fresh lime juice

½ oz [15 ml] sweet vermouth

½ oz [15 ml] orange liqueur

Mint leaf, for garnish

DIRECTIONS

*To a shaker, add the bourbon, lime juice,
vermouth, orange liqueur, and ice. Shake and
strain into a chilled coupe glass. Garnish with
a mint leaf and serve.*

CHAPTER 5

TEQUILA

AS MUCH AS WE BELIEVE THAT ORANGE LIQUEUR IS AN IMPORTANT PART OF YOUR HOME BAR FOR A WIDE VARIETY OF REASONS, we'd be lying if we said we didn't include it so early on in part so that you'd be able to make one specific cocktail in the chapter that followed. That chapter is this one. And that cocktail is the margarita. That's right—after four grueling chapters of making drinks that are not margaritas, it's finally time to buy a bottle of tequila, crank up some Jimmy Buffet, and relax in the knowledge that your home bar is now well within the city limits of Margaritaville.

As exciting as that is, it's worth pausing for a moment to observe just how much the margarita dominates the way people think about tequila cocktails. Though it's a wonderful drink, viewing tequila solely through the lens of the margarita is far too limiting.

The problem is compounded by the fact that tequila was essentially absent from the early decades of publishing cocktail recipes. Our goal in this chapter is to showcase tequila in a wide variety of recipes, so that next time it occurs to you that it is indeed five o'clock somewhere, you have myriad options to choose from. Including, of course, a damn good margarita.

Tequila is an offshoot of a Mexican spirit historically known as vino de mezcal. The word *mezcal* is a combination of two indigenous words loosely meaning cooked agave, and *vino* was the Spanish term for pretty much anything with booze in it. Thus, *vino de mezcal* referred to any distilled, cooked agave product. Due to a combination of economic, cultural, and geographic forces, in the mid-eighteenth century vino de mezcal produced in and around the town of Tequila, Jalisco, started becoming more widely known. Its prominence increased when, in 1795, the king of Spain granted the Cuervo family a permit to distill, creating the first commercially produced "mezcal de Tequila," as it was known at the time. Commercialization led to investment, industrialization, and increased yields, setting up mezcal de Tequila to become the dominant player in the category.

As the spirit's popularity grew, it soon became known simply as tequila. In 1974 the Mexican government established an official "Denomination of Origin" (D.O.), which protected tequila's name and defined regulations for its production. The most significant of those rules was that, of the dozens of agave varietals that are distilled within Mexico, tequila can be made from only one, tequilana Weber, blue variety, more commonly known as blue agave. The regulations also established the state of Jalisco as the epicenter of tequila production, but it can also be produced in municipalities in Guanajuato, Michoacán, Nayarit, and Tamaulipas.

The process of turning blue agave into tequila starts in the field. The agaves take five to ten years to reach maturity, at which point the plant is harvested by hand: its long, sharp leaves are cut off with a sharp tool called a *coa*, revealing the core (or piña), the dense, 22 to 200 lb [10 to 90 kg] heart of the plant that is severed from its roots and transported to the distillery. There, the agaves are split in half and roasted, either in traditional brick steam ovens or a device called an autoclave, essentially a giant pressure cooker the size of a semi-truck trailer. Oven roasting typically takes two to three days, while the autoclave can do it in as few as twelve hours. Cooking is important because raw agave contains complex starches that are broken down into simpler, fermentable sugars when heated, similar to how an onion becomes sweeter when you cook it. After roasting, the agave is crushed or shredded to extract sugars from the fibrous core. Crushing is done by a large volcanic rock called a tahona, whereas shredding happens on a machine called a roller mill that chops the agave while rinsing the sugar from the fiber with water.

Once the sugars are extracted from the cooked agaves, production resembles the process of making other spirits. The extracted sugar is pumped to fermentation tanks where it will ferment for one to seven days, becoming alcohol. Then the juice (called *mosto*) is distilled twice in column or pot stills. It is then cut to proof (typically 40 percent ABV in the United States) and either bottled or put into barrels for aging.

TEQUILA 101

AN HISTORICAL OFFSHOOT OF MEZCAL (SEE PAGE 262), TEQUILA IS MADE FROM ONLY ONE TYPE OF AGAVE: TEQUILANA WEBER, ALSO KNOWN AS BLUE AGAVE. Some tequilas, known as mixto, are made from a mix of agave and other sugars—but with rare exceptions, we generally avoid them. Like all spirits, tequila is clear when it comes off the still. After distillation, tequila may be bottled right away or aged in metal or oak barrels (most often ex-bourbon barrels).

THE MOST COMMON CLASSIFICATIONS OF TEQUILA

BLANCO

Blanco is typically clear, and is either bottled directly after distillation or after a very brief period (fewer than 60 days) of resting in stainless steel or neutral oak barrels.

REPOSADO

Aged in oak barrels for at least 60 days.

AÑEJO

Aged in oak barrels for at least one year.

EXTRA AÑEJO

Aged in oak barrels for at least three years.

TWO OTHER CLASSIFICATIONS

You may come across are joven and cristalino. Joven tequilas may be blends of unaged and aged tequilas, or may simply be unaged tequila with additives to simulate aging. Cristilano tequila is tequila that has been aged and then filtered or redistilled to remove the color imparted by barrels; this process also strips out some of the character.

SINCE WE LOVE FULL FLAVOR OF PURE AGAVE, WE GENERALLY RECOMMEND STOCKING YOUR BAR WITH A HIGH-QUALITY 100% AGAVE BLANCO TEQUILA. You may also want to seek out brands that are free of additives such as caramel coloring, glycerin, oak extract, and sweeteners; these additives won't necessarily be mentioned on the label, but you can find a listing of additive-free brands on the website Tequila Matchmaker. Or, of course, see the bottles we reach for below.

BOTTLES WE REACH FOR

EL TESORO/TAPATIO

El Tesoro is remarkable in its commitment to cutting no corners in production. Agaves are roasted in traditional brick ovens, crushed with a volcanic rock tahona, fermented with the fibers, and distilled in copper pot stills. It's a lot of work, but the end result is worth it. Also keep an eye out for Tapatio, made at the same distillery.

CIMARRON/DON FULANO

Cimarron has an earthy, vegetal character that is a great example of tequila made from agave harvested in the valley of Jalisco. If you can find Don Fulano (the higher-end expression made at the same distillery) in your market, we highly recommend you make it part of your home collection.

G4

Produced at the incredible El Pandillo distillery, G4 is made with a combination of spring and rain water and exhibits incredible minerality and depth. It will add a bright, peppery complexity to cocktails and is absolutely wonderful to sip on neat.

EL TEQUILEÑO

Family owned and responsibly run, El Tequileño tequilas are extremely deserving of a spot in your bar. Their 100% agave release is about as good as blanco tequila gets. They also make a surprisingly good mixto. It uses a high proportion of agave, is additive-free, and is genuinely good. Making great tasting, inexpensive tequila while harvesting less agave is a goal we can get behind.

PUEBLO VIEJO

A mainstay in the well of basically every bar we've worked in, Pueblo Viejo is just about the best deal in tequila: rich, fruity agave flavor at a price that is shockingly affordable. If you feel like treating yourself, we highly recommend their high-end expression, San Matias Tahona.

MARGARITA

THERE ARE COMPETING ORIGIN STORIES SURROUNDING THE INVENTION OF THE MAR-GARITA, but none is as compelling to us as the simple fact that the drink is essentially a Daisy (page 78) made with tequila—and, would you look at that, the word for daisy in Spanish is . . . *margarita*. Coincidence? Possibly, but it's certainly suggestive. The Tequila Daisy was a known drink by the 1930s, perhaps the product of American bartenders and tourists making their way to Mexico during Prohibition and inevitably leading someone to adapt the Daisy to the local spirit. The drink appeared under the name *margarita* in a 1953 issue of *Esquire* magazine. It took about a decade more for the United States to thoroughly catch on, but once people got their first taste of the margarita, they never let go.

Like every classic cocktail, the Margarita, and in turn the Margarita drinker, has suffered the abuse of low-quality ingredients being used to make it. The offenders in question here are bad tequila and so-called margarita mix. We've hopefully convinced you already to avoid bad tequila. As for margarita mix, don't go anywhere near it. By making it this far in the book, you've already proven adept at juicing a lime and pouring a measure of orange liqueur. Since the mix is simply a poor imitation of those two things, you can, thankfully, abstain from its horrid sweetness and enamel-stripping acidity. You deserve a real Margarita made with fresh lime juice and good orange liqueur.

INGREDIENTS

1 lime

Kosher salt, for garnish

2 oz [60 ml] tequila

¾ oz [22.5 ml] orange liqueur

¾ oz [22.5 ml] fresh lime juice

DIRECTIONS

Using the cut side of a lime, wet half the exterior edge of a rocks glass or chilled coupe glass and then dip it into a shallow dish filled with salt so that the salt sticks to the rim. To a shaker, add the tequila, orange liqueur, lime juice, and ice. Shake and strain into the prepared glass.

VARIATIONS

Our recipe here fits the classic format, but it's not uncommon to see margaritas rounded out with a little extra sweetness. If you'd like yours a little less tart, consider adding a barspoon of Rich Simple Syrup (page 33) or agave nectar. The margarita can be served up or on the rocks, depending on your preference.

PALOMA

SQUIRT SODA WAS FIRST EXPORTED TO MEXICO IN THE 1950S, and although no one lays claim to the invention of the Paloma, it was likely conceived very soon after the first shipment arrived. A combination of tequila, lime, and grapefruit soda, the paloma is fantastically easy to make and even easier to enjoy. Take a few sips from a can of Squirt, add a shot of tequila and a squeeze of lime, and you've got one of the better backyard barbecue beverages. That said, if you feel like freshening up the Paloma a bit, we love trading out the grapefruit soda for fresh juice, as in the recipe below.

INGREDIENTS

1½ oz [45 ml] tequila

1½ oz [45 ml] fresh grapefruit juice

½ oz [15 ml] fresh lime juice

Scant ½ oz [15 ml] Rich Simple Syrup

Soda water, for topping

Grapefruit slice, for garnish

DIRECTIONS

To a shaker, add the tequila, grapefruit and lime juices, syrup, and ice. Shake and strain into a highball glass filled with ice. Top with soda and stir gently to incorporate. Garnish with a grapefruit slice and serve.

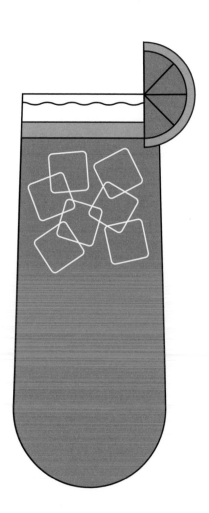

MEXICAN FIRING SQUAD

THE MEXICAN FIRING SQUAD WAS THE CREATION OF AMERICAN FOOD AND DRINK WRITER CHARLES H. BAKER. The story has it that he was in Mexico City with friends, and after growing tired of cocktails he deemed inferior, the group went to a bar and "ordered things in [their] own way." Oh, the wonderful history of Americans going to Mexico only to demand that it be more like America. Nevertheless, this anthropologically unsound moment did lead to a pretty good drink.

Like the margarita, this is a tequila-based take on the Daisy (page 78). Early Daisy recipes called for orange liqueur, later ones for grenadine. The Mexican Firing Squad then is simply a bitter tequila Daisy in the more contemporary tradition, or at least contemporary to Baker's day. The original recipe doesn't call for soda water, though it is a frequent addition and we're somewhere in between not judging and fully supporting inviting it to party with the squad.

INGREDIENTS

2 oz [60 ml] tequila

¾ oz [22.5 ml] grenadine

¾ oz [22.5 ml] fresh lime juice

2 dashes Angostura bitters

Soda water, for topping (optional)

Cocktail cherry, pineapple, and orange, for garnish (optional)

DIRECTIONS

To a shaker, add the tequila, grenadine, lime juice, bitters, and ice. Shake and strain into a rocks glass filled with ice. If including soda, make it a highball glass and top with the soda. The original garnish was a cherry, a slice of pineapple, and a slice of orange; feel free to choose your own level of commitment to this. Serve.

TEQUILA SUNRISE

THE 1970S ARE NOT GENERALLY REGARDED AS A HIGH WATERMARK IN AMERICAN CULTURE, AND THE ERA'S MIXOLOGY WAS NO EXCEPTION. Cocktails of the time tended to be simple and sweet, designed for social lubrication at the singles bar more than quiet appreciation in a dark cocktail lounge. The Tequila Sunrise fit this motif perfectly. Served in a tall glass, it featured tequila and orange juice with a little bit of grenadine poured down to the bottom. If you squinted, and drank enough agave spirits or consumed other mind-altering substances, the contrast between the grenadine and the orange juice might remind you of a sunrise.

We've maintained the aesthetic of the drink but revamped it to a fresher and more compact format. Make it with good tequila, fresh orange juice, a jolt of lemon for acidity, and real grenadine, and the Tequila Sunrise can hold its own in the modern cocktail era.

INGREDIENTS

1½ oz [45 ml] tequila

2 oz [60 ml] fresh orange juice

½ oz [15 ml] fresh lemon juice

Scant ¼ oz [7.5 ml] grenadine

DIRECTIONS

To a shaker, add the tequila, orange and lemon juices, and ice. Shake and strain into a chilled coupe glass. Pour the grenadine through the cocktail so it settles at the bottom, and serve.

ONE CHANCE FANCY

ONE CHANCE FANCY IS A DRINK THAT, HAD TEQUILA BEEN INVITED TO THE AMERICAN COCKTAIL PARTY BACK IN THE 1800S, WOULD PROBABLY ALREADY EXIST. It drinks like a classic cocktail: simple, subtle, spirit driven. It's not a classic though, but a creation of ours, a modern drink imitating an old one. It's like the cocktail version of that period in the late 1990s when car companies borrowed aesthetically from the '30s and '40s. This is our Plymouth Prowler, made with tequila.

Give this a shot if you're looking for a tequila Old-Fashioned with a bit of a twist. Though its namesake is a song by Bobbie Gentry, the inspiration is the Fancy Cocktail (page 77), which is an Old-Fashioned laced with orange liqueur. Tequila is the star of the show here, but vermouth and orange liqueur add just enough sweet and bitter elements to keep things interesting. A richer vermouth works particularly well, as does a cognac-based orange liqueur if you have one.

INGREDIENTS

2 oz [60 ml] tequila

¼ oz [7.5 ml] orange liqueur

¼ oz [7.5 ml] sweet vermouth

2 dashes Angostura bitters

Orange peel, for garnish

DIRECTIONS

To a mixing glass, add the tequila, orange liqueur, vermouth, bitters, and ice. Stir and strain into a rocks glass filled with ice or a single large cube. Garnish with an orange peel and serve.

TEQUILA SOUR

WHILE THERE'S NO DENYING THAT TEQUILA AND LIME WORK EXCEPTIONALLY WELL TOGETHER, LIME ISN'T THE ONLY OPTION WHEN MAKING A SOUR TEQUILA DRINK. Lemon partners well with pepper, and works when matched with the spice of tequila. Here is just one example of that potential, where we sub tequila for whiskey in a sour. This particular recipe was inspired by Los Angeles bartender Dan Sabo's competition-winning Whiskey Sour recipe, in which he brings a bit of orange juice into the mix. It's a perfect addition here, working with the egg white to make the drink incredibly luscious.

INGREDIENTS

2 oz [60 ml] tequila

¾ oz [22.5 ml] fresh lemon juice

½ oz [15 ml] fresh orange juice

½ oz [15 ml] Rich Demerara Syrup (page 33)

1 egg white

1 dash orange bitters

Orange peel, for garnish

DIRECTIONS

To a shaker without ice, add the tequila, lemon and orange juices, syrup, egg white, and bitters. Dry shake to aerate the egg white. Add ice and shake again, then strain into a chilled coupe glass. Garnish with an orange peel and serve.

TIKI MARGARITA

THE TIKI MARGARITA WAS CREATED AT BAR TIKI IN MEXICO CITY IN THE MID-AUGHTS, A GLORIOUS TIME IN COCKTAIL HISTORY WHEN YOU COULD INVENT AN ENTIRE NEW COCKTAIL SIMPLY BY SWAPPING OUT A SINGLE INGREDIENT. Here, orange liqueur is replaced with orgeat, resulting in a truly great drink that pairs well with yacht rock and shoes without socks. Be aware that different orgeats can vary widely in sweetness, so adjust this drink to your taste and to the bottle you have on hand. You also can't go wrong with a few dashes of bitters mixed in or splashed on top as garnish.

INGREDIENTS

2 oz [60 ml] tequila
1 oz [30 ml] fresh lime juice
½ oz [15 ml] orgeat
Crushed ice (optional)
Mint, pineapple, and cocktail cherries, for garnish

DIRECTIONS

To a shaker, add the tequila, lime juice, orgeat, and cubed ice. Shake and strain into a rocks glass, ideally filled with crushed ice. Garnish with mint, pineapple, cherries, a little umbrella—really just go for it here—and serve.

VERMOUTH-ARITA

THE VERMOUTH-ARITA IS A TAKE ON THE CYNAR-GARITA (PAGE 213), ITSELF A BITTER TAKE ON THE CLASSIC MARGARITA (PAGE 87). The basic premise holds in either case: You carve out a bit of space in the standard Margarita recipe, fill it in with something bitter and sweet, and you end up with a really delicious cocktail. This is a great option for when the weather gets a bit colder, and a good reminder that a Margarita can be modified with unexpected flavors beyond the fruity ones you tend to see in restaurants.

INGREDIENTS

1½ oz [45 ml] tequila

1 oz [30 ml] sweet vermouth

½ oz [15 ml] orange liqueur

½ oz [15 ml] fresh lime juice

Orange peel, for garnish

DIRECTIONS

To a shaker, add the tequila, vermouth, orange liqueur, lime juice, and ice. Shake and strain into a rocks glass filled with ice. Garnish with an orange peel and serve.

STINGLESS BEE

FOR THOUSANDS OF YEARS, A SPECIES OF STINGLESS BEE CALLED *MELIPONA* HAS BEEN CULTIVATED IN THE YUCATÁN FOR ITS SWEET, CITRUSY HONEY. This is our take on a Bee's Knees (page 61) made with tequila, and we think you'll agree that it goes down without any sting at all.

INGREDIENTS

2 oz [60 ml] tequila

¾ oz [22.5 ml] Honey Syrup (page 33)

½ oz [15 ml] fresh lime juice

½ oz [15 ml] fresh lemon juice

1 egg white

Peychaud's bitters, for garnish (optional)

DIRECTIONS

To a shaker without ice, add the tequila, syrup, lime and lemon juices, and egg white. Dry shake to aerate the egg white. Add ice and shake again, then strain into a chilled coupe glass. If desired, place a few drops of bitters onto the surface of the drink and etch into a design. Serve.

CHAPTER 6

LIGHT RUM

RUM IS SIMULTANEOUSLY ONE OF THE SIMPLEST SPIRITS TO DEFINE AS WELL AS ONE OF THE MOST COMPLICATED TO UNDERSTAND. Let's start with the simple part. At the broadest level of definition, rum is a spirit distilled from sugars derived from sugar cane. Easy, right? It's when we start delving into the particulars that things get confusing. There are a ton of variables that go into rum production and many different styles of rum. What's more, those styles are rarely rigidly defined. That makes buying a bottle of rum quite different from buying a bottle of whiskey. When you see the word *bourbon* on a label, for example, that alone tells you a lot about how that whiskey was made. With rum you often need to do a bit more digging.

We talk about sugar when discussing rum, but most of the time we're really talking about molasses. Sugar is made by skimming out the crystals that form when you boil the juice from sugar cane stalks; molasses is the stuff that's left over. Historically, sugar was the valuable part and molasses was just a by-product. But if you dilute that molasses with a little water and let yeast work its magic, you get alcohol. And if you run that alcohol through a still, you get rum. Thus, rum production tended to follow as a complementary business to the sugar industry, particularly in the Caribbean.

This is also a good time to clear up a popular misconception about rum, which is that it must be sweet because it is made from sugar. In reality, all spirits are made from sugar in some form, whether that sugar is derived from sugar cane, sugar beets, fresh fruit, agave, grains, or something else entirely. Any sugar that doesn't ferment into alcohol is left behind in the still, so all distilled spirits are naturally dry. If there is any sugar in a bottle of rum, it was added after distillation—a topic we'll return to later.

Among the factors that influence the qualities of a rum are the type of sugar used to produce it, the way it is fermented, the method of distillation, and how the spirit is handled post-distillation through barrel aging and other practices. The world of rum is so diverse that we can really only scratch the surface in this book, highlighting a few styles that are particularly versatile in cocktails. We begin with light rum, a modern style that cemented its place in the cocktail canon with crowd-pleasing favorites like the daiquiri and mojito (or, if you want to keep things really simple, the rum and Coke).

When we say "light" in this context, we don't just mean a lack of color. We also mean that these rums are light in body and flavor. They typically begin with molasses, are fermented quickly, and are distilled through modern column stills that take the spirit to a high degree of purity, resulting in a very clean taste profile. This is in marked contrast to heavier-bodied rums made on Old-Fashioned pot stills, which express much more of the flavor of their raw ingredients.

Despite the lack of color, many light rums are aged in barrels. Rum right off the still generally needs some time to rest, mellow out, and smooth its rough edges. Distillers will age their rums for a few years, often in used barrels that don't contribute much flavor, to accomplish this. The spirit is then filtered through charcoal to remove any color imparted by the wood, resulting in a spirit with a little bit of oak influence and perfect visual clarity. This was the method pioneered by the Bacardi family in Cuba and since copied many times over, with particular commercial success in Puerto Rico thanks to favorable tax treatment and the embargo on Cuban rums in the United States. Due to their origins in former Spanish colonies, these rums are often referred to as "Spanish style," although you'll now find them made in many countries with no connection to Spain.

Compared to other styles of rum, light rum tends to be less assertive in cocktails. It's also wonderfully easy to drink, especially when mixed with rum's favorite fellow travelers, sugar and lime. Get to know that enticing combination while imbibing the cocktails in this chapter, and you'll appreciate it even more when we delve into different styles of rum later on.

BACARDI SUPERIOR

Ubiquitous and affordable, there's a reason you'll find Bacardi everywhere. Its light, clean flavor profile with hints of creaminess and vanilla plays reliably well with lime, sugar, and mint.

HAMILTON 87 WHITE 'STACHE

Renowned rum expert Ed Hamilton blended this rum to re-create the profile of rums from the past aged in oak casks and filtered to clarity with no additives. Sourced primarily from Trinidad with additions from Guyana and the Dominican Republic, it's distinguished by its purity, higher proof, and excellence in a daiquiri.

BRUGAL ESPECIAL EXTRA DRY

A clean rum with inviting notes of vanilla on the nose, Brugal is exactly what the label suggests: a dry rum ideal for mixing.

FLOR DE CAÑA EXTRA SECO

Surprisingly complex with hints of honeysuckle and butterscotch, this Nicaraguan rum offers excellent balance while contributing character to cocktails.

REAL MCCOY 3

Made at the highly respected Foursquare distillery in Barbados, Real McCoy 3 retains the brown sugar and toffee notes from the bourbon barrels in which it is aged. Flavorful enough to sip or serve in stirred cocktails, it also won't distract in drinks like the Mojito (page 99) or Paradise (page 245).

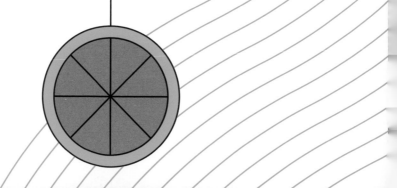

DAIQUIRI

RUM. LIME. SUGAR. It's one of the most sublime combinations in the entire cocktail canon, and we know it as the Daiquiri. No one knows precisely where it originated, although the drink is indelibly linked to Cuba. Historic predecessors include the British punch or grog, which had British sailors mixing their rum ration with lime and sugar, and the Cuban Canchanchara, which mixed rum or aguardiente with citrus and either molasses or honey. Sometime in the twentieth century, a cocktail known as the daiquiri took shape in the thriving Cuban bar culture and eventually made its way to the United States, albeit with significant variations in the ingredients used. Better historians than us have attempted to disentangle the knot of various recipes bearing the name, and we won't attempt to pin down a one true original. We'll simply recommend that you mix one up as soon as you get your hands on a bottle of light rum. It's a perfect cocktail, and there's not much you can do to top it.

INGREDIENTS

2 oz [60 ml] rum

Generous ¾ oz [22.5 ml] fresh lime juice

½ oz [15 ml] Rich Simple Syrup (page 33)

DIRECTIONS

To a shaker, add the rum, lime juice, syrup, and ice. Shake, strain into a chilled coupe glass, and serve.

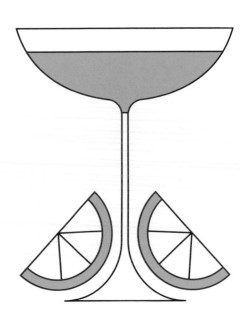

MOJITO

WE DON'T PRESUME TO KNOW YOUR LIFE, BUT WE WILL TAKE A GUESS AT SOMETHING: YOU DON'T MAKE YOURSELF NEARLY ENOUGH MOJITOS. The Mojito must be one of the most unfairly maligned cocktails in history. When the cocktail renaissance took off, snobby bartenders tended to look down on this drink. We know this because we were snobby bartenders ourselves. "I'm sorry, we're out of mint," became a common refrain among bartenders who didn't want to be bothered making a Mojito. Because it was simple. Because it was popular. And most of all, because it was a bit of work. Don't let any of that deter you. The reason people keep ordering Mojitos even in the fanciest cocktail bars is that they are delightful.

Like the Daiquiri, the Mojito evolved to perfection in the pre-revolutionary cocktail bars of Cuba. Also like the Daiquiri, its exact origins are too murky for us to attempt a definitive history. What we will tell you is that the Mojito is worth the effort of making correctly. A slapdash Mojito does no one any favors. A well-made Mojito, on the other hand, is among the finest of leisure drinks. Reward yourself with the real deal.

INGREDIENTS
8 to 10 mint leaves
½ oz [15 ml] Rich Simple Syrup (page 33)
2 oz [60 ml] white rum
¾ oz [22.5 ml] fresh lime juice
Crushed ice
1½ to 2 oz [45 to 60 ml] soda water
Mint sprigs, for garnish

DIRECTIONS
In the bottom of a highball glass, gently muddle the mint leaves and syrup, lightly pressing the leaves to extract their flavor. Add the rum and lime juice, rinsing the muddler with them as you pour. Fill with crushed ice, top with soda, and give it a gentle stir to combine. Garnish generously with a bouquet of mint and serve.

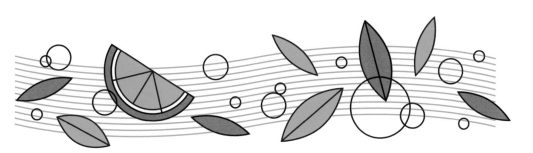

MOJITO CABALLITO

TROPICAL DRINKS HISTORIAN JEFF "BEACHBUM" BERRY TRACES THIS FUN MOJITO RIFF TO SLOPPY JOE'S, A HAVANA BAR THAT SERVED AS A MUST-VISIT CUBAN DESTINATION FOR VACATIONING AMERICANS DURING THE DRY PROHIBITION YEARS. Two things set it apart from the standard recipe. First, the addition of dry vermouth brings a little more flavor than using only rum. Second, it's garnished with a "horse's neck" of lime: not just the standard strip of citrus peel, but a long spiral made by peeling continuously along the entire skin of the fruit. It's visually striking and aromatic. When you grow bored of the classic Mojito—perish the thought!—change things up with this one.

INGREDIENTS

8 to 10 mint leaves

½ oz [15 ml] Rich Simple Syrup (page 33)

1½ oz [45 ml] light rum

¾ oz [15 ml] dry vermouth

¾ oz [22.5 ml] fresh lime juice

Crushed ice

2 oz [60 ml] soda water

Mint sprigs, for garnish

Long strip of lime peel, for garnish

DIRECTIONS

In the bottom of a highball glass, gently muddle the mint leaves and syrup, lightly pressing the leaves to extract their flavor. Add the rum, vermouth, and lime juice, rinsing the muddler with them as you pour. Fill with crushed ice, top with soda, and give it a gentle stir to combine. Garnish with a generous bouquet of mint and a long, spiral strip of lime peel and serve.

HONEYSUCKLE

IS THE HONEYSUCKLE A VARIATION ON THE DAIQUIRI (PAGE 98), SUBSTITUTING HONEY FOR SUGAR, OR A VARIATION ON THE BEE'S KNEES (PAGE 61), WITH RUM IN PLACE OF GIN? You can ponder this mystery while you mix one, and mix one you should. Whichever way you decide to think about it, it's one of the best versions of a basic sour you could ask for.

INGREDIENTS

2 oz [60 ml] light rum

¾ oz [22.5 ml] fresh lime juice

¾ oz [22.5 ml] Honey Syrup (page 33)

DIRECTIONS

To a shaker, add the rum, lime juice, syrup, and ice. Shake, strain into a chilled coupe glass, and serve.

NEVADA

WHAT DOES THIS COCKTAIL HAVE TO DO WITH THE STATE OF NEVADA? Heck if we know, but the addition of grapefruit juice to this daiquiri riff results in a juicy, easy-drinking refresher, with a softer edge than the original. Some recipes include a dash of bitters, while others omit it. We think a dash of Peychaud's goes rather nicely here, but feel free to leave it out if you're looking to keep things simple.

INGREDIENTS

1½ oz [45 ml] light rum

1 oz [30 ml] fresh grapefruit juice

¾ oz [22.5 ml] fresh lime juice

Scant ½ oz [15 ml] Rich Simple Syrup (page 33)

1 dash Peychaud's bitters (optional)

DIRECTIONS

To a shaker, add the rum, grapefruit and lime juices, syrup, bitters, and ice. Shake, strain into a chilled coupe glass, and serve.

SANTIAGO

IN 1936, AFTER WHAT MUST HAVE BEEN ONE OF ITS MORE ENTERTAINING DAYS OF
ORAL ARGUMENTS, THE NEW YORK SUPREME COURT OFFICIALLY DETERMINED THAT A
"BACARDI COCKTAIL," WHEN ORDERED BY NAME, MUST BE MADE WITH BACARDI RUM.
But what is a Bacardi Cocktail? That's a little harder to answer, although modern convention has settled on this simple combination of light rum, lime juice, and grenadine. Historical sources provide similar recipes under the names *daiquiri* and *Santiago* too. In the interest
of avoiding both confusion and lawsuits, we choose to call it the latter of these and recommend shaking it up with whichever light rum you prefer.

INGREDIENTS
2 oz [60 ml] light rum
¾ oz [22.5 ml] fresh lime juice
½ oz [15 ml] grenadine

DIRECTIONS
*To a shaker, add the rum, lime juice,
grenadine, and ice. Shake, strain into
a chilled coupe glass, and serve.*

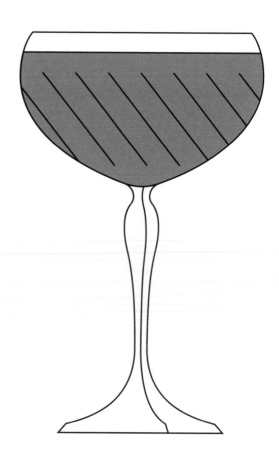

STAN LEE

IF YOU LOOK THROUGH ENOUGH OLD BAR BOOKS, YOU CAN FIND COMBINATIONS OF JUST ABOUT EVERYTHING. One that pops up surprisingly frequently is light rum and gin. It doesn't seem like it should work, and indeed, it often doesn't. Yet with so many vintage cocktails marrying these spirits together, such as the Stanley in *The Savoy Cocktail Book*, we figured there must be something to this union. This is our homage to those cocktails, the product of much experimentation and many prototypes poured down the kitchen sink. The rum nicely mellows out the botanicals of the gin, with the bitters providing a touch of spice.

INGREDIENTS
1½ oz [45 ml] light rum

¾ oz [22.5 ml] gin

¾ oz [22.5 ml] fresh lime juice

½ oz [15 ml] grenadine

1 dash Angostura bitters

DIRECTIONS
To a shaker, add the rum, gin, lime juice, grenadine, bitters, and ice. Shake, strain into a chilled coupe glass, and serve.

COUNTRY CLUB

THERE AREN'T A TON OF STIRRED COCKTAILS CALLING FOR LIGHT RUM, GIVEN THAT SPIRIT'S NATURAL AFFINITY FOR CITRUS AND ITS LOW-KEY FLAVOR PROFILE. To show that it is possible to use it that way, however, here's one called the Country Club from the 1930 book *Cocktails by Jimmy*. We've tweaked the recipe for modern proportions, and you can see the resemblance to a martini with the combination of base spirit, dry vermouth, and accents of citrus.

INGREDIENTS
1½ oz [45 ml] light rum

1 oz [30 ml] dry vermouth

½ oz [15 ml] orange liqueur

1 dash orange bitters

Lemon peel, for garnish

DIRECTIONS
To a mixing glass, add the rum, vermouth, orange liqueur, bitters, and ice. Stir and strain into a chilled coupe. Garnish with a lemon peel and serve.

CHAPTER 7

COGNAC

WHEN WE MENTION COGNAC, YOU MAY THINK OF SUPPLE LEATHER CHAIRS, POTENT CIGARS, AND SNIFTERS OF RICH, EXPENSIVE SPIRIT. Or perhaps it brings to mind bottle service poured from crystal decanters at a nightclub. In this chapter we'll ask you to think of cognac in a different way: as just another ingredient for your cocktails that unlocks some excellent drinks.

Cognac—or, more generically, brandy—was among the spirits that were widely available during the early days of the American cocktail, so it's right at home in the classic canon. Alongside whiskey, rum, and gin, it was one of the bottles that would make its way into all kinds of cocktail standards. It works in mixed drinks for much the same reason that whiskey does: It's a distilled spirit that expresses the character of its base ingredients but also layers them with the appealing influence of oak. If you enjoy whiskey cocktails, you'll likely enjoy cognac cocktails too.

The category of brandy encompasses any spirit distilled from fruit. That includes spirits like cognac but also grape brandies produced elsewhere in the world, such as the grape brandies of South America known as pisco or singani, distillates like grappa and marc made from the grape matter left over from winemaking, and brandies or eaux de vies from various fruits, including apple, apricot, plum, or raspberry. Name a fruit, and there's a decent chance that someone, somewhere, has fermented and distilled it into brandy.

Brandy is one of the earliest commercially distilled spirits, which makes sense when you think about it. Whereas grain can be stored indefinitely, fruit will spoil soon after harvest. Transforming it into alcohol is a smart way to preserve it (and it just so happens to have some enjoyable side effects!). Indeed, the word *brandy* is shortened from *brandywine*, which in its original etymology meant burned wine. The "burning" referred to the process of distillation, and to this day you'll see similar terms used in other languages, such as *branntwein* for brandy in German or *brännvin* as a generic term for liquor in Swedish.

Although the category of fruit spirits is extremely broad, when we use the word *brandy* we typically mean a spirit distilled from grapes and aged in oak barrels. In the cocktail context, that often means cognac. You don't have to use cognac for the drinks in this book, but in much the same way that bourbon from Kentucky or gin from London set the standards for their styles of spirits, the brandies from the Cognac region of France defined the way we tend to think about oak-aged brandies used in cocktails. Yes, there are very good brandies made elsewhere, from California to Armenia to Australia, but if you're going to pick up one bottle to start mixing, cognac is a reliable way to begin. As such, we'll use the words *brandy* and *cognac* more or less interchangeably, leaving the decision to roll the dice on brandy from some other location entirely up to you.

The basic process for making brandy begins the same as making wine. A producer starts with grapes, presses out the juice, and ferments it to produce alcohol. They then distill it and put it in a barrel. In the case of cognac, the grapes must be grown in a small region north of Bordeaux, and they consist primarily of ugni blanc, folle blanche, and colombard. (A few other varietals are allowed to comprise a fraction of the blend.) The wine from these grapes is too thin and tart for enjoyable drinking, but it is transformed via distillation. After two runs through copper pot stills, the spirit is transferred into Limousin oak casks.

Cognac must be aged for at least two years, though it generally spends a great deal longer than that in wood. It will almost always be blended, often with older stocks that add character to younger distillates. We suggest you begin with a mid-priced bottle, preferably one with a little oomph beyond the standard 40 percent ABV you most commonly see today. Ideally it will be a cognac or other brandy you'd happily sip on its own, but that will also bring notes of fruit and vanilla to the cocktails that follow.

COGNAC 101

IN MUCH THE SAME WAY THAT BOURBON IS A STRICTLY DEFINED TYPE OF WHISKEY, COGNAC IS A STRICTLY DEFINED TYPE OF BRANDY. All cognac is produced from grapes in a small region near Bordeaux. This region is further broken down into six areas, or *crus*: Grand Champagne, Petite Champagne, Borderies, Fins Bois, Bons Bois, and Bois Ordinaires. You may occasionally see these regions noted on labels. The main grape used in cognac production is ugni blanc, although a few other high-acid white wine grapes are employed as well.

After fermentation, this wine will be distilled twice in copper pot stills and then aged for a minimum of two years in French oak. Age classifications for cognac refer to the youngest brandy in the blend; artful blending is one of the hallmarks of cognac production, and many cognacs will include portions of spirit aged considerably longer than the minimum. Current legal classifications of cognac are highly detailed, but three to know are:

VS: Also known as "three stars" or "very special," VS cognac is aged for a minimum of two years.

VSOP: Also known as "very superior old pale," VSOP cognac is aged for a minimum of four years.

XO: Also known as "Hors d'age" or "Extra Old," XO cognac has been aged for a minimum of 10 years.

BOTTLES WE REACH FOR

PIERRE FERRAND 1840

Designed specifically for classic cocktails, this expression boasts a higher than typical strength (45 percent ABV), an excellent balance of fruity, floral, and oaky qualities, and an affordable price that makes it a reliable option for mixing.

H BY HINE

Try this VSOP from Hine for a cognac that's equally well-suited for performing in cocktails as it is for enjoying neat. Fruit-forward, bright, and with notes of oak and vanilla, it's wonderfully versatile in many cocktails.

PARK VS CARTE BLANCHE

Blended from two regions and offering a fruity, floral character, Park VS is a fantastic choice when looking for a cognac that shares the stage well with other ingredients.

SIDECAR

IN MOTORCYCLE TERMINOLOGY, A SIDECAR IS AN ATTACHMENT THAT ALLOWS A PAS-
SENGER TO RIDE ALONGSIDE THE VEHICLE. We're not quite sure how the name also came
to refer to the most famous cognac cocktail, but ordering a Sidecar does sound zippier and
more modern than asking for a Brandy Crusta (page 146), its closest predecessor in the
drink world. The formula for a Sidecar is strikingly similar to that of a Margarita, and it's
no coincidence that we choose to open this and the tequila chapter with those cocktails.
They're both wonderfully approachable introductions to their respective spirits, mixing
superbly with orange liqueur and citrus. The Sidecar trades young tequila for oaky cognac,
lime for lemon, and a salt rim for sugar. The sugared rim helps balance the tartness of the
drink, though you can leave it off if you choose. We typically coat about half the rim, allowing the imbiber to decide for themselves whether to sip with or without the touch of added
sweetness.

INGREDIENTS

1 lemon wedge

Sugar, for garnish

1½ oz [45 ml] cognac

1 oz [30 ml] orange liqueur

¾ oz [22.5 ml] fresh lemon juice

DIRECTIONS

*Using the cut side of a lemon wedge, wet half
the exterior edge of a chilled coupe glass and
then dip it into a shallow dish filled with sugar
so that the sugar sticks to the rim. To a shaker,
add the cognac, orange liqueur, lemon juice,
and ice. Shake, strain into the prepared glass,
and serve.*

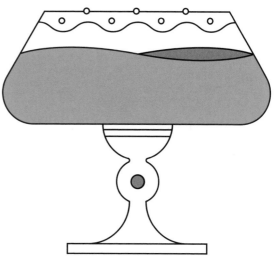

BRANDY OLD-FASHIONED

WE OBVIOUSLY LOVE THE OLD-FASHIONED (PAGE 45). HECK, WE MADE IT THE VERY FIRST DRINK IN THE BOOK. And in forty-nine of the fifty United States, if you walk into a reputable cocktail bar and ask for one, you'll get a cocktail more or less like we described it: made with bourbon, on a single perfect ice cube, with a slice of orange peel for aromatics.

And then there's Wisconsin. The Brandy Old-Fashioned is the unofficial state drink there, and they make it a little differently. First of all, they use brandy instead of whiskey (usually California brandy, but cognac will do just fine). Second, they give the fruit a more active role, muddling cherry and orange into a pulp at the bottom of the glass. Finally, they typically top the drink with a splash of soda; Sprite or 7UP if you want it "sweet," or just a little seltzer otherwise.

You could, of course, just make a standard Old-Fashioned with brandy in place of bourbon and end up with a perfectly good cocktail, but Wisconsin's version is the state drink for a reason. It's worthy of your attention, and much more sessionable than the spirit-forward Old-Fashioned you'll find everywhere else.

INGREDIENTS

1 barspoon (⅙ oz [5 ml]) Rich Demerara Syrup (page 33)

½ orange wheel

1 or 2 cocktail cherries

2 oz [60 ml] cognac

2 dashes Angostura bitters

1 oz [30 ml] soda water

Orange wheel and cocktail cherry, for garnish

DIRECTIONS

In the bottom of a rocks glass, muddle the syrup, ½ orange wheel, and 1 or 2 cherries to a pulp. Add the cognac and bitters, rinsing the muddler with them as you pour. Add ice and stir to combine. Top with the soda, garnish with an orange wheel and cherry, and serve.

METROPOLE

THIS COCKTAIL READS LIKE A MANHATTAN, AND INDEED, IT HAILS FROM THE OLD HOTEL METROPOLE IN TIMES SQUARE. The hotel is long gone, so your best bet to revisit it now is via its namesake drink. It's rather dry, but that allows the fruitier notes of cognac to shine through all the more. When the mood strikes for a strong, dry, spirit-forward cocktail, give this one a try.

INGREDIENTS
1½ oz [45 ml] cognac

1½ oz [45 ml] dry vermouth

2 dashes Peychaud's bitters

1 dash orange bitters

Cocktail cherry, for garnish

DIRECTIONS
To a mixing glass, add the brandy, vermouth, both bitters, and ice. Stir and strain into a chilled coupe glass. Garnish with a cherry and serve.

PALACE HOTEL

THE PALACE HOTEL, named after the hotel in San Francisco, hews a little closer to the Manhattan (page 68) recipe than the Metropole (above), made with equal parts brandy and sweet vermouth. The original specs don't call for bitters, but if you're tempted to add a dash or two, be our guest.

INGREDIENTS
1½ oz [45 ml] cognac

1½ oz [45 ml] sweet vermouth

1 barspoon (⅙ oz [5 ml]) orange liqueur

Lemon peel, for garnish

DIRECTIONS
To a mixing glass, add the cognac, vermouth, orange liqueur, and ice. Stir and strain into a chilled coupe glass. Garnish with a lemon peel and serve.

BURNT FUSELAGE

WHEN YOU'RE IN NEED OF A "STIFF STEADIER," THE BURNT FUSELAGE WILL DO THE
TRICK. According to Harry MacElhone's 1927 book *Barflies and Cocktails*, this equal-parts mix
of cognac, dry vermouth, and orange liqueur was the favorite of Philadelphia pilot Chuck
Kerwood, known as the "wild man of aviation." The original recipe specifically called for
Grand Marnier, which is on the richer, sweeter side of the spectrum of orange liqueurs. Use a
rich liqueur if you have it, but we find the drink also works nicely with a quality triple sec.

INGREDIENTS
1 oz [30 ml] cognac

1 oz [30 ml] dry vermouth

1 oz [30 ml] orange liqueur

Lemon peel

DIRECTIONS
*To a mixing glass, add the cognac, vermouth,
orange liqueur, and ice. Stir and strain into a
chilled coupe glass. Express the lemon peel over
the drink, discard the peel, and serve.*

JAPANESE COCKTAIL

THERE'S NOT ANYTHING OBVIOUSLY JAPANESE IN THE JAPANESE COCKTAIL, WHICH
APPEARED IN JERRY THOMAS'S *HOW TO MIX DRINKS*. Perplexing name aside, it's a very
pleasing concoction. Orgeat is used primarily in citrusy shaken drinks, but here it acts as
subtle sweetener in a more Old-Fashioned-style cocktail, accenting cognac with a touch of
almond. Depending on your brand of orgeat, your cocktail may end up a little cloudy. If this
bothers you, close your eyes when you sip.

INGREDIENTS
2 oz [60 ml] cognac

¼ oz [7.5 ml] orgeat

2 dashes Angostura bitters

Lemon peel, for garnish

DIRECTIONS
*To a mixing glass, add the cognac, orgeat,
bitters, and ice. Stir and strain into a chilled
coupe glass. Garnish with a lemon peel and
serve.*

IMPROVED JAPANESE COCKTAIL

IF YOU READ THE RECIPE FOR THE JAPANESE COCKTAIL (PAGE 110) AND THOUGHT, HMM, IT SEEMS LIKE LEMON JUICE WOULD BE A GOOD ADDITION TO THIS DRINK, YOU'RE NOT ALONE. The same idea occurred to Toby Cecchini of the Long Island Bar in Brooklyn, New York. Toby's rendition transforms the Japanese Cocktail into a citrusy drink, a sort of mashup with the sidecar. There's still nothing Japanese about it, but don't let that stop you from making it. It's a great example of how adapting a classic can make a cocktail that's even better than the original.

INGREDIENTS
2 oz [60 ml] cognac
1 oz [30 ml] fresh lemon juice
½ oz [15 ml] orgeat
½ oz [15 ml] orange liqueur
3 dashes Peychaud's bitters

DIRECTIONS
To a shaker, add the cognac, lemon juice, orgeat, orange liqueur, bitters, and ice. Shake, strain into a chilled coupe glass, and serve.

BETWEEN THE SHEETS

THE SUGGESTIVELY NAMED BETWEEN THE SHEETS (WE ASSUME IT DOESN'T ALLUDE TO SLEEPING) SEEMS LIKE AN UNLIKELY COMBINATION OF INGREDIENTS, but it's really just a sidecar with light rum in place of some of the brandy. This cuts back on the oak and vanilla notes, resulting in a lighter, brighter drink.

INGREDIENTS
¾ oz [22.5 ml] cognac
¾ oz [22.5 ml] light rum
¾ oz [22.5 ml] orange liqueur
½ oz [15 ml] fresh lemon juice

DIRECTIONS
To a shaker, add the cognac, rum, orange liqueur, lemon juice, and ice. Shake, strain into a chilled coupe glass, and serve.

BRANDY FLIP

FEW TERMS IN MIXOLOGY ARE AS HISTORICALLY FLUID AS THE *FLIP.* Originally a hot ale drink heated with a metal loggerhead, it gradually took on the addition of an egg. Then the ale eventually disappeared, as did the heat. Nowadays, we think of flips as any cocktail made with a whole egg, typically shaken with ice until cold.

Flips, at least in their modern meaning, are usually consumed as an after-dinner drink or nightcap. Thanks to the egg, they're very rich, and it's not the kind of cocktail you'd often turn to on a summer day or to begin an evening. You could make them with just about anything, but we think brandy is a good entry point into the style. Oak and vanilla are welcome in flips, as are hints of spice, provided in this recipe by the Angostura bitters. The key to a good flip is to shake it very hard, fully incorporating the egg to produce a velvety, creamy texture. Oh, and don't forget the nutmeg. The aromatics of fresh spice take this cocktail over the top.

INGREDIENTS

2 oz [60 ml] cognac

½ oz [15 ml] Rich Demerara Syrup (page 33)

2 dashes Angostura bitters

1 whole egg

Freshly grated nutmeg, for garnish

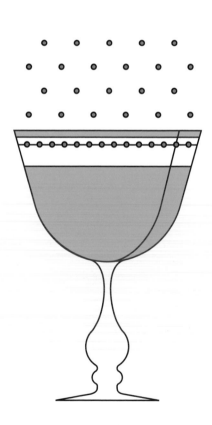

DIRECTIONS

To a shaker, add the cognac, syrup, bitters, egg, and ice. Shake hard and strain into your preferred cocktail glass or small wineglass. Garnish with grated nutmeg and serve.

CHAPTER 8

BENEDICTINE

IN 1510, AN ITALIAN BENEDICTINE MONK NAMED DOM BERNARDO VINCELLI DEVELOPED A UNIQUE RECIPE FOR A MEDICINAL LIQUEUR WHILE STAYING AT AN ABBEY IN NORMANDY, FRANCE. Flavored with more than two dozen herbs and sweetened with honey, the liqueur was immediately regarded as exceptional, even winning praise from King François on a royal visit to the abbey. The recipe was kept a closely guarded secret, handed down through generations until, tragically, the monks had to flee to safety during the French Revolution. The liqueur would have been lost forever if not for Alexandre Le Grand, a wine merchant who came across the recipe in a book in his grandfather's library in 1863. Intrigued, he re-created the liqueur and was astonished by its remarkable taste. Soon after, he constructed a beautiful distillery and brought the centuries-old Benedictine liqueur back from the brink of obscurity.

Well, that's the story anyway. And it was certainly a successful one, helping turn Benedictine into a popular spirit in France and beyond. Did Le Grand actually come across a long-lost recipe, or was he just a brilliant marketer? Regardless, the most important truth here is that Benedictine is a delicious and extremely useful liqueur, and it deserves a spot on your bar.

Benedictine is an herbal liqueur, the first of many you'll encounter in this book. Like gin and vermouth, herbal liqueurs are flavored with botanicals, which contribute their tastes and aromas through maceration, distillation, or both. They're also sweet; much like orange liqueur, they can replace the use of syrups in a cocktail. Sometimes they are intensely bitter too. Benedictine, however, is an extremely approachable one to start with. Made from twenty-seven herbs and spices, the famous liqueur ends up tasting a bit like an intriguingly complex chamomile tea.

Though its popularity has seen peaks and valleys over the last century and a half, Benedictine has established itself as an essential component of some of the most beloved cocktails of all time. Because it's gently flavored, you can use just a splash for complexity or a more generous pour without overwhelming other ingredients. Though its sweetness is pronounced, it's easily balanced when mixed. It's typically used to complement other spirits, but there are a few cocktails in which it plays a starring role. This chapter has a handful of great drinks to get you started, but as the book progresses, we'll have you reaching for that bottle of Benedictine again and again.

IF YOU LIKE BENEDICTINE, TRY...

DRAMBUIE
While there aren't any direct replacements for Benedictine, there are some bottles that exhibit similar combinations of botanicals and honey or offer a comparable balance of sweetness and herbaceousness. Case in point: Drambuie, which combines a scotch whisky base with honey and herbs. It's a bar standby primarily for use in the rusty nail cocktail.

BÄRENJÄGER
This German liqueur pushes the honey flavor even more to the fore than Benedictine and can make a fantastic addition to hot toddies.

AMARETTO
With intense nutty notes and subtle floral qualities, good amaretto is underrated for providing depth and complexity in cocktails. Forget the overly sweet amaretto sours you may have had in the past and look up Jeffrey Morgenthaler's contemporary rendition, or try it mixed with scotch in a godfather. We suggest the bottlings from Lazzaroni, Caffo, and Luxardo.

AMARO NONINO
Although it's an amaro rather than a honeyed herbal liqueur, we think that the gentle balance and complexity of Amaro Nonino makes it a sensible recommendation here. Made with a grappa base, Amaro Nonino is a great after-dinner sipper, pairs fantastically with cognac, and is essential in a modern classic cocktail, the paper plane.

FRISCO

WE MENTIONED THAT BENEDICTINE IS A SUPREMELY VERSATILE INGREDIENT, and what better way to illustrate that than with two versions of the same cocktail? The Frisco and Frisco Sour (page 116) both call for whiskey and Benedictine, the latter bringing in citrus juice as well. The original Frisco appears in cocktail guides of the 1930s in the guise of an Old-Fashioned variation. In essence, the drink replaces the bitters and sugar in a traditional Old-Fashioned with the aromatic botanicals and sweet honey of Benedictine. What you end up with is an incredibly simple-to-make, surprisingly delicious drink.

There are nights when you get out all your bar tools to make an elaborate cocktail, and then there are nights when you barely manage to measure some booze into an ice-filled glass and stir with your finger. The Frisco is for those latter nights. The original recipe simply called for "whisky," and while it's common to find this made with rye, we love it with bourbon, the higher proof the better.

INGREDIENTS
2 oz [60 ml] bourbon
½ oz [15 ml] Benedictine
Lemon peel, for garnish

DIRECTIONS
To a mixing glass, add the bourbon, Benedictine, and ice. Stir and strain into a rocks glass filled with ice or a single large cube. Garnish with a lemon peel and serve.

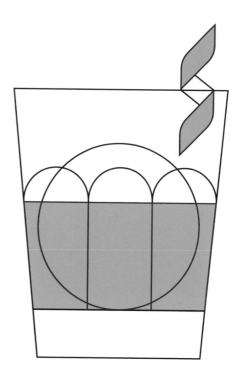

FRISCO SOUR

YOU TRIED THE FRISCO; NOW TRY THE REMIX. As often happens in the cocktail world, bartenders took the very simple Frisco recipe and added another layer. Though the drink began as an Old-Fashioned variation, by the late 1940s many recipes were adding lemon, transforming it into a riff on the Whiskey Sour. Nowadays the Frisco is almost always made as a sour, while the stirred version has been largely overtaken by the Monte Carlo (which we'll encounter in the rye chapter, page 154). The Frisco sour is a great drink in and of itself, and considering Benedictine's honeyed sweetness, you can think of it as a sort of proto–Gold Rush (page 50).

INGREDIENTS

2 oz [60 ml] bourbon

¾ oz [22.5 ml] Benedictine

¾ oz [22.5 ml] fresh lemon juice

Lemon peel, for garnish

DIRECTIONS

To a shaker, add the bourbon, Benedictine, lemon juice, and ice. Shake and strain into a chilled coupe glass. Garnish with a lemon peel and serve.

FORD COCKTAIL

THE FORD COCKTAIL WAS FIRST PUBLISHED IN 1895 AND REPRESENTS AN EARLY TAKE ON THE DRY MARTINI (A COCKTAIL THAT ITSELF WAS STILL FINDING ITS FOOTING IN THE WORLD OF MIXOLOGY). Originally calling for sweeter Old Tom gin and just a few dashes of Benedictine, this drink works wonderfully with a touch more liqueur and a quality London dry. This is one of the better martini variations. Sip it and sing its praises from the rooftops.

INGREDIENTS

1½ oz [45 ml] gin

1½ oz [45 ml] dry vermouth

¼ oz [7.5 ml] Benedictine

2 dashes orange bitters

Orange peel, for garnish

DIRECTIONS

To a mixing glass, add the gin, vermouth, Benedictine, bitters, and ice. Stir and strain into a chilled coupe glass. Garnish with an orange peel and serve.

QUEEN ELIZABETH

THE TRADITION OF LIQUOR BRANDS HOLDING COCKTAIL COMPETITIONS IN ORDER TO DEVELOP RECIPES IS A LONG ONE, AND FROM ONE SUCH CONTEST AROSE THE QUEEN ELIZABETH. Created in 1934 by Philadelphia bartender Herbert L. Quick for a competition sponsored by Benedictine, the drink was actually named for Quick's wife, not the monarch. The drink is built like a standard sour, except that it doesn't contain a strong spirit. With a foundation of dry vermouth instead, it's refreshingly light while still maintaining impressive complexity. The Queen Elizabeth is the perfect drink when the occasion calls for a low-proof cocktail. It may not look like much on paper, but don't pass this one by. It's literally a winner.

INGREDIENTS

1½ oz [45 ml] dry vermouth

¾ oz [22.5 ml] Benedictine

¾ oz [22.5 ml] fresh lime juice

DIRECTIONS

To a shaker, add the vermouth, Benedictine, lime juice, and ice. Shake, strain into a chilled coupe glass, and serve.

TIP TOP

IT'S NICE TO KNOW THAT IF, FOR EXAMPLE, YOUR ROOMMATE HAS CONSUMED ALL THE HARD SPIRITS IN YOUR CAREFULLY STOCKED HOME BAR, YOU CAN STILL MAKE A DELICIOUSLY ROBUST COCKTAIL. The Tip Top, a dry vermouth–based Old-Fashioned of sorts from the famous Waldorf-Astoria bar in New York, is a great drink for when you're short on standard spirits. It's all about using vermouth's subtle acidity to dry out Benedictine's richness while not getting in the way of its complex herbal profile. It works wonderfully. While your roommate is out replacing your bottle of bourbon, make yourself a Tip Top.

INGREDIENTS

2 oz [60 ml] dry vermouth

¾ oz [22.5 ml] Benedictine

2 dashes orange bitters

Lemon twist, for garnish

DIRECTIONS

To a mixing glass, add the vermouth, Benedictine, bitters, and ice. Stir and strain into a chilled coupe glass. Garnish with a lemon twist and serve.

VANCOUVER

JUST AS MANHATTAN HAS ITS NAMESAKE COCKTAIL, VANCOUVER, BRITISH COLUMBIA,
HAS ONE TOO. They're both stirred drinks made with vermouth. But which vermouth for
the Vancouver? That turns out to be a vexing question. It was thought for a long time to be
made with sweet vermouth, and often served as such, but a recently discovered older text
has revealed that it was originally made with dry. First published in the *About Town Cocktail
Book* (that town being, of course, Vancouver), not one word was devoted to describing or
elaborating on this drink that ostensibly represents the entire city. It's essentially hidden in
the text.

Even if you happened to notice it, the Vancouver reads like a redundant variation of the Ford
Cocktail (page 116). The latter, created three decades prior, already did a wonderful job with
the same ingredients. The Vancouver seems like the cocktail version of a Hollywood reboot
that never needed to happen. Except that the Vancouver is fantastic and worthy of its city's
name. Think of the Ford and the Vancouver like brioche and croissants: identical ingredients
can yield strikingly different, and delicious, results. It's also worth noting that the Vancouver
is among the vintage cocktails with a perfectly conceived original recipe. Many have the right
concept but need adjustment for modern tastes. The Vancouver has been spot-on for one
hundred years. We also like that it's garnished with an olive, an underrated garnish that adds
just a slight touch of salt to balance out the sweeter Benedictine as the drink warms.

INGREDIENTS
1½ oz [45 ml] gin
¾ oz [22.5 ml] dry vermouth
½ oz [15 ml] Benedictine
1 dash orange bitters
Olive, for garnish

DIRECTIONS

*To a mixing glass, add the gin, vermouth,
Benedictine, bitters, and ice. Stir and strain
into a chilled coupe glass. Garnish with an
olive and serve.*

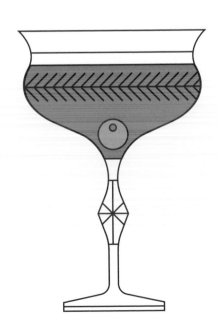

LANI-HONI

WHEN YOU BUY A BOTTLE OF LIQUEUR THAT'S USED PRIMARILY IN SMALL AMOUNTS, SUCH AS BENEDICTINE, IT TENDS TO STICK AROUND YOUR BAR FOR A LONG TIME. That's both a blessing and a curse. It's great that you don't have to restock it every week, but you might also find yourself thinking, "Gosh, it sure would be nice if I could put this to use more than a splash at a time." That's where the Lani-Honi comes in. This obscure cocktail was reportedly served on the Matson cruise ship line in the 1960s, and as you can imagine from such an origin, the recipe was rather sweet. We've adjusted it slightly, increasing the lemon and dialing back the liqueur, but we nonetheless call for a substantial pour of Benedictine. That's not something you see every day. But as this drink proves, maybe you should see it more often.

INGREDIENTS

1¼ oz [37.5 ml] Benedictine

1¼ oz [37.5 ml] light rum

¾ oz [22.5 ml] fresh lemon juice

DIRECTIONS

To a shaker, add the Benedictine, rum, lemon juice, and ice. Shake, strain into a rocks glass filled with ice, and serve.

FITCHETT

AN INTERNET SEARCH FOR THE VANCOUVER (PAGE 118) WILL OFTEN BRING UP A RECIPE SIMILAR TO THIS ONE, BUT WE NOW KNOW THAT THIS BEGAN A TWIST ON THE ORIGINAL VANCOUVER. It also appears in the *About Town Cocktail Book*, credited specifically to Joseph Fitchett, head bar steward of the Vancouver Club. Fitchett's recipe called for sweet vermouth and an olive or cherry, for garnish. In this case we suggest the latter, with perhaps a twist of lemon too.

INGREDIENTS

1½ oz [45 ml] gin

¾ oz [22.5 ml] sweet vermouth

¼ oz [7.5 ml] Benedictine

1 dash orange bitters

Cocktail cherry, for garnish

Lemon twist, for garnish

DIRECTIONS

To a mixing glass, add the gin, vermouth, Benedictine, bitters, and ice. Stir and strain into a chilled coupe glass. Garnish with a cherry and a lemon twist and serve.

COCK 'N' BULL SPECIAL

AS YOU BECOME MORE FAMILIAR WITH COCKTAILS, YOU'LL BEGIN TO RECOGNIZE THAT SOME RECIPES READ BETTER ON THE PAGE THAN OTHERS. Just looking at the ingredients, you'll be able to make a pretty accurate guess as to what the drink will taste like and whether it will be balanced. The Cock 'n' Bull Special defies such expectations. This is a mostly forgotten post-Prohibition Old-Fashioned riff from the bar of the same name, and we suspect that one reason people pass it over is that it reads too sweet. With an ounce combined of Benedictine and orange liqueur, it seems like it should be tooth-achingly saccharine, yet it's perfectly balanced.

This is aided by the addition of a dash of bitters, absent from the original recipe, but mostly it's a testament to how the complexity of Benedictine keeps the drink's sweetness in check. This drink is by no means dry, but it embraces sugar in a way that's entirely enjoyable. If you or someone you know is a bit apprehensive about spirit-forward cocktails, there is no easier entry point than a Cock 'n' Bull Special. Think of it as a Whiskey Sour drinker's favorite Old-Fashioned and a worthwhile recipe to have in your back pocket.

INGREDIENTS

¾ oz [22.5 ml] bourbon

¾ oz [22.5 ml] Benedictine

½ oz [15 ml] cognac

¼ oz [7.5 ml] orange liqueur

1 dash Angostura bitters

Orange peel, for garnish

DIRECTIONS

To a mixing glass, add the bourbon, Benedictine, cognac, orange liqueur, bitters, and ice. Stir and strain into a rocks glass filled with ice or a single large cube. Garnish with an orange peel and serve.

JUBILANT

AS YOU'VE LIKELY NOTICED IN THIS CHAPTER, BENEDICTINE TENDS TO SHINE IN
STIRRED COCKTAILS IN WHICH IT ADDS A SUBTLE HONEYED COMPLEXITY. That said,
it's not exclusively for the world of stirred drinks, as the Jubilant demonstrates wonderfully. In the neighborhood of a White Lady (page 79) or a gin sour (page 59), the Jubilant deftly incorporates orange juice, giving the drink extra weight, but keeps just enough lemon in the game to ensure that everything is bright.

INGREDIENTS

1½ oz [45 ml] gin

¾ oz [22.5 ml] Benedictine

½ oz [15 ml] fresh orange juice

½ oz [15 ml] fresh lemon juice

1 egg white

Lemon twist, for garnish

DIRECTIONS

To a shaker without ice, add the gin, Benedictine, orange and lemon juices, and egg white. Dry shake to aerate the egg white. Add ice and shake again, then strain into a chilled coupe glass. Garnish with a lemon twist and serve.

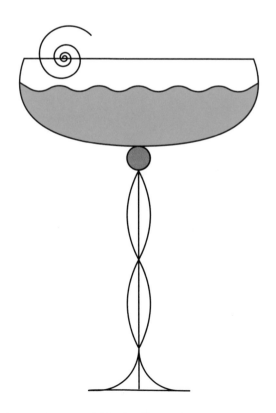

BENNY AND HOT

THE BURNLEY MINERS SOCIAL CLUB IN LANCASHIRE, ENGLAND, HAS THE PECULIAR DISTINCTION OF BEING THE NUMBER ONE BAR IN THE WORLD FOR SALES OF BENEDICTINE. The reason why is this wonderfully simple combination of Benedictine, hot water, and lemon, known as the Benny and Hot (or, in local dialect, "Bene 'n' Hot"). As the story goes, soldiers from Lancashire fell in love with the drink while recuperating in France during the First World War, and they brought it back with them to England. Patrons are still enjoying it a century later, and whereas most bars use Benedictine a bottle or two at a time, the Burnley Miners Social Club churns through it by the case.

The original recipe is served with equal parts Benedictine and hot water, but we suggest using a little more water. It's a great way to showcase Benedictine, brightened with just a touch of lemon. It's a superbly warming drink on a cold winter night. Just heat some water in a kettle, slice a lemon, and you're good to go.

INGREDIENTS
1½ oz [45 ml] Benedictine
3 oz [90 ml] hot water
1 lemon wheel

DIRECTIONS
In a small warmed mug or heatproof glass, combine the Benedictine and hot water. Drop in a lemon wheel and serve.

CECILIA

SEEING AS HOW THE JUBILANT (PAGE 121) IS A REIMAGINING OF A FEW GIN COCKTAILS, WE DECIDED TO REWORK THE JUBILANT ITSELF. Simply swapping out the gin for tequila, and lemon for lime, resulted in a pretty delicious drink. We added just a touch more acidity and a small dose of Rich Demerara Syrup (page 33) to give the drink more top notes and bottom end. The end result is a margarita riff by way of a gin sour, and we just may like it even better than the original Jubilant.

INGREDIENTS

1½ oz [45 ml] tequila

¾ oz [22.5 ml] Benedictine

¾ oz [22.5 ml] fresh lime juice

½ oz [15 ml] fresh orange juice

1 barspoon (⅙ oz [5 ml]) Rich Demerara Syrup (page 33)

½ oz [15 ml] egg white

Orange peel, for garnish

DIRECTIONS

To a shaker without ice, add the tequila, Benedictine, lime and orange juices, syrup, and egg white. Dry shake to aerate the egg white. Add ice and shake again, then strain into a chilled coupe glass. Garnish with an orange peel and serve.

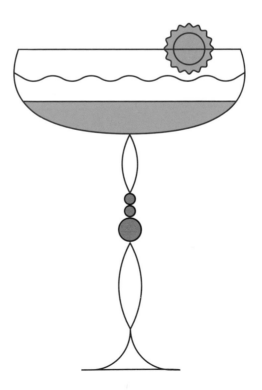

BRANDY LIFT

THE BRANDY LIFT SOUNDS LIKE IT BELONGS IN A COLLECTION OF VINTAGE COCK-TAILS, SOMETHING FROM THE ERA OF FLIPS, FIZZES, AND SLINGS. Actually, though, it's a modern drink from San Francisco bartender and Small Hand Foods proprietor Jennifer Colliau, created for a party at Portland Cocktail Week in 2011. This would naturally fall into the fizz category of drinks if it contained an egg white, but since there wasn't an existing name for drinks made with cream and soda, Jennifer christened it a *lift*. Other bartenders have since followed suit with their own creations, turning the lift into a potentially nascent cocktail category. Try this one out and we think you'll agree she's onto something.

INGREDIENTS

1½ oz [45 ml] cognac

½ oz [15 ml] Benedictine

½ oz [15 ml] orgeat

½ oz [15 ml] cream

2 to 3 oz [60 to 90 ml] soda water

DIRECTIONS

To a shaker, add the cognac, Benedictine, orgeat, cream, and ice. Shake and strain into a chilled rocks or fizz glass. Top with the soda, building up a head of foam, and serve. If you're using a short, narrow glass, the foam will extend above the lip and hold firm.

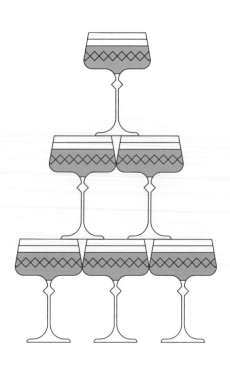

CHAPTER 9

CAMPARI

AND NOW FOR SOMETHING COMPLETELY DIFFERENT. IN OUR COCKTAIL JOUR-
NEY SO FAR, WE'VE BEEN USING BITTER FLAVORS AS AN ACCENT: A DASH
HERE OR A DROP THERE TO COMPLEMENT THE SWEET, STRONG, AND SOUR
NOTES IN DRINKS. In this chapter, bitter finally takes center stage. The bottle we're
asking you to buy now is unapologetically bitter, and we're going to be using whole
ounces of it in cocktails. Depending on your preferences, this may sound really exciting or awfully intimidating. If it's the latter, fear not; we'll ease you into it. And who
knows? By the time this chapter is over, you may find a new favorite ingredient.

Why drink bitter things to begin with? In nature, the perception of bitterness is
believed to be a kind of warning system, the body's way of saying, "Don't eat this,
it might be poison!" Yet many of us tend to be attracted to bitter tastes despite
that, hence the popularity of things like dark chocolate, black coffee, hoppy beers,
and Brussels sprouts. As you become accustomed to bitter tastes, you start to see
through the bitterness to the other flavors that go along with it, like the hints of
citrus peel in an espresso or the piney notes of an IPA. You may even start to crave
bitterness. (Then again, you may not. The capacity to perceive bitterness is at
least partially determined by genetics, and those with a high density of bitter taste
receptors—so-called supertasters—may find the bitterness of such things overwhelming. There's nothing unsophisticated about that. Indeed, supertasters can
take it as a point of pride that they are blessed with exquisitely sensitive palates!)

As we discussed in the vermouth chapter, people have been infusing bitter roots and barks into wine and spirits for centuries. This tradition is particularly rich in Italy, a country that gives us a broad array of bitter liqueurs as well as the catchall name to describe them, *amaro*. *Amaro* (plural *amari*) simply means "bitter" and it refers to an entire category of spirits that are flavored with botanicals, including distinctively bitter ones, and are at least somewhat sweetened. Just like when mixing a cocktail, the sugar is included to balance the bitter elements. When made well, amari are bitter, complex, herbaceous, and a touch sweet.

Broadly speaking, amari are classified as either *aperitivi* or *digestivi*. The former are meant to be enjoyed before a meal to stimulate the appetite, the latter to aid digestion afterward. The lines are a bit subjective, but a *digestivo* is typically darker, richer, and heavier. An *aperitivo*, in contrast, tends to be low-proof, citrusy, and bright, with a bitter edge. That brings us at last to the subject of this chapter, the most famous aperitivo of them all: Campari.

Campari is the creation of Gaspare Campari, who as a young man ventured to Torino and learned the arts of café hospitality and of how to flavor liqueurs. He eventually struck out on his own, first in his hometown of Novara, and then in Milan. It was there that he achieved commercial success with his Campari bitter, a bitter red cordial that the Milanese began asking for by name. His family continued growing the company after his death, turning Campari into a worldwide brand.

Precisely what goes into Campari is a trade secret, though it has strong notes of bitter orange. Until recently it was also dyed with cochineal, a red dye extracted from beetles, but it has now switched to non–animal-derived sources. As to the rest, we can only guess.

Like any other ingredient, we suggest you taste Campari by itself to get a feel for it, but that's rarely how we actually drink it. Perhaps the best way to get acquainted with it is by simply mixing an ounce or so of Campari with ice and several ounces of soda, garnished with a slice of orange. The soda cuts the bitterness and the combination is perfect for low-proof café drinking on a sunny day. Then try the drinks that follow. As we'll see in this chapter and beyond, Campari is a significant player in cocktails and, in our opinion, a must for a well-stocked bar.

APEROL

You could think of Aperol as a more approach-able cousin of Campari, and indeed it's made by the same company. Lighter in color, lower in proof, and not nearly as bitter, it offers an easy introduction to aperitivi and is popularly served in a spritz.

GRAN CLASSICO

With a similar level of bitterness, we reach for Gran Classico when we want to swap some of Campari's citrus flavors for earthier, subtle dark berry notes.

APERITIVO CAPPELLETTI

This is a wonderful option for spritzes or for when you want less intense bitters. Because it is naturally colored and based on wine instead of spirits, you may also be able to find this bottle in places where distilled spirits aren't licensed for sale.

SUZE

There's a whole category of gentian-forward bitter liqueurs that tend to be golden-hued with a sharp edge of bitterness. They play a similar role to Campari in cocktails. Suze is perhaps the most well-known example, but also look for others such as Aveze and Salers.

MEZZODI APERITIVO

Though less widely known, Mezzodi exists somewhere in between Gran Classico and Cappelletti and has a slight hint of strawberry that makes it a very good friend to tequila.

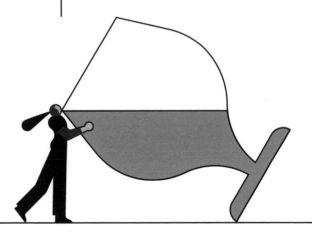

AMERICANO

JAMES BOND'S COCKTAIL PREDILECTIONS ARE MOST FAMOUSLY ASSOCIATED WITH
A MARTINI, SHAKEN NOT STIRRED, BUT HIS FIRST ORDER IN IAN FLEMING'S SERIES
OF BOOKS IS ACTUALLY AN AMERICANO. We think it's also one of the first cocktails you
should try with Campari. As we'll see throughout this chapter, Campari and vermouth are
a natural pairing. One of the earliest drinks to combine them was the Milano-Torino, or
Mi-To, named after the cities of origin for these two products. The Americano simply adds
soda water, which stretches out the flavors and makes a lighter, more refreshing beverage.
The only complicated thing about this drink is making sure you don't accidentally end up
with the Americano espresso beverage instead—not something you'll have to worry about
at home, but a confusion that can arise if you order it at a bar.

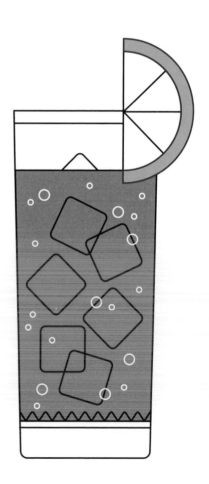

INGREDIENTS

1 oz [30 ml] Campari

1 oz [30 ml] sweet vermouth

4 to 5 oz [120 to 150 ml] soda water

Orange slice, for garnish

DIRECTIONS

*In a rocks or highball glass filled with ice,
pour the Campari, vermouth, and soda.
Gently stir to combine the ingredients,
garnish with an orange slice, and serve.*

VARIATION

*To make the Milano-Torino, simply omit
the soda and serve equal parts Campari
and sweet vermouth over ice. Garnish with
a twist of orange peel.*

NEGRONI

NOW THAT WE'VE EASED INTO CAMPARI WITH AN EASY-DRINKING AMERICANO, IT'S TIME TO KICK OFF THE TRAINING WHEELS AND TAKE A NEGRONI FOR A SPIN. The story behind this drink is that sometime around 1919 in Florence, Italy, Count Camillo Negroni asked a bartender to make him an Americano fortified with gin instead of diluted with soda. With that simple substitution, one of the greatest cocktails in history came to be.

It's not just that the Negroni is deliciously strong and bitter, although it certainly is that. The Negroni's importance also stems from the fact that its simple three-part formula lends itself to almost infinite variation. By switching out one or more of the ingredients with a somewhat similar product, it's possible to make a brand-new cocktail, often meeting with success. In Portland, Oregon, our friend Douglas Derrick took this so far as to create an entire week devoted to Negronis, during which bartenders all over the world serve both the classic formula and creative variations while raising money for charity. We'll encounter some of those variations soon, but let's start with the classic. It's beautiful in its simplicity and a must for any fan of bitter cocktails.

INGREDIENTS
1 oz [30 ml] Campari
1 oz [30 ml] gin
1 oz [30 ml] sweet vermouth
Orange peel, for garnish

DIRECTIONS
To a mixing glass, add the Campari, vermouth, and ice. Stir and strain into a rocks glass filled with ice or a big cube. Garnish with an orange peel and serve.

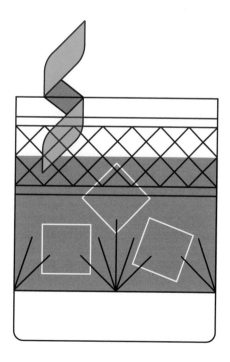

BOULEVARDIER

IT'S PERHAPS UNFAIR TO CALL THE BOULEVARDIER A VARIATION ON THE NEGRONI, GIVEN THAT IT WAS CREATED SUFFICIENTLY EARLY IN TIME TO HAVE POSSIBLY BEEN AN INDEPENDENT CREATION. It is firmly in the Negroni style, however. This excellent cocktail appeared in the 1927 book *Barflies and Cocktails*, and is associated with Erskine Gwynne, publisher of an expatriate magazine in Paris called *The Boulevardier*. The word *boulevardier* refers to someone who's a fashionable person about town, which seems very fitting for this cocktail. It's simply a Negroni with whiskey in place of gin, although given the relatively softer touch of bourbon, we tend to bump up that spirit's role in the recipe relative to the Campari and vermouth, departing from the typical equal-parts formula. We enjoy this drink with rye in place of bourbon too.

INGREDIENTS

1½ oz [45 ml] bourbon

1 oz [30 ml] Campari

1 oz [30 ml] sweet vermouth

Orange peel, for garnish

DIRECTIONS

To a mixing glass, add the bourbon, Campari, vermouth, and ice. Stir and strain into a rocks glass filled with ice or a big cube. Garnish with an orange peel and serve.

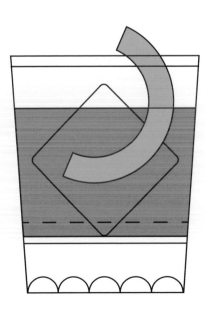

JASMINE

CAMPARI ISN'T JUST FOR STIRRED COCKTAILS. As you might expect from its affinity for orange peel, it also plays wonderfully with citrus. The Jasmine is the creation of Paul Harrington, one of the bartenders and writers who helped usher in the modern cocktail renaissance in the 1990s from a bar called Townhouse in Emeryville, California. Like the Pegu Club (page 76), the Jasmine is crisp, tart, and bitter in the most alluring way possible, and it illustrates how cocktails in the sour family can become increasingly complex as we bring more ingredients into play.

INGREDIENTS

1½ oz [45 ml] gin

¾ oz [22.5 ml] fresh lemon juice

¼ oz [7.5 ml] Campari

¼ oz [7.5 ml] orange liqueur

Lemon peel, for garnish

DIRECTIONS

To a shaker, add the gin, lemon juice, Campari, orange liqueur, and ice. Shake and strain into a chilled coupe glass. Garnish with a lemon twist and serve.

SIESTA

THE CITRUS NOTES OF CAMPARI COME TO THE FORE IN THIS BRILLIANT TEQUILA COCKTAIL FROM KATIE STIPE, WHO CREATED IT WHILE WORKING IN NEW YORK. Grapefruit, orange peel, and lime all pair very well with tequila, and this cocktail brings all three together in one glass (with the orange notes coming from Campari). Think of this as a margarita with a bitter edge. It's excellent.

INGREDIENTS

2 oz [60 ml] tequila

½ oz [15 ml] Campari

½ oz [15 ml] fresh lime juice

½ oz [15 ml] fresh grapefruit juice

Generous ¼ oz [7.5 ml] Rich Simple Syrup (page 33)

Grapefruit twist, for garnish

DIRECTIONS

To a shaker, add the tequila, Campari, lime and grapefruit juices, syrup, and ice. Shake and strain into a rocks glass filled with ice. Garnish with a grapefruit twist and serve.

ROSITA

THE ROSITA TRACES BACK TO 1974, WHEN IT APPEARED IN THE *MR. BOSTON OFFICIAL BARTENDER'S GUIDE*, ALTHOUGH IT OWES ITS PERFECTION TO LEGENDARY COCKTAIL WRITER GAZ REGAN. Regan included his version in his 1991 book *The Bartender's Bible*, then promptly forgot about it until a friend reintroduced him to his own recipe sometime well into the twenty-first century. It's hardly a forgettable cocktail, but we can attest from experience that things can get a bit blurry when you're testing hundreds of recipes. The next time you find yourself staring down a bottle of tequila and a bottle of Campari, we hope you'll remember the Rosita.

INGREDIENTS

1½ oz [45 ml] tequila

1 oz [30 ml] Campari

½ oz [15 ml] sweet vermouth

½ oz [15 ml] dry vermouth

1 dash Angostura bitters

Lemon or orange peel, for garnish

DIRECTIONS

To a mixing glass, add the tequila, Campari, sweet and dry vermouths, bitters, and ice. Stir and strain into a rocks glass filled with ice. Garnish with a lemon or orange peel and serve.

THE RUM DRINK

WE WISH WE HAD A MORE DISTINCTIVE NAME FOR THIS ONE, BUT THE LATE JOHN LERMAYER OF MIAMI COCKTAIL BAR SWEET LIBERTY PUBLISHED IT SIMPLY AS "THE RUM DRINK." The cocktail is equally straightforward, a classic daiquiri accented with just a whisper of Campari. Lermayer used Campari essentially like a dash of bitters here: not so much that it takes over, but just enough to add a bit of interest.

INGREDIENTS

2 oz [60 ml] light rum

¾ oz [22.5 ml] fresh lime juice

½ oz [15 ml] Rich Simple Syrup (page 33)

1 barspoon (⅙ oz [5 ml]) Campari

DIRECTIONS

To a shaker, add the rum, lime juice, syrup, Campari, and ice. Shake, strain into a chilled coupe glass, and serve.

LUCIEN GAUDIN

THE LUCIEN GUADIN IS NAMED AFTER AN ACCLAIMED FRENCH FENCER OF THE 1920S, THOUGH WE DARESAY THAT HISTORY HAS RECORDED HIS NAMESAKE COCKTAIL MORE PROMINENTLY THAN HIS SWORDSMANSHIP. Another close relative of the Negroni, this is a slightly different way of combining gin, Campari, and vermouth and brings in an additional citrus component with the orange liqueur.

INGREDIENTS

1 oz [30 ml] gin

½ oz [15 ml] Campari

½ oz [15 ml] dry vermouth

½ oz [15 ml] orange liqueur

Orange peel, for garnish

DIRECTIONS

To a mixing glass, add the gin, Campari, vermouth, orange liqueur, and ice. Stir and strain into a chilled coupe glass. Garnish with an orange peel and serve.

GARIBALDI

CAMPARI AND ORANGE JUICE? That's it? Well, technically yes, but there's more to this drink than meets the eye. The key is to make your orange juice extra frothy. As popularized at the bar Dante in New York City, this cocktail is made with an especially fluffy juice that comes from their mechanical juicer. You probably don't have that at home, but you can make a quality Garibaldi nonetheless. One way to go about it is to simply pulse the juice with an immersion blender. You can also whisk it by hand. The key is to use very fresh juice and incorporate some air. It's a little bit of extra work, but oh so worth it. Pull out this drink when you want to elevate your brunch game.

INGREDIENTS

4 oz [120 ml] fresh orange juice

1½ oz [45 ml] Campari

Orange wedge, for garnish

DIRECTIONS

Aerate your orange juice with an immersion blender or whisk. In a rocks or highball glass filled with ice, add the Campari and half of the orange juice. Stir gently to combine, then add the remainder of the juice. Garnish with an orange wedge and serve.

CHAPTER 10

VODKA

IF WE WERE WRITING THIS BOOK AT THE BEGINNING OF OUR BARTENDING CAREERS, THERE'S A GOOD CHANCE THAT THIS WOULD HAVE BEEN THE VERY FIRST CHAPTER IN THE BOOK. Vodka dominated cocktail menus in the early years of the twentieth century, and even today it remains the best-selling category of spirits in the United States.

So given its popularity, why not place it first? One reason is that vodka was a relative latecomer to the cocktail world. The classic canon was developed in the nineteenth and early twentieth centuries when this Eastern European spirit was at best a curiosity in the bars that were driving interest in cocktails. It wasn't until the 1930s that vodka began to take hold in cosmopolitan New York City, and it would take a few decades more for it to spread throughout the rest of the country. As a result, it just doesn't appear in many vintage and classic recipes.

The other reason is that vodka is at its best in cocktails when it has other ingredients to work with. By definition, vodka is a neutral spirit. Until very recently, American regulations required vodka "to be without distinctive character, aroma, taste, or color." Current rules aren't quite as restrictive, acknowledging that different vodkas do have subtly different characteristics. Nonetheless, vodka by itself doesn't contribute much flavor to a cocktail. It's essentially a clean slate on which you can write with other spirits, syrups, juices, and bitters. Thus, if you started with just a

bottle of vodka, there wouldn't be very many cocktails worth mixing with it. Once you've built up your bar with bottles like orange liqueur, Benedictine, vermouth, and Campari, the possibilities for mixing with vodka open up considerably.

We don't say that to be dismissive of vodka, which by itself has a great history and culture behind it. That history just isn't focused on cocktails. In the countries where vodka originated, it was intended to be consumed socially or with food, typically served neat and often chilled (or, in some circumstances, infused with local fruits, herbs, and other botanicals). To think of vodka solely as a cocktail ingredient underrates the delights of its traditional uses. If you haven't spent a night downing shots of ice-cold vodka with rye bread, caviar, and various pickles and fish, you're really missing out!

Vodka can be made from just about anything, although wheat, rye, and potatoes are some of the more traditional base ingredients. Some less common ones include honey, milk, grapes, maple syrup, and quinoa. If you can ferment it, you can proba-bly turn it into vodka. What all vodkas have in common is that they are distilled to a very high degree of purity. The spirit came into its modern form with the devel-opment of the column still, which made it possible to distill alcohol to a very high proof. This is what gives it its neutral character; at such a high proof, the flavors of its base ingredients are vastly diminished if not altogether erased.

That said, not all vodkas are made the same, and there are subtle differences among them. Some of this can come from the ingredients used to make them, but distillers are also permitted to make tiny additions of sugar or citric acid and to introduce some congeners produced early in the distillation process (known as *backset*). The method of filtration also affects the final flavor. The differences between brands won't be as stark as between, say, two gins that use lots of differ-ent botanicals, but they will be noticeable if you taste them side by side.

One factor you can comfortably ignore is whether vodka has gone through many distillations. Boasting a high number of distillations makes for good marketing copy, but it doesn't necessarily imply anything about the quality of the spirit. Col-umn stills are referred to as continuous stills for a reason: you can operate them without stopping. Unlike pot stills, which demand multiple batch distillations to increase the purity of alcohol, column stills are made for efficiency. How a producer operates their stills is more important than the simple number of distillations.

VODKA 101

WHAT SHOULD YOU LOOK FOR WHEN BUYING VODKA? We recommend some wariness of the cheapest brands, which can be rough and hot, but we'd also advise against spending money on super-upscale brands that derive their reputation more from marketing than from real differences in quality. And in truth, the differences between brands will be most apparent when tasting them neat. Once you start mixing them with strongly flavored ingredients in cocktails, differences between decent brands will tend to wash out.

We've listed a few of our go-to bottles, but this is also a great category to begin exploring craft distillers. There's a good chance you can find someone making vodka in your local area that's every bit as good as the big brands. Once you get a bottle, the first thing you should do is try it neat. Then, if you're curious, we'd suggest sticking it in the freezer until it is ice cold, then sip it again for a real vodka experience. For mixing, keep a bottle out on your home bar or bar cart and start exploring the drinks in this chapter.

BOTTLES WE REACH FOR

REYKA
Distilled in Iceland, filtered through lava rocks, and cut with glacial water, Reyka certainly has what it takes to be marketed as a clean, pure spirit. Frankly, we don't know how much of a difference all of that makes, but it's a solid, affordable vodka that we're happy to keep on hand.

KETEL ONE
One of the early luxury vodkas imported to the US, Ketel One holds a regular spot in our bars. Distilled from winter wheat in Holland, with portions of the distillate redistilled in pot stills and blended back into the final product, it's smooth and pleasantly silky.

TIMBERLINE
There are plenty of big brands in vodka, but as a category it's a prime candidate for supporting your local distilleries. In that spirit, we recommend Timberline Vodka from Hood River, Oregon. Made at Clear Creek Distillery, this batch-distilled vodka is partially derived from Pacific Northwest apples, which gives it a unique, very subtle fruity note while still maintaining a classic, clean vodka profile.

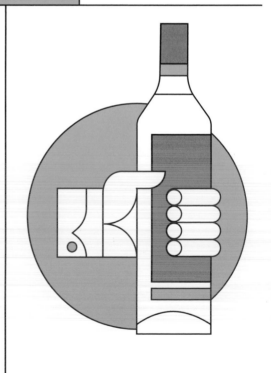

MOSCOW MULE

THE MOSCOW MULE ISN'T JUST THIS BOOK'S FIRST COCKTAIL WITH VODKA, IT'S
ALSO THE COCKTAIL THAT DID MORE THAN ANY OTHER TO INTRODUCE VODKA TO THE
UNITED STATES. IN 1941, IT WAS STILL A NICHE SPIRIT IN AMERICA, LITTLE KNOWN
OUTSIDE OF RUSSIAN CUISINE. It was around this time that the inspired combination of
the Moscow Mule came together at the Cock 'n' Bull restaurant in Los Angeles. In one of
the great sales collaborations in the history of drinking, Smirnoff vodka and Cock 'n' Bull
ginger beer found an alluring partnership. The drink became a favorite of Hollywood and
spread throughout the country, popularizing vodka as it went.

The Moscow Mule has enjoyed a revival alongside more spirit-forward and complex cocktails to become one of today's most popular drinks. Simplicity is part of its appeal, offering
an easy-drinking break from the Old-Fashioneds, martinis, and Negronis that have typified
the modern cocktail movement. The copper mugs that it's often served in are also hard
to resist. When you see that frosty mug full of crushed ice and ginger beer, who wouldn't
want to order one on the spot? You don't have to use a copper cup when making it at home,
although you'll earn extra points from guests if you do.

INGREDIENTS
Crushed ice
4 to 5 oz [120 to 150 ml] ginger beer
1½ oz [45 ml] vodka
Lime wedge

DIRECTIONS

*In a copper mug or rocks or highball
glass filled with crushed ice, add the
ginger beer and vodka. Squeeze in the
lime and drop it into the drink. Gently
stir to combine and serve.*

CAIPIROSKA

**THE CAIPIROSKA IS A VARIATION ON ONE OF THE WORLD'S MOST POPULAR COCK-
TAILS, THE BRAZILIAN CAIPIRINHA (PAGE 276).** We'll spend some time with that one in
the chapter on cachaça. In the meantime, we'll do what people have done for decades when
they feel like drinking a Caipirinha but don't happen to have any cachaça on hand: make it
with vodka instead.

The key to both drinks is muddling fresh lime. This is a technique that relies more on feel
than on measured precision; ideally you want a fresh, vibrant lime that will yield lots of
juice when you press it with the muddler. It's also one of the few drinks in which we recommend using granulated sugar instead of syrup. This is a rustic cocktail, and sipping on the
not quite fully dissolved grains of sugar along with the lime pulp is one of the pleasures of
the drink.

INGREDIENTS

½ lime, cut into 3 or 4 wedges

1 Tbsp sugar, or ½ oz [15 ml] Rich Simple Syrup
 (page 33)

2 oz [60 ml] vodka

DIRECTIONS

*In a shaker, muddle the lime and sugar,
pressing to extract juice from the lime. Add
the vodka, rinsing the muddler as you pour.
Add ice and shake. Pour everything, without
straining, directly into a rocks glass and serve.*

LEMON DROP

WHEN WE BEGAN OUR BARTENDING CAREERS, WE WERE MAKING LEMON DROPS EVERY NIGHT. These days we get asked for them pretty rarely (in part because we work in fancier bars now than we did back then). As cocktails like the Old-Fashioned and Negroni began displacing '90s-era drinks like this one, the Lemon Drop fell out of fashion and was dismissed by bartenders. But you know what? It's a perfectly fine drink, hewing closely to the classic sour format. Sure, a lot of the Lemon Drops served in chain restaurants with flavored vodka and sour mix are overly sweet, but when made with good ingredients and proper proportions, the drink is pleasantly tart and enjoyable.

Standard recipes call for lemon-flavored vodka. We'd argue that between the fresh lemon juice and orange liqueur, there's plenty of citrus to go around without it. That said, if you find yourself making Lemon Drops on the regular, feel free to pick up a bottle.

INGREDIENTS

1 lemon

Sugar, for garnish

2 oz [60 ml] vodka

¾ oz [22.5 ml] orange liqueur

1 oz [30 ml] fresh lemon juice

1 barspoon (⅙ oz [5 ml]) Rich Simple Syrup (page 33)

DIRECTIONS

Using the cut side of a lemon, wet half the exterior of a chilled coupe glass and then dip it into a shallow dish filled with sugar so that the sugar sticks to the rim. To a shaker, add the vodka, orange liqueur, lemon juice, syrup, and ice. Shake, strain into the prepared glass, and serve.

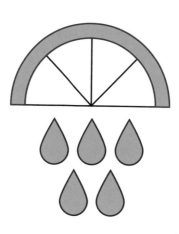

GREYHOUND

THE GREYHOUND IS ONE OF THE SIMPLEST DRINKS IN THE BOOK, PERFECT FOR WHEN YOU WANT TO EXPEND THE MINIMUM AMOUNT OF EFFORT ON A REFRESHING COCK-TAIL. Related recipes go back to at least the early twentieth century, although those renditions likely would have been made with gin rather than vodka. As vodka rose in popularity in the United States, this two-ingredient preparation became a staple, including finding a fitting home at bus terminal restaurants. One point where we differ with the old recipes: They often called for canned grapefruit juice, but we'd strongly advise you to squeeze it fresh.

INGREDIENTS

1½ oz [45 ml] vodka

4 to 5 oz [120 to 150 ml] fresh grapefruit juice

Grapefruit peel, for garnish

DIRECTIONS

In a rocks glass filled with ice, add the vodka and grapefruit juice and stir gently to combine. Garnish with a strip of grapefruit peel and serve.

VARIATIONS

As mentioned above, you can make this just as easily with gin (or tequila, or any other white spirit). Serve this in a glass with a salted rim and you have yourself a Salty Dog.

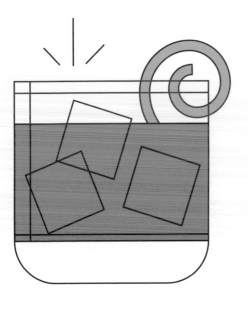

ITALIAN GREYHOUND

ALTHOUGH IT GETS POINTS FOR CONVENIENCE, THE GREYHOUND IS ADMITTEDLY NOT THE MOST EXCITING COCKTAIL. One way to add interest is by bringing in a bitter note. As you know from the previous chapter, a great way to bring bitter and citrus flavors together is with a pour of Campari. It's an easy addition, but it elevates the standard Greyhound into a sleeker and more stylish breed.

INGREDIENTS

1 oz [30 ml] vodka

1 oz [30 ml] Campari

4 to 5 oz [120 to 150 ml] fresh grapefruit juice

Grapefruit peel, for garnish

DIRECTIONS

In a rocks glass filled with ice, add the vodka, Campari, and grapefruit juice. Stir gently to combine, garnish with a grapefruit peel, and serve.

HAWAIIAN SUNSET

AS FURTHER PROOF THAT TROPICAL DRINKS DON'T HAVE TO BE MADE WITH RUM, WE OFFER THE HAWAIIAN SUNSET. A cocktail from the Aku Aku Polynesian Restaurant in 1960s Las Vegas, this drink wraps Russian vodka in the tropical accoutrements of tiki culture: fresh citrus juices, grenadine, and orgeat. It's sweet, flavorful, and superbly easy-drinking.

INGREDIENTS

1½ oz [45 ml] vodka

½ oz [15 ml] fresh lemon juice

½ oz [15 ml] fresh lime juice

½ oz [15 ml] orgeat

1 barspoon (⅙ oz [5 ml]) grenadine

Lime peel, for garnish

DIRECTIONS

To a shaker, add the vodka, lemon and lime juices, orgeat, grenadine, and ice. Shake and strain into a chilled coupe glass. Garnish with a lime peel and serve.

TIPSY COACHMAN

SO FAR IN THIS CHAPTER, WE'VE EXPLORED HOW VODKA MIXES HARMONIOUSLY WITH CITRUS OR GINGER BEER, USING THOSE INGREDIENTS TO TAKE THE EDGE OFF THE SPIRIT. Here we employ it in a slightly different way, using the neutral character of vodka to stretch out and soften the intensely complex flavors of our old friend Benedictine. Taken on its own, Benedictine is overpoweringly sweet and herbaceous. But open it up with a pour of vodka, a dash of bitters, and the chilling and diluting effects of ice, and you have yourself a proper cocktail. This is in fact one of the earliest American vodka cocktails, dating back to the 1930s at the Russian Tea Room in New York City. Originally called the "gypsy queen," we've taken the liberty of renaming it for modern sensibilities. If you've been reading this chapter and wondering when we'd get to a strong, spirit-forward vodka cocktail that would satisfy even the most demanding mixology nerds, look no further.

INGREDIENTS

1½ oz [45 ml] vodka

¾ oz [22.5 ml] Benedictine

1 dash Angostura bitters

Lemon peel, for garnish

DIRECTIONS

To a mixing glass, add the vodka, Benedictine, bitters, and ice. Stir and strain into a rocks glass filled with ice or a single large cube. Garnish with a lemon peel and serve.

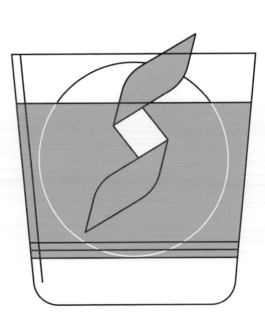

VODKA MARTINI

THERE ARE SOME QUESTIONS THAT MAY NEVER BEGET A CERTAIN ANSWER, AMONG THEM, "WHAT IS THE CORRECT WAY TO MAKE A VODKA MARTINI?" James Bond liked his shaken, not stirred, breaking all the rules of mixing spirit-forward cocktails. The classic Martini is defined in part by the inclusion of vermouth, yet many people who order vodka martinis don't want any vermouth at all. Blue cheese–stuffed olives aren't part of the cocktail canon either, but if you ask nicely and tip well, you might talk your bartender into making a few for your cocktail. And then there's the espresso martini, the chocolate martini, the appletini . . . the list of drinks combining vodka and the suffix -tini is seemingly endless. The point is, the Vodka Martini is pretty much whatever you want it to be.

For modern drinkers, that often means a hefty pour of vodka shaken with ice until very cold, and we can't deny that there's some appeal to a bracing glass of frosty vodka. To make a drink that more approximates the classic Martini, try the recipe below. Some purists insist on calling this a Kangaroo. That's the name the combination of vodka and dry vermouth went under in some vintage bar books, but good luck ordering one today. The Venn diagram of imbibers who know enough about cocktail history to ask for a Kangaroo and who prefer it to a classic gin martini is essentially two separate circles, so if you're in the mood for a Vodka Martini, just ask for one by name and specify the way you like it prepared.

INGREDIENTS

2 oz [60 ml] vodka

½ oz [15 ml] dry vermouth

Lemon peel or olive, for garnish

DIRECTIONS

To a mixing glass, add the vodka, vermouth, and ice. Stir and strain into a chilled coupe or martini glass. Garnish with a lemon peel or olive and serve.

VARIATIONS

When not using vermouth, you may want to shake this to make it as cold as possible. You can even skip the fine strainer, letting the tiny ice shards float atop the drink. To make a "dirty" vodka martini, use about ½ oz [15 ml] of olive brine for every 2½ oz [75 ml] of vodka, and definitely shake.

CHAPTER 11

MARASCHINO LIQUEUR

WHEN WE SAY "MARASCHINO," THE FIRST THING THAT COMES TO MANY PEOPLE'S MINDS IS THE BRIGHT RED CHERRIES THAT YOU SEE TOPPING ICE CREAM SUNDAES OR SKEWERED INTO SHIRLEY TEMPLES. This chapter is not about how to make cocktails with the syrup from those cherry jars. It's about an elegant, flavorful liqueur that's played an outsized role in cocktail history. The liqueur is made with cherries, though only distantly related to the ones you nibbled on as a kid.

Maraschino liqueur is made by macerating sour marasca cherries, including the pits and stems, in distilled spirits; those spirits may or may not be distilled from cherries themselves. This mixture is then distilled again, rested, and finally sweetened. That makes it distinct from ordinary cherry liqueur, which would typically be made just by macerating cherries in a spirit, filtering, and adding sugar. Unlike a cherry liqueur, which is typically cherry-colored, maraschino liqueur is completely clear. The liqueur is also distinct from cherry brandy, also known as kirsch or cherry eau de vie, which is unsweetened and made by distilling fermented cherry juice. Maraschino liqueur is very much its own thing.

144

The liqueur form of maraschino dates back to the sixteenth century in the region of present-day Zadar, Croatia, home to its key ingredient, bitter marasca cherries. Commercial production began in the mid-eighteenth century, and the liqueur gained notoriety throughout Europe. After the Second World War, many maraschino distillers—including one of the largest producers, Luxardo—moved across the Adriatic Sea to Italy and resumed production there.

When it comes to mixing up cocktails, what's most important to know about maraschino liqueur is that, although it is made from cherries, it tastes distinctly different than the fruit. The reasons for this are twofold. First, much of the flavor comes from the pits, not just the fruity part of the cherry. These add unmistakable almond and rose notes to the spirit. Second, the distillation after maceration transforms the spirit, creating an entirely unique product. It's like the difference between fermented corn water and a finished whiskey: Distillation changes things drastically so that they taste of, but not entirely like, the ingredients they're made from.

The proliferation of maraschino liqueur throughout Europe led to it being a very early addition to classic cocktails, showing up in all sorts of drinks that have stood the test of time. A little bit goes a long way, contributing complex floral, nutty, and cherry notes all at once, along with significant sweetness. It's not a spirit we ever pour to drink by itself, but it's one whose absence we'd lament in any bar without it. You'll find it essential for re-creating classic cocktails.

BOTTLES WE REACH FOR

LUXARDO

The go-to in cocktail bars, Luxardo is distinguished by its classic straw-wrapped bottle and its burly aroma. Its cherry flavor is complemented by woody and nutty notes that ensure it will stand up to other strong ingredients in a mixed drink.

MARASKA

Bright, sweet, and more gentle than Luxardo, Maraska delivers distinctly sweet notes of fresh cherry.

VERGNANO

There's no mistaking the almondy, marzipan flavor in this aromatic maraschino liqueur, which brings out the nutty notes of cherry pits as much as those of the fruit itself.

BRANDY CRUSTA

THE BRANDY CRUSTA IS ONE OF THE EARLIEST COCKTAILS EVER PUBLISHED, APPEARING IN JERRY THOMAS'S *BAR-TENDER'S GUIDE* WAY BACK IN 1862. Though many today see this drink as simply a predecessor to the more famous Sidecar (page 107), looking at the early recipes leads us to view it as a flourish on an Old-Fashioned. Thomas's recipe was " . . . the same as a fancy cocktail, with a little lemon juice and a small lump of ice added." This implies that the Crusta began as a Brandy Old-Fashioned with the addition of a small amount of lemon juice, served on the rocks in an elaborately garnished glass. When made with this approach, the Brandy Crusta is a unique cocktail in its own right.

Twenty years after the original recipe was published, Harry Johnson updated the Crusta by calling for maraschino in place of orange curaçao. Nearly all subsequent recipes followed suit, and having tried both versions, we tend to agree with Johnson's take. That said, if you want to try the original, simply use orange liqueur in place of maraschino in the following recipe. Although the garnishes for this cocktail may seem absurdly over the top, they truly do make the drink more delicious. The extreme amount of lemon peel adds acidity to the drink that develops as you enjoy it, while the sugared rim balances this out.

INGREDIENTS

2 lemons

Sugar, for garnish

2 oz [60 ml] cognac

¼ oz [7.5 ml] maraschino liqueur

¼ oz [7.5 ml] Rich Demerara Syrup (page 33)

¼ oz [7.5 ml] lemon juice

2 dashes Angostura bitters

DIRECTIONS

Using the cut side of 1 of the lemons, wet the exterior edge of a rocks glass and then dip it into a shallow dish filled sugar so that the sugar sticks to the rim. Peel the remaining entire lemon in one strip and wrap the peel around the interior of the glass. Fill with ice to secure the peel, ideally with a single large cube. To a mixing glass, add the cognac, maraschino liqueur, syrup, lemon juice, bitters, and ice. Stir and strain into the prepared glass and serve.

HEMINGWAY DAIQUIRI

ERNEST HEMINGWAY LIKED SUGAR IN HIS COCKTAILS THE WAY HE LIKED PUNCTU-ATION IN HIS SENTENCES: SPARSE, IF AT ALL. Though his facility with direct prose is something we aspire to as writers, we cannot say the same for his approach to balancing a cocktail. The original Hemingway Daiquiri, created for him at the Floridita Bar in Cuba where he was a regular, is bracingly tart. Rum, lime, and grapefruit juice were offset by maraschino liqueur. Though none of the drinks at the Floridita were particularly sweet, this one is particularly bereft of sugar. The motivation for this was Hemingway's diabetes, which required that he limit his intake.

Health effects aside, the general consensus now is that Hemingway's Daiquiri is better with a bit more sweetness. Common approaches to making this drink today all increase both the maraschino and the grapefruit, resulting in a cocktail worth writing home about. The grapefruit adds a fruity bitterness that works perfectly with maraschino's floral and nutty aromas.

INGREDIENTS
2 oz [60 ml] light rum
½ oz [15 ml] maraschino liqueur
¾ oz [22.5 ml] fresh lime juice
½ oz [15 ml] fresh grapefruit juice

DIRECTIONS
To a shaker, add the rum, maraschino liqueur, lime and grapefruit juices, and ice. Shake, strain into a chilled coupe glass, and serve.

THE CLASSIC BAR *Maraschino Liqueur*

147

RENDEZVOUS

ONE OF THE PROMINENT COCKTAILS IN THE TWENTY-FIRST-CENTURY MIXOLOGY REVIVAL WAS THE AVIATION, A DRINK WHOSE ORIGINAL RECIPE CALLED FOR A FLORAL LIQUEUR KNOWN AS CRÈME DE VIOLETTE. For some unknown reason, however, when Harry Craddock wrote his *Savoy Cocktail Book*, he omitted that ingredient and gave the recipe as a simple combination of gin, lemon juice, and maraschino liqueur. That's the way the Aviation was made for years to come, and although we prefer the original, we can't deny that it's a smart way of using maraschino.

A subtle variation on Craddock's Aviation appeared in Ted Saucier's 1951 book *Bottoms Up*. He swapped out lemon for lime and called the new drink a Rendezvous. Cocktails have a lot in common with pasta, in that tiny variations in form are awarded with entirely new names. Make this recipe with lemon juice if you'd like to try Craddock's version of the Aviation, or stick to the formula below if you'd like to make Saucier's adaptation. As for crème de violette (see page 256)? We don't call for it in this book so you'll have to rendezvous with that bottle another time.

INGREDIENTS
1½ oz [45 ml] gin
½ oz [15 ml] maraschino liqueur
½ oz [15 ml] fresh lime juice

DIRECTIONS
To a shaker, add the gin, maraschino liqueur, lime juice, and ice. Shake, strain into a chilled coupe glass, and serve.

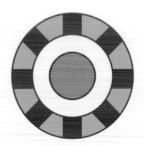

CASINO

THE CASINO COCKTAIL PRESENTS AN OPPORTUNITY TO TALK ABOUT HOW CLAS-SIC RECIPES FREQUENTLY FAIL TO LIVE UP TO MODERN STANDARDS. Whether that's because the ingredients are different now, palates have changed, bartender's skills have adapted, or some combination of the three, we often don't make drinks the ways we used to. More often than not, that's a good thing. Take the Casino, for example. The original recipe from *The Savoy Cocktail Book* called for 2 oz [60 ml] of gin with just a couple dashes of lemon juice, maraschino, and orange bitters. The gin overwhelms every other ingredient. It's not at all how modern bartenders would build a drink, and it isn't something that a modern bar patron would happily pay for.

That said, within this strange recipe is a really good idea. There's no reason that gin, lemon, maraschino, and bitters can't taste wonderful when mixed together. The question is, how should we mix them? The Casino presents a fork in the road. On one hand it contains juice and thus could easily be interpreted as a sour; on the other, the specs are very booze forward and the instructions state that it should be stirred. So is the Casino a sour or an Old-Fashioned? We answer that question with a question of our own: Why can't it be both? To make it as sour, simply add a couple dashes of orange bitters to Craddock's Aviation (page 148). To take it in a more spirit-forward direction, try the recipe below.

INGREDIENTS
2 oz [60 ml] gin
½ oz [15 ml] maraschino liqueur
2 dashes orange bitters
Lemon peel
Cocktail cherry, for garnish

DIRECTIONS
To a mixing glass, add the gin, maraschino liqueur, bitters, lemon peel, and ice. Stir and strain into a chilled rocks glass filled with ice or a single large cube. Garnish with a cherry and serve.

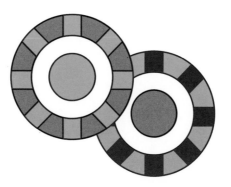

KING'S JUBILEE

HARRY CRADDOCK CAME UP WITH THE KING'S JUBILEE TO CELEBRATE THE TWENTY-FIFTH YEAR OF REGNANCY FOR KING GEORGE V. Although an American by birth, Craddock was working and living in London and was thus obliged to honor his king, which he did by going to such great lengths as . . . switching out the gin in his Aviation recipe for rum. Despite being a simple variation, the King's Jubilee drinks quite differently, with rum providing a broader and blunter flavor profile than a nuanced gin. It pushes the maraschino a bit more to the fore and results in a refreshing drink that falls between a Daiquiri and an Aviation.

INGREDIENTS

1½ oz [45 ml] light rum

½ oz [15 ml] maraschino liqueur

½ oz [15 ml] fresh lemon juice

Cocktail cherry, for garnish

DIRECTIONS

To a shaker, add the rum, maraschino liqueur, lemon juice, and ice. Shake and strain into a chilled coupe glass. Garnish with a cherry and serve.

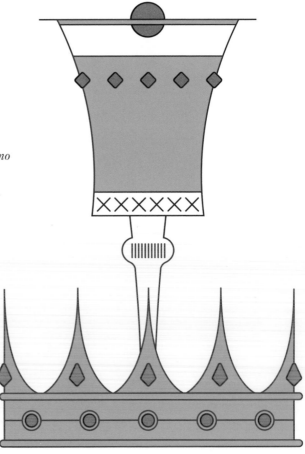

MARTINEZ

FIRST PUBLISHED IN 1884, THE MARTINEZ RECIPE READ, IN ITS ENTIRETY, "SAME AS MANHATTAN, ONLY YOU SUBSTITUTE GIN FOR WHISKY." The Manhattan it was referencing included a few dashes of curaçao, and it's generally agreed that the gin in question was Dutch genever. But the Martinez wouldn't stay static for long. Three years later, when it resurfaced in an updated version of Jerry Thomas's *Bar-Tender's Guide*, the curaçao had been swapped out for maraschino and the gin specified was the increasingly popular Old Tom style.

After that, the history of the Martinez gets confusing. A few decades into the twentieth century, cocktail books regularly called for the recently available dry vermouth, while the similarly fashionable London dry gin often stood in for Old Tom. Sometimes orange curaçao was listed as an option, though mostly it wasn't, while orange, Angostura, and Boker's bitters all made appearances in various recipes. Throughout the nearly 140-year history of the Martinez, what has been most apparent is how the drink adapts to trends, tastes, and availability of products. At its core, it's a Manhattan made with gin, but which and how much gin, vermouth, liqueur, and bitters one should use has been open to interpretation.

We're going to carry on with that tradition and recommend that you make a Martinez that suits the contemporary palate and utilizes what's available in your increasingly well-stocked home bar. While the early Martinez recipes called for equal parts vermouth and gin, or even twice as much of the former as the latter, the gin became more dominant as time progressed. We lean toward an equal-parts rendition while embracing both dry and sweet vermouth. This raises the acidity of the cocktail, moderates the sweetness, and keeps the strength of gin in check. As a nod to the recipes that called for orange liqueur, we add just one dash of orange bitters along with Angostura. By such a circuitous route we arrive at our ideal Martinez.

INGREDIENTS

1½ oz [45 ml] gin

1 oz [30 ml] sweet vermouth

½ oz [15 ml] dry vermouth

¼ oz [7.5 ml] maraschino liqueur

1 dash orange bitters

1 dash Angostura bitters

Orange peel, for garnish

DIRECTIONS

To a mixing glass, add the gin, sweet and dry vermouths, maraschino liqueur, both bitters, and ice. Stir and strain into a chilled coupe glass. Garnish with an orange peel and serve.

DIPLOMAT

WE LOVE A GOOD LOW-PROOF COCKTAIL FOR THOSE OCCASIONS WHEN WE WANT TO
ENJOY A WELL-MADE DRINK BUT DON'T FEEL LIKE CONSUMING A SIZEABLE POUR OF
FULL-STRENGTH SPIRITS. The Diplomat, borrowed from Robert Vermeire's 1922 book
Cocktails: How to Mix Them, is an excellent predinner drink. It's reminiscent of the Duplex and
the Vermouth Panache (page 71) from earlier in the book, but with maraschino standing in
for bitters to add extra depth.

INGREDIENTS

2 oz [60 ml] dry vermouth

1 oz [30 ml] sweet vermouth

¼ oz [7.5 ml] maraschino liqueur

Lemon twist, for garnish

Cocktail cherry, for garnish

DIRECTIONS

*To a mixing glass, add the dry and sweet
vermouths, maraschino liqueur, and ice.
Stir and strain into in a chilled coupe glass.
Garnish with a lemon twist and cherry and
serve.*

FANCY FREE

IF YOU RECALL THE FANCY (PAGE 77) AND FRISCO (PAGE 115) COCKTAILS, YOU'RE
HOPEFULLY RECOGNIZING A TREND. Take a slug of whiskey, a small pour of liqueur, and
perhaps a dash or two of bitters, and you'll likely end up with a pretty good drink. The
Fancy Free is another testament to the success of this simple formula. A straightforward
mixture of bourbon, maraschino liqueur, and a couple dashes of bitters, it's a drink for
those nights when you want an Old-Fashioned with an interesting twist or, if you're like us,
are just out of Rich Demerara Syrup and can't be bothered to make more.

INGREDIENTS

2 oz [60 ml] bourbon

½ oz [15 ml] maraschino liqueur

1 dash Angostura bitters

1 dash orange bitters

Orange peel, for garnish

DIRECTIONS

*To a mixing glass, add the bourbon,
maraschino liqueur, both bitters, and ice. Stir
and strain into a rocks glass filled with ice or a
single large cube. Garnish with an orange peel
and serve.*

RITZ

THE APTLY NAMED RITZ IS THE CREATION OF DALE DEGROFF, ONE OF THE LEGENDARY BARTENDERS WHO HELPED USHER IN THE CONTEMPORARY COCKTAIL REVIVAL. With champagne and cognac, it's an instantly appealing drink that helped introduce maraschino to a modern audience. The flair of finishing the drink with a shock of flamed orange peel (page 26) is another nice touch and one that surely attracted notice in a crowded bar.

INGREDIENTS

¾ oz [22.5 ml] cognac

½ oz [15 ml] orange liqueur

¼ oz [7.5 ml] maraschino liqueur

¼ oz [7.5 ml] fresh lemon juice

2 to 3 oz [60 to 90 ml] sparkling wine

Flamed orange peel, for garnish

DIRECTIONS

To a mixing glass, add the cognac, orange and maraschino liqueurs, lemon juice, and ice. Stir and strain into a chilled coupe glass. Top with the sparkling wine, garnish with flamed orange peel, and serve.

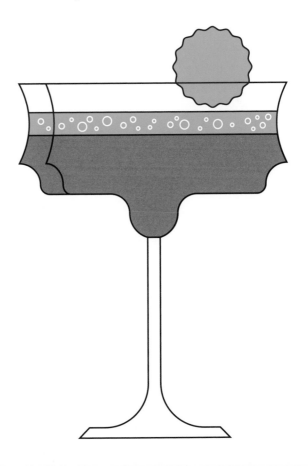

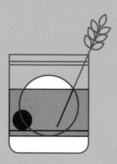

CHAPTER 12

RYE

THE BOTTLES YOU'VE ACQUIRED SO FAR HAVE BEEN ALL ABOUT ADDING
BREADTH TO YOUR HOME BAR. NOW, BY PICKING UP A BOTTLE OF RYE WHIS-
KEY, YOU'RE ADDING DEPTH. This chapter is less about expanding outward and
more about learning to appreciate nuance. That's because rye is very similar to
bourbon. Most everything you learned about the rules of bourbon production—
how it's distilled, aged, and blended—applies to rye as well. The rules are almost
entirely the same. What's different is the recipe. Whereas bourbon must be made
with at least 51 percent corn, rye must be made with a majority of . . . wait for it . . .
rye. Because the production processes are so similar, comparing rye and bourbon
will teach you to appreciate the influence of grain on whiskey, how it compounds
or contrasts with the influence of the barrel, and how all that gives you more con-
trol over the final flavor of the cocktail you're mixing up.

Regarding those differences, broadly speaking, bourbon tends to be sweeter and rounder
while rye is spicier and sharper. Bourbon often provides a larger sounding board for the
flavors and aromas contributed by the barrel itself, and so it's common to taste vanilla,
caramel, butterscotch, and cinnamon. Rye contains those same flavors, but notes of
baking spices, mint, herbs, banana, and pepper often work their way to the fore.

It's worth noting that most bourbons contain some amount of rye, and most ryes
contain some amount of corn, so these contrasts are less about absolutes and more
about emphasis. A rock band and a jazz band might both have drums and electric

guitars, but the overall impression you get from listening will be quite different. The same is true for bourbon and rye.

Rye emerged from near oblivion in the early aughts, and though it may seem like a modern trend, it was once the dominant American whiskey. First produced well before the American Revolution, rye was distilled primarily in Pennsylvania and Maryland. This proximity to the populous northeastern states gave it an advantage over bourbon, a still-nascent spirit produced in a then-difficult-to-access region soon to be known as Kentucky. After America's independence cut off its access to the British rum trade, rye was heartily embraced by former rum-loving patriots. By the early twentieth century, when cocktail culture was coming into its own, rye outsold bourbon by about three to one.

What killed rye was Prohibition. During those dark years, American distillers closed down and cheap Canadian rye (which technically doesn't have to contain any rye at all) flooded the black market. When Prohibition ended, Depression-era corn subsidies made bourbon much cheaper to produce. Rye distillers, already struggling to compete with lower-quality foreign spirits, often couldn't cope. Most closed for good while others struggled to remain profitable as Americans' preferences shifted toward gin and vodka starting in the middle of the century. Brands that remained were bought up by bourbon companies and moved to Kentucky. By the end of the century, only a handful of rye distillers remained active.

Luckily, that all changed in the early aughts when bartenders, looking to the past for inspiration, began to mix drinks calling for America's former preeminent spirit. It didn't take long for the demand for rye to spread all across the country. From 2009 to 2019, rye whiskey sales increased by a staggering 1,200 percent. Though it's still nowhere near the popularity of bourbon, rye once again commands the attention and appreciation it has always deserved.

We have reserved some rye-specific cocktails for this chapter, but while you're getting acquainted with them, we also recommend revisiting some of your favorite bourbon drinks and seeing how they change with rye as the base spirit. The Manhattan (page 68) in particular is worthy of a second look, and the rye version is what you're more likely to encounter in today's cocktail bars. You may discover that there are drinks where you prefer rye to bourbon and vice versa, but we'd encourage you to focus less on which is better and more on how they're different. This is a mapping expedition and it's early for drawing borders. We believe you're up to the challenge.

RYE 101

THE RULES GOVERNING AMERICAN RYE WHISKEY CLOSELY PARALLEL THOSE FOR BOURBON, SO WE WON'T GO INTO TOO MUCH DETAIL ON THEM HERE (REFER BACK TO PAGE 42 FOR THE REGULATIONS ON BOURBON). The main difference is in the mashbill. Whereas bourbon is made with at least 51 percent corn, rye is made with at least 51 percent rye. Rules governing the proofs to which the spirits can be distilled, barrelled, and bottled, as well as the requirement to use new, charred oak containers for aging, are otherwise the same. (Rye from other countries, including Canada, is governed by different standards.) Generally speaking, American rye will tend to have a spicier profile compared to bourbon, though of course this varies from brand to brand.

When it comes to buying rye, our advice is much the same as bourbon. Pick up a straight rye of at least 45 percent ABV. The state of origin is less important, although you'll likely end up with something from Kentucky or Indiana. The goal, as before, is to end up with a whiskey with the strength to stand up in cocktails but that you'd also happily sip neat or on the rocks.

BOTTLES WE REACH FOR

RITTENHOUSE

With a balanced rye spice and caramel profile, bolstered by a 50 percent ABV strength, Rittenhouse Rye is the go-to in quite a few cocktail bars. It's a versatile, well-priced bottle that you can always depend on. For a few bucks more, check out it's longer-aged, higher-proof sibling from the Heaven Hill Distillery, Pikesville Rye.

WILD TURKEY RYE 101

If you want a rye with a sharper edge, we recommend Wild Turkey Rye 101. It's an excellent go-to with the strength to stand up to other bold ingredients.

OLD FORESTER RYE

A relatively new entrant to the market, Old Forester has a bold rye profile that is softened by a subtle tropical banana note. We love it shaken in Whiskey Sours or complex tropics-inspired drinks.

HIGH WEST DOUBLE RYE

Made from a blend of High West's own Utah-distilled rye and some sourced from Indiana, Double Rye is one to grab when you want a peppery, vegetal rye spice in your cocktails.

SAZERAC RYE

For a gentler, lower-proof rye, the Sazerac rye from Buffalo Trace Distillery is a very good option. Vanilla and spicy notes of clove stand out on the finish.

WARD EIGHT

ALCOHOL AND POLITICS HAVE A LONG RELATIONSHIP, THOUGH WHETHER DRINK
DRIVES ONE TO POLITICS OR POLITICS DRIVES ONE TO DRINK VARIES BY THE PERSON.
The most popular story behind the creation of the Ward Eight suggests that it was created
to commemorate an 1898 election victory for Martin Lomasney, a heavy-hitter in Boston
politics. The historic details are vague, but it is generally agreed to be one of Boston's best
contributions to cocktail culture.

The Ward Eight is a perfect example of how to successfully mix with orange juice. Though
recipes vary, they include enough lemon juice to give the drink some spark. What many
early versions lacked was sweetness, with only a tiny bit of grenadine to offset all that
citrus. Even with orange juice, the cocktail needs a little more sugar than those early renditions provide. We like the idea of keeping true to the original juiciness of the drink but
bump up the grenadine to give it body and balance.

INGREDIENTS

2 oz [60 ml] rye
¾ oz [22.5 ml] fresh lemon juice
¾ oz [22.5 ml] fresh orange juice
½ oz [15 ml] grenadine
Cocktail cherry, for garnish

DIRECTIONS

*To a shaker, add the rye, lemon and orange
juices, grenadine, and ice. Shake and strain
into a chilled coupe glass. Garnish with a
cherry and serve.*

MONTE CARLO

THE MONTE CARLO IS AN OLD-FASHIONED VARIATION THAT TRADES IN SIMPLE SYRUP FOR BENEDICTINE. If that sounds remarkably similar to the Frisco we covered a few chapters back (page 115), well, that's because it is. Even so, there are a few key points of difference that make the Monte Carlo worth spending some time on. First, the Monte Carlo specifically calls for the use of rye. Second, it adds a dash of bitters. These are subtle changes, but they make for a unique drink and provide a different approach to balancing Benedictine and whiskey in a stirred cocktail. As we'll see in this and in several cocktails coming up soon, rye and Benedictine are a match made in heaven.

The first published mention of the Monte Carlo we found is in the 1944 edition of *Bartender's Friend* by Nick Thomas. The original recipe called for equal parts rye and Benedictine, which is delicious if served for dessert but otherwise overly sweet. We like the balance of the specs below, which allows all the ingredients to show without overpowering each other.

INGREDIENTS
1¾ oz [22.5 ml] rye
½ oz [15 ml] Benedictine
1 dash Angostura bitters

DIRECTIONS
To a mixing glass, add the rye, Benedictine, bitters, and ice. Stir, strain into a rocks glass filled with ice or a single large cube, and serve.

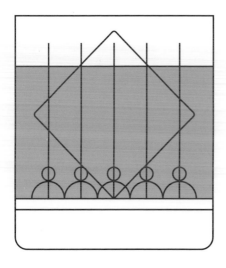

VIEUX CARRÉ

THE VIEUX CARRÉ IS ONE OF THE QUINTESSENTIAL NEW ORLEANS COCKTAILS, CRE-ATED IN 1938 BY LOCAL BARTENDER WALTER BERGERON. The name itself (pronounced "voo caw-ray") translates to "old square," a reference to New Orleans's lively French Quarter. Enjoying one at its place of origin in the rotating Carousel Bar in the Monteleone Hotel is a must whenever you're in the city.

The Vieux Carré is essentially a complex spin on the Manhattan, multilayered and approachable at the same time. Each component works to balance the others, the spice of rye offsetting the suppleness of cognac, the honey in Benedictine brightening the dark aromatics in sweet vermouth, the mild anise note of Peychaud's complementing the cinnamon of Angostura. All this leads to a drink that appeals regardless of one's level of experience in the world of cocktails; it's one of our favorites to introduce to Old-Fashioned or Manhattan drinkers who are ready to move on to something new. To say more about the Vieux Carré would only delay you further from making one right now. That seems tragic. Here's the recipe.

INGREDIENTS

¾ oz [22.5 ml] rye

¾ oz [22.5 ml] cognac

¾ oz [22.5 ml] sweet vermouth

1 generous barspoon (⅙ oz [5 ml]) Benedictine

1 dash Angostura bitters

1 dash Peychauds bitters

Lemon peel, for garnish

DIRECTIONS

To a mixing glass, add the rye, cognac, vermouth, Benedictine, both bitters, and ice. Stir and strain into a rocks glass over ice or a single large cube. Garnish with a lemon peel and serve.

SARATOGA

THERE'S A FANTASTIC OLD INTERVIEW WITH VANILLA ICE IN WHICH HE ARGUES THAT THE BEAT FOR "ICE ICE BABY" IS NOT A COPY OF QUEEN'S "UNDER PRESSURE" BUT INSTEAD ABSOLUTELY UNIQUE. The argument rests on the fact that at the end of the measure, a single note is different. It's not a convincing argument; it's absurd to take credit for the whole thing when really all you did was change one thing. Well, unless we're talking cocktails. Many uniquely named drinks are the mixology equivalent of a Vanilla Ice sample. Case in point, the Saratoga, created in the late 1880s. The Saratoga is the "Ice Ice Baby" to the Manhattan's "Under Pressure," subbing out some of the whiskey for a bit of cognac. Think of this drink when you want to bring a minor changeup to your usual Manhattan, or when you're in the mood for a Vieux Carré but are out of Benedictine.

INGREDIENTS
1 oz [30 ml] rye
1 oz [30 ml] cognac
1 oz [30 ml] sweet vermouth
2 dashes Angostura bitters
Lemon peel, for garnish

DIRECTIONS
To a mixing glass, add the rye, cognac, vermouth, bitters, and ice. Stir and strain into a chilled coupe glass. Garnish with a lemon peel and serve.

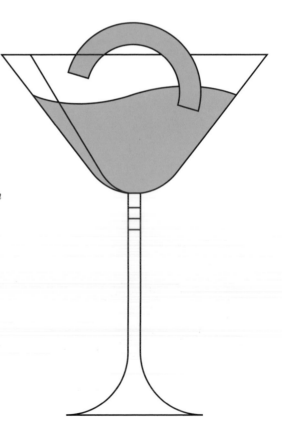

SCOFFLAW

IN 1924 A BANKER AND PROHIBITION SUPPORTER NAMED DELCEVARE KING HELD A NATIONWIDE CONTEST TO COME UP WITH A TERM TO DENOTE PEOPLE WHO BROKE THE LAW BY IMBIBING. (To be fair, it had to be hard going through life named Delcevare.) The winning entry was the compound word *scofflaw*, as in one who scoffs at the law. It should come as no surprise that said law scoffers enthusiastically embraced the name and even made a drink in its honor. The Scofflaw was created at Harry's New York Bar in Paris by a "genial bartender" named Jock, and it was described as Paris's "wet answer" to America's dry word. It quickly became a favorite of traveling Americans.

The Scofflaw has seen a lot of modern interpretations, but frankly we think the original recipe is pretty good. It's admittedly a touch sweet, but when we tried to offset this with more booze or lemon, the drink lost the richness and depth that makes it delicious. This is one of those drinks that simply tastes best on the sweeter side. We recommend taking it on the rocks, but we cannot, our lawyers inform us, recommend scoffing at any laws while you sip it.

INGREDIENTS

1 oz [30 ml] rye

1 oz [30 ml] dry vermouth

½ oz [15 ml] grenadine

Generous ½ oz [15 ml] fresh lemon juice

1 dash orange bitters

Orange peel, for garnish

DIRECTIONS

To a shaker, add the rye, vermouth, grenadine, lemon juice, bitters, and ice. Shake and strain into a rocks glass. Garnish with an orange peel and serve.

OLD PAL

OUR RECIPE FOR THE OLD PAL IS A BIT DIFFERENT THAN WHAT YOU'LL FIND IN MOST COCKTAIL GUIDES, WHICH IS AN EQUAL-PARTS DRINK OF RYE WHISKEY, Campari, and dry vermouth. If that sounds like a bracingly dry and bitter cocktail to you, well, you're right. Going back to its origins in Harry MacElhone's *ABC of Mixing Cocktails*, however, we note that he called for Canadian Club whisky. Although Canadian whisky is often referred to as rye, it's often considerably sweeter than what we know as rye whiskey in the United States. To our palates, that suggests that the drink would benefit from adding a touch of demerara sugar. Doing so rounds it out without sacrificing the acidity of dry vermouth or the robust flavor of American rye whiskey. You get the best of modern interpretations of the drink with the balance of the original.

INGREDIENTS

1 oz [30 ml] rye

1 oz [30 ml] Campari

1 oz [30 ml] dry vermouth

1 barspoon (⅙ oz [5 ml]) Rich Demerara Syrup (page 33)

DIRECTIONS

To a mixing glass, add the rye, Campari, vermouth, syrup, and ice. Stir, strain into a rocks glass filled with ice or a large ice cube, and serve.

TWELVE MILE LIMIT

IF WE LEARNED ANYTHING FROM THE SCOFFLAW, IT'S THAT WHEN THE GOVERN-MENT TRIES TO MAKE THINGS LESS FUN, BARTENDERS MAKE FUN OF THE GOVERN-MENT. This is a tradition we're very proud of and we hope it endures forever. The Twelve Mile Limit is another wonderful example. When Prohibition first began, the ban on liquor extended three miles out to sea. Enterprising businesspeople therefore anchored ships just a bit farther than three miles out and ferried thirsty Americans to a floating party. What followed was a cocktail commemorating this achievement called the Three Mile Limit, then a quadrupling of said limit out to twelve miles by a less-than-amused government.

The distance of twelve miles may have been too much for party barges to contend with, but it nonetheless inspired another commemorative cocktail, the Twelve Mile Limit. It was a stronger version of the Three Mile Limit that also happens to taste a lot better. This blend of rum, cognac, and rye manages to be welcoming, smooth, and refreshing, exactly the kind of drink you'd be thirsty for after sailing a dozen miles. Luckily you simply need to travel the very short distance to your home bar to shake up one of these and raise a toast to combining boating and drinking solely on your own terms.

INGREDIENTS
1 oz [30 ml] light rum
½ oz [15 ml] rye
½ oz [15 ml] cognac
½ oz [15 ml] grenadine
½ oz [15 ml] fresh lemon juice
Lemon peel, for garnish

DIRECTIONS
To a shaker, add the rum, rye, cognac, grenadine, lemon juice, and ice. Shake and strain into a chilled coupe glass. Garnish with a lemon peel and serve.

RED HOOK

CONSIDERING THAT IT'S A SIMPLE, THREE-INGREDIENT TAKE ON THE MANHATTAN, ONE MIGHT ASSUME THAT THE RED HOOK IS A CLASSIC COCKTAIL. But one would be wrong, because the Red Hook is actually a modern invention. Created in 2003 at the influential Milk & Honey in Manhattan by Vincenzo Errico, the Red Hook is a throwback to a time before every New York City neighborhood had a cocktail named after it. More important though, coming from an era when bartenders were particularly enamored with bitter flavors, the Red Hook shows an admirable amount of restraint. Instead of accenting a Manhattan with bitters, it brings in maraschino liqueur. The rose, almond, and cherry notes work perfectly with the earthier botanicals in sweet vermouth.

About that vermouth, though: The original recipe calls for Punt e Mes, which is a particularly bitter and strong brand. (The name means "point and a half," the half referring to the extra bitterness.) We try to avoid calling for specific brands in this book, but this is one drink where you may want to seek it out or at least use a richer, full-flavored vermouth. With a light vermouth, you may want to scale back the maraschino a bit. However you decide to make it, stir up a Red Hook, put on OutKast's "Hey Ya!," and toast to the modern classics of 2003.

INGREDIENTS
2 oz [60 ml] rye
½ oz [15 ml] sweet vermouth
½ oz [15 ml] maraschino liqueur
Cocktail cherry, for garnish

DIRECTIONS
To a mixing glass, add the rye, vermouth, maraschino liqueur, and ice. Stir and strain into a chilled coupe glass. Garnish with a cherry and serve.

TRINIDAD SOUR

IF THE RED HOOK WAS ABOUT HOW TO USE BITTER FLAVORS WITH RESTRAINT, THE TRINIDAD SOUR IS ITS POLAR OPPOSITE. It uses more than an ounce of Angostura bitters. Given that Angostura bitters are technically classified as nonpotable, that's quite a feat! It also makes this one of the more expensive cocktails in this book to make. Bitters are very affordable when you're just using them a dash or two at a time, but when you start turning them into the main ingredient, the cost adds up quickly. So, this probably won't be a drink you make every night, but it's very much worth trying.

The Trinidad Sour pushes the envelope of how much bitters can palatably go into a drink. It arose in a period in which bartenders and cocktail lovers had a major infatuation with bitters, with this drink being the equivalent of writing your crush's name over and over again in your notebook. Though we look back on some crushes with embarrassment, others we realize were completely valid. The Trinidad Sour is one of the latter. Maybe it won't turn out to be your long-term partner, but it's a wonderful fling. It's the kind of drink that shows you what's possible way out on the edge of mixology, which may also lead one to appreciate the simple pleasure of a subtly balanced classic all the more. (There are conflicting stories about the origins of this drink and various versions of the recipe; this one comes to us from Damon Dyer, creator of the Monte Cassino cocktail [page 188].)

INGREDIENTS
1¼ oz [37 ml] Angostura bitters
1¼ oz [37 ml] orgeat
¾ oz [22.5 ml] fresh lemon juice
½ oz [15 ml] rye
Lemon peel, for garnish

DIRECTIONS

To a shaker, add the bitters, orgeat, lemon juice, rye, and ice. Shake and strain into a chilled coupe glass. Garnish with a lemon peel and serve.

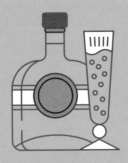

CHAPTER 13

ABSINTHE

MANY OF THE THINGS YOU MAY HAVE HEARD ABOUT ABSINTHE ARE NOT QUITE TRUE. It's not illegal. You're not supposed to set it on fire. And, in all likelihood, it won't make you hallucinate green fairies. (If that's the sort of experience you're looking for, we're afraid our book won't be of much help.)

Now that we've taken all the fun out of absinthe, let's talk about what it is and why you should pick up a bottle for your home bar, even without the promise of dancing fairies. In a story that should sound familiar by now, absinthe began as an allegedly medicinal mixture of high-proof spirits and potent botanicals, with production focused in Switzerland and France. Its signature ingredient will also be familiar: wormwood, the same root that gave its name to vermouth and that gives absinthe a slightly bitter edge. Like gin, absinthes can be made with a wide variety of other botanicals, often chosen to give the spirit notes of anise. Common inclusions are anise, fennel, and hyssop, as well as mint or coriander.

Wormwood gives absinthe part of its flavor, but it also contributed to the spirit's bad reputation. Bohemian artists in the Belle Époque took heartily to absinthe, and lurid tales of mad behavior under its influence led to it being banned in the United States, parts of Europe, and elsewhere in the early twentieth century. In truth, any issues were likely due to the spirits' high alcohol content, potentially toxic additions from disreputable producers, or the use of other psychoactive substances.

As with many drug scares, the dangers were inflated, but wormwood took the fall. Absinthe mostly disappeared or was driven underground, with drinkers turning to less complex substitutes such as pastis.

Luckily for us, governments eventually came to their senses and made absinthe legal again. In France and Switzerland, that meant explicitly lifting the ban. In the United States, it was legalized sort of accidentally. Modernization of laws focused on thujone, a specific compound in wormwood that can be toxic in extremely high quantities. Most traditionally made absinthes fall well below the legal level, so old-school absinthes came back to the United States in 2007, to much rejoicing among American bartenders. That's because absinthe is both interesting in its own right and an absolutely essential ingredient in classic cocktails.

Absinthe by itself is a rough beast, coming in at a very high strength (often around 60 percent ABV) and a strong concentration of botanical notes. Its anise-forward taste can also be challenging, and your appreciation of absinthe may depend on how receptive you are to those kinds of flavors. In any case, it's not intended to be consumed straight out of the bottle. In traditional absinthe service, the spirit is diluted with cold water and perhaps a bit of sugar. In cocktails, we often employ just a whisper of absinthe to subtly provide depth, complexity, and hints of anise.

Once you get your bottle of absinthe, we suggest getting to know it the traditional way: dilute it with 3 to 5 times the volume of ice cold water to absinthe, and add a sugar cube (or a teaspoon or so of Rich Simple Syrup, page 33) for every ounce [30 ml] of absinthe. Then dive into the cocktails that follow, which range from those offering just a subtle absinthe note to others featuring the spirit front and center.

ABSINTHE 101

A RICH MYTHOLOGY SURROUNDS THE CONSUMPTION OF ABSINTHE, BUT ITS PRODUCTION IS RELATIVELY STRAIGHTFORWARD. It's a botanical spirit, typically made by macerating botanicals in alcohol and then redistilling it to produce a clear spirit. The one herb that's absolutely essential to its production is grand wormwood, also known as Artemisia absinthium. Traditionally it will also include herbs such as anise, fennel, or hyssop. There are two main classifications to know and seek out:

BLANCHE: Produced entirely via distillation, blanche absinthes are completely clear.

VERTE: Verte absinthes undergo a second maceration after distillation in which additional herbs and botanicals are added, contributing a green hue to the finished spirit. An absinthe made with actual herbs will be colored a natural shade of green; if it glows like a neon sign, the sign is telling you to stay away.

Traditional absinthe is a high-proof spirit, intended to be consumed either diluted with cold water or as a component in cocktails. When absinthe is diluted with water, some oils within the spirit will fall out of solution, producing a cloudy effect called *louche*.

When selecting absinthe for your bar, it's worth investing in a quality spirit. A bottle of absinthe will likely last you a long time, so get a good one. (If you want to economize, look for a smaller bottle.)

BOTTLES WE REACH FOR

LUCID

The first genuine absinthe available in the United States in the contemporary era, Lucid helped revive the category. It's an excellent introduction to absinthe, with a bittersweet edge that avoids leaning too far into anise. Its availability in 375 ml bottles is an added feature, allowing one to dip a toe into absinthe without committing to a full-size bottle.

KÜBLER

On the other hand, if you find yourself running through absinthe too quickly, Kübler is a great option. A Swiss blanche absinthe, it louches to an appealing shade of pearl and offers sweet notes of licorice. Its liter bottle should last even the most ardent absinthe devotee a decent amount of time.

VIEUX PONTARLIER

A wonderful absinthe in the verte style from the "absinthe capital" of France, this is one of our go-to picks for sipping in a traditional absinthe service. It will, of course, also show very well in cocktails.

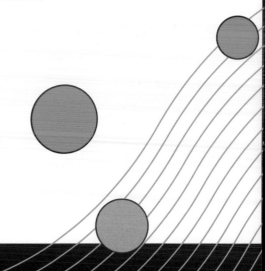

SAZERAC

AH, THE SAZERAC. If not for this one cocktail, we may have filed away the bottle of absinthe for a bit later in this book. But to advise you to purchase a bottle of rye and then not proceed forthwith to the means of making a Sazerac would be unthinkable. It's one of the all-time greats, enough to justify the splurge on absinthe all by itself, even though we use it here only to rinse the serving glass to contribute subtle flavor and aromatics.

The Sazerac is synonymous with New Orleans, and there's no other city in the United States where you can find a well-made Sazerac in so many places. As a local friend advised on how to survive the summer heat and humidity there, "walk on the shady side of the street and stop for a Sazerac on every corner." The Sazerac is firmly in the tradition of Old-Fashioned or improved whiskey cocktails, yet it stands alone, having achieved its own sort of perfection.

Precisely how you make it is up to you. Like the martini, this is a cocktail where personal conviction and argumentation come into play. Peychaud's bitters are absolutely essential. An ongoing debate is whether to augment them with Angostura too. We are ourselves bitterly divided on the question and so can't provide a definitive answer. A convincing argument can be made that the original recipe called for both, and that Angostura adds depth and complexity; a counterargument can be made that many top New Orleans bartenders stick with just the Peychaud's, and that this gives the drink a clarity of expression. To settle the question for yourself, try it both ways. You'll end up with two Sazeracs—hardly the worst of outcomes.

INGREDIENTS

Absinthe, for rinse

2 oz [60 ml] rye

1 barspoon (⅙ oz [5 ml]) Rich Simple Syrup (page 33)

4 dashes Peychaud's bitters, or 3 dashes Peychaud's bitters plus 1 dash Angostura bitters

Lemon peel

DIRECTIONS

Coat a small, chilled rocks glass with a little absinthe, discarding the excess, or spritz the glass with absinthe from an atomizer. To a mixing glass, add the rye, syrup, bitters, and ice. Stir and strain into the prepared rocks glass. Express the lemon peel over the drink, discard the peel, and serve.

ABSINTHE FRAPPÉ

NOW THAT WE'VE EASED INTO ABSINTHE WITH THE SAZERAC, WHICH CALLS FOR A MERE WHISPER OF THE GREEN STUFF, LET'S DIVE RIGHT INTO A TRUE ABSINTHE LOVERS' COCKTAIL. The Absinthe Frappé is another authentic New Orleans drink, originating in the 1870s at the bar now known as the Old Absinthe House. At its simplest, it's just absinthe served with a little sugar over crushed ice. Other recipes bring a little something else to the drink: soda, citrus, anisette, cream, or even Benedictine. As you can guess by now, we're keen to that last option. That said, we also really like the version below, which brings refreshing mint into play. It's a strong, intensely flavorful cocktail, and it's irresistible in a sweltering New Orleans summer.

As the name suggests, the frappé needs to be made with crushed ice or a blender. We generally opt for the former, breaking out our ice-smashing hammers to reduce the cubes into tiny pebbles. Feel free to choose your own method, but finely crushed ice is an absolute must.

INGREDIENTS

6 to 8 mint leaves

¼ oz [7.5 ml] Rich Simple Syrup (page 33)

1½ oz [45 ml] absinthe

2 oz [60 ml] soda water

Mint sprigs, for garnish

DIRECTIONS

In the bottom of a shaker, gently muddle the mint leaves and syrup, lightly pressing the leaves to extract their flavor. Add the absinthe, rinsing the muddler with it as you pour. Add crushed ice, shake, and pour everything (without straining) into a rocks glass. Add soda, stir to combine, and top with additional crushed ice. Garnish with a bouquet of mint and serve.

ABSINTHE SUISSESSE

THE ABSINTHE SUISSESSE IS ANOTHER NEW ORLEANS CLASSIC, THIS ONE MADE FOR BRUNCHING. There are two schools of thought when it comes to brunch cocktails. One is to keep things light and low-proof so that you can go on to have a reasonably productive day. The other is, well, this one. The Suissesse calls for a full 1½ oz [45 ml] of absinthe, and given that absinthe tends to weigh in between 50 and 60 percent ABV, that's a serious drink. Add in cream and orgeat, and the forecast for an afternoon nap is looking mighty certain. Pick the right day to try this, is what we're saying. But definitely do try it. It's stupid delicious.

INGREDIENTS

¾ oz [22.5 ml] cream

½ oz [15 ml] orgeat

1 egg white

1½ oz [45 ml] absinthe

DIRECTIONS

To a shaker without ice, add the cream, orgeat, and egg white. Dry shake to aerate the egg white. Add absinthe and crushed ice and shake again, pour into a rocks glass without straining, and serve.

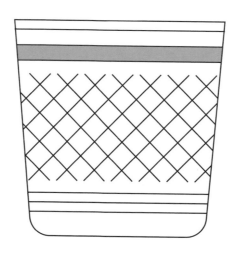

IMPROVED COCKTAIL

YOU'VE SIPPED THE "OLD-FASHIONED" COCKTAIL (PAGE 45), YOU'VE IMBIBED THE "FANCY" COCKTAIL (PAGE 77), AND NOW IT'S TIME FOR THE "IMPROVED" COCKTAIL. These drinks harken back to a simpler time in mixology when there weren't so many ingredients to work with. A cocktail was just spirits, sugar, and bitters. If you added a little something to it, you had something new. By the 1870s, one popular way to "improve" a cocktail was to add a touch of maraschino and absinthe. As for the primary spirit to be used, it could be just about anything. Whiskey, cognac, or genever are three winning options. We've given it here with rye, but pick your poison.

We mentioned in the very beginning of the book that you may want to hold on to your empty bitters bottles. Here we get to the reason why. Absinthe is such a powerful ingredient that you can use it in small amounts just like bitters. We like to keep an empty bitters bottle full of absinthe in our home bars for drinks like this so that we can add it a dash at a time. (You can also purchase stylish dasher bottles from specialty barware shops.) If you don't have the right bottle, just pour a tiny amount in a barspoon and add it to your drink, or rinse the glass as when making a Sazerac (page 169).

INGREDIENTS

2 oz [60 ml] rye

1 scant barspoon (⅙ oz [5 ml]) maraschino liqueur

1 dash absinthe

1 barspoon (⅙ oz [5 ml]) Rich Simple Syrup (page 33)

2 dashes Angostura bitters

Lemon peel, for garnish

DIRECTIONS

To a mixing glass, add the rye, maraschino liqueur, absinthe, syrup, bitters, and ice. Stir and strain into a rocks glass filled with ice or a large ice cube. Garnish with a lemon peel and serve.

TUXEDO #2

IF THIS WERE A BOOK OF COCKTAIL ARCHAEOLOGY, WE WOULD ENTER HERE INTO A LONG DISCOURSE ON THE EVOLUTION OF THE TUXEDO COCKTAIL, THE TUXEDO #2, AND THE CLOSELY RELATED TURF CLUB. Since we're focused more on the practicalities of mixing drinks, we'll keep it brief. The Tuxedo #2 is named for the actual Tuxedo Club in New York, the same one that lent its name to the formal dinner jacket. The cocktail is comfortably in the martini tradition but dressed up with a touch of maraschino and a rinse of absinthe. These additions make the drink even more elegant, achieving a superb balance. Trust us, this is a seriously good cocktail—the kind you'd want to imbibe while donning your fanciest tuxedo.

INGREDIENTS

Absinthe, for rinse

2 oz [60 ml] gin

¾ oz [22.5 ml] dry vermouth

¼ oz [7.5 ml] maraschino liqueur

3 dashes orange bitters

Orange peel, for garnish

DIRECTIONS

Coat a chilled coupe glass with a little absinthe, discarding the excess. To a mixing glass, add the gin, vermouth, maraschino liqueur, bitters, and ice. Stir and strain into the prepared coupe. Garnish with an orange peel and serve.

COCKTAIL DE LA LOUISIANE

THIS WAS THE HOUSE COCKTAIL OF THE DE LA LOUISIANE RESTAURANT IN NEW ORLE-
ANS, AND WITH ONE SIP YOU'LL KNOW WHY THIS SEDUCTIVE DRINK HELD THE HONOR.
Recorded in the 1937 book *Famous New Orleans Drinks and How to Mix 'Em* by Stanley Clisby
Arthur, it was long forgotten until it enjoyed a minor revival among twenty-first-century
bartenders. Nowadays they tend to fiddle with the proportions, making it more like a
Manhattan with some flavorful accents. We prefer the magic of the original recipe, which
is luscious, rich, and complex. We brighten it up just the slightest bit with a twist of lemon
peel. (Remember when we said that rye and Benedictine are a match made in heaven? This
is the kind of drink that proves it.)

INGREDIENTS

¾ oz [22.5 ml] rye

¾ oz [22.5 ml] sweet vermouth

¾ oz [22.5 ml] Benedictine

2 barspoons (⅓ oz [10 ml]) absinthe

3 dashes Peychaud's bitters

Lemon peel, for garnish

Cocktail cherry, for garnish

DIRECTIONS

*To a mixing glass, add the rye, vermouth,
Benedictine, absinthe, bitters, and ice. Stir
and strain into a chilled coupe glass. Garnish
with a lemon peel and cherry and serve.*

WALDORF

SPEAKING OF SIGNATURE DRINKS, THIS WAS AT ONE TIME THE NAMESAKE COCKTAIL OF THE WALDORF HOTEL IN NEW YORK. The original was made in equal parts and served on crushed ice, but we prefer to serve it more like a Manhattan rendered beguilingly complex with a little absinthe.

INGREDIENTS

2 oz [60 ml] rye

¾ oz [22.5 ml] sweet vermouth

¼ oz [7.5 ml] absinthe

2 dashes Angostura bitters

Cocktail cherry, for garnish

DIRECTIONS

To a mixing glass, add the rye, vermouth, absinthe, bitters, and ice. Stir and strain into a chilled coupe glass. Garnish with a cherry and serve.

QUILL

NEGRONIS ARE ALREADY MADE WITH THREE ASSERTIVELY FLAVORED INGREDIENTS, SO WHY NOT ADD A FOURTH? Absinthe is one of the few spirits that can stand up to gin and Campari even when employed in a small amount. There's only ¼ oz [7.5 ml] in the Quill, but that's enough to transform the drink. It's a subtle addition that brings a pleasant note of anise to the classic Negroni.

INGREDIENTS

1 oz [30 ml] gin

1 oz [30 ml] Campari

1 oz [30 ml] sweet vermouth

¼ oz [7.5 ml] absinthe

Orange peel, for garnish

DIRECTIONS

To a mixing glass, add the gin, Campari, vermouth, absinthe, and ice. Stir and strain into a rocks glass filled with ice or a single large cube. Garnish with an orange peel and serve.

WIFFIN

COCKTAIL HISTORIAN DAVID WONDRICH HAS A REPUTATION FOR DIGGING UP RECIPES FROM LONG-FORGOTTEN SOURCES, BUT THIS DRINK DOESN'T EVEN COME FROM AN ACTUAL BAR OR COCKTAIL BOOK. He found it described by P. G. Wodehouse in his short story "The Passing of Ambrose," in which character Ambrose Wiffin longs for a cocktail made with "gin blended smoothly against Italian vermouth and the spot of old brandy nestled in like a trusting child against the dash of absinthe." The drink may have originated in fiction, but it's worth mixing up in the real world.

INGREDIENTS

1½ oz [45 ml] gin

¾ oz [22.5 ml] sweet vermouth

½ oz [15 ml] cognac

1 dash absinthe

Lemon peel, for garnish

DIRECTIONS

To a mixing glass, add the gin, vermouth, cognac, absinthe, and ice. Stir and strain into a chilled coupe glass. Garnish with a lemon peel and serve.

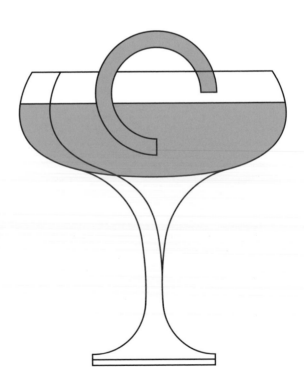

CHRYSANTHEMUM

WE LIKE A GOOD STIFF DRINK AS MUCH AS ANYONE, BUT IT'S ALWAYS A GOOD IDEA TO HAVE AT LEAST A FEW LOW-PROOF COCKTAIL RECIPES IN YOUR REPERTOIRE FOR WHEN YOU'RE TRYING TO STAY COOL AND COLLECTED. The Chrysanthemum fits the bill perfectly. It's mostly vermouth, but accents of absinthe and Benedictine give it the depth of a much boozier concoction. Our version is a bit drier than the original; if you feel like adding a dash of orange bitters too, that won't do the drink or the drinker any harm.

INGREDIENTS
2 oz [60 ml] dry vermouth

½ oz [15 ml] Benedictine

2 barspoons (⅓ oz [10 ml]) absinthe

Orange peel, for garnish

DIRECTIONS
To a mixing glass, add the vermouth, Benedictine, absinthe, and ice. Stir and strain into a chilled coupe glass. Garnish with an orange peel and serve.

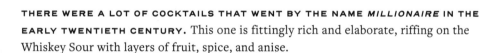

MILLIONAIRE

THERE WERE A LOT OF COCKTAILS THAT WENT BY THE NAME *MILLIONAIRE* IN THE EARLY TWENTIETH CENTURY. This one is fittingly rich and elaborate, riffing on the Whiskey Sour with layers of fruit, spice, and anise.

INGREDIENTS
2 oz [60 ml] bourbon

½ oz [15 ml] orange liqueur

¼ oz [7.5 ml] absinthe

½ oz [15 ml] fresh lemon juice

½ oz [15 ml] grenadine

1 egg white

Freshly grated nutmeg, for garnish

DIRECTIONS
To a shaker, add the bourbon, orange liqueur, absinthe, lemon juice, grenadine, egg white, and ice. Shake hard, or try the reverse shake as detailed in the directions for the White Lady (page 79). Strain into a chilled coupe glass. Grate fresh nutmeg over the surface and serve.

CHAPTER 14

CHARTREUSE

WE ARE VERY EXCITED ABOUT THE BOTTLE WE'RE INTRODUCING YOU TO IN THIS CHAPTER. Chartreuse is one of the world's greatest spirits as well as one of our personal favorites. Chartreuse will expand your bar's range of herbal liqueurs. The first herbal liqueur you added to your bar, Benedictine (page 113), was a perfect introduction to the category; its herbal profile is complex but approachable, wrapped up in a cozy dose of delicious honey. If trying Benedictine is like wading slowly into the pool of herbal liqueurs, drinking Chartreuse is backing up, taking a running start, and doing a cannonball into the deep end. Chartreuse is an experience.

The story of Chartreuse began in 1605 when Carthusian monks in the Chartreuse mountains of France were given an alchemist's recipe for an "elixir of long life." That complex recipe, containing 130 different ingredients, took time to perfect. It wasn't until 1764 that the first official bottlings of "Elixir Vegetal de la Grande-Chartreuse" were available for medicinal use. Coming in at a staggering 71 percent ABV, these early elixirs were guaranteed to either cure you or at least render you entirely unaware of your ailments. It wasn't until 1840 that the monks lowered the strength of their original formulation to a strong but palatable 55 percent ABV now known as "green Chartreuse." They also developed a sweeter, milder yellow version that's now bottled at 43 percent ABV.

Just as we suggested that you simultaneously pick up sweet and dry vermouths, we recommend you acquire both green and yellow Chartreuse for this chapter. Although Chartreuse is one of the more expensive spirits in the book, it is fortunately available in half-size (375 ml) bottles, so you can sample them without breaking the bank. If your tastes are anything like ours, however, it won't be long before you're committing to full-size bottles.

Since it's produced by monks who are committed to piety and helping the greater good, you might assume that once the recipe for Chartreuse was perfected, they immediately made their medicinal formula widely known so that as many people as possible could benefit from its use. Alas, the recipe for Chartreuse is in fact an extremely tightly guarded secret. Even within the monastery, only two people know the precise measurements of each of the 130 ingredients. In the old bakery at the monastery, those two monks blend by hand every single batch of herbs and botanicals used in the making of the liqueur. Those blends are then sent to the nearby distillery where the botanicals are macerated in alcohol, distilled, and aged underground in wooden casks for three to five years. After this period, they are naturally colored green or yellow, sweetened, and bottled for sale.

The flavor of Chartreuse is, as one might expect of a liqueur made with more than a hundred ingredients, extremely complex. The green expression is dense with flavor. Aided by the higher proof, it's a full-on assault of vegetal herbs, baking spice, citrus, and slight bitterness. Much like Campari, Chartreuse makes a strong first impression. The yellow bottling is a little more approachable thanks to its lower proof, though it's still potently herbaceous. You may not immediately take to sipping Chartreuse neat as a nightcap, but once you fall in love with it, there's nothing else in the world that quite compares.

Luckily, an easy way to get to know Chartreuse is in cocktails, and the spirit is an essential ingredient in some of the most delicious drinks ever created. When mixed, its complex tapestry of botanicals adds incredible depth. Much like Campari adds unmistakable bitterness to cocktails, Chartreuse brings intense herbal flavors. It pushes in that direction much further than ingredients like vermouth or Benedictine and creates irresistible layers of flavor that have been beloved by bartenders for well over a century. (We should also mention that green Chartreuse is one of the best things ever in hot chocolate.) It can be a challenging addition to your home bar, but once you taste the peerless character it brings to cocktails, we think you'll see why it earns its place.

STREGA

This golden Italian bitter is made from around seventy botanicals including fennel, mint, juniper, and saffron. Though it can be used as a potentially intriguing substitute in cocktails that call for yellow Chartreuse, we find it a touch sharper and particularly well suited for pairing with gin and mezcal.

GENEPY

Genepy is another green, herbal liqueur with a complex profile, named for an Alpine herb of the Artemisia genus. The rendition made by Dolin (of vermouth fame) is one of the most widely available. With notes of sage and mint, and a light floral character, it can be swapped for Chartreuse with different, but often pleasing, results.

CENTERBA

If you find yourself drawn to complex herbal liqueurs, you may want to challenge yourself with Centerba. Distilled with 100 herbs, very dry, and bottled at 70 percent alcohol, Centerba is an extreme herbal spirit. We love it in small quantities, balanced with honey or other rich, sweet flavors.

CHARTREUSE VEP

The VEP stands for vieillissement exceptionnellement prolongé, or "exceptionally long aging." These bottlings of Chartreuse, which also come in green and yellow varieties, are distinguished by years of aging in large, mostly neutral casks that allow the flavors to marry.

LAST WORD

THE LAST WORD IS ONE OF THE MOST INFLUENTIAL DRINKS OF THE MODERN COCKTAIL RENAISSANCE, YET ITS ORIGINS GO BACK MUCH FURTHER. It was reportedly created at the Detroit Athletic Club sometime during Prohibition and somehow made its way into Ted Saucier's 1951 book *Bottoms Up*. From there it languished in obscurity for fifty years until beloved Seattle bartender Murray Stenson of the venerable Zig Zag Café found it, made it, and put it on the menu. From there it spread around the world, securing its status as a new classic.

There are a few reasons for its influence. One is that it's damn delicious. Another is that it's easy to remember the recipe, which is just four equal parts. Lastly, it's the rare kind of drink that lends itself to infinite variation, inspiring new riffs by swapping out one or two of the ingredients. Switch the gin for whiskey, or the Chartreuse for some other herbal liqueur, et voilà, you've got a whole new cocktail. The method doesn't always work, but you'd be surprised how often it does. First, though, introduce your palate to the original.

INGREDIENTS

¾ oz [22.5 ml] green Chartreuse

¾ oz [22.5 ml] gin

¾ oz [22.5 ml] maraschino liqueur

¾ oz [22.5 ml] fresh lime juice

Cocktail cherry, for garnish

DIRECTIONS

To a shaker, add the Chartreuse, gin, maraschino liqueur, lime juice, and ice. Shake and strain into a chilled coupe glass. Garnish with a cherry and serve.

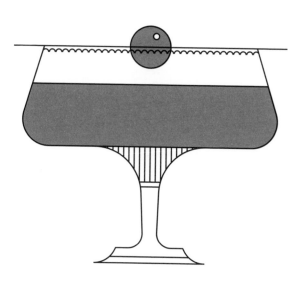

CLOISTER

FOR A MORE RESTRAINED AND APPROACHABLE COCKTAIL WITH GIN AND CHAR-
TREUSE, TRY THE CLOISTER, A DRINK THAT APPEARED IN THE 1970S BUT FEELS LIKE
A MUCH OLDER CLASSIC. We follow the lead of PDT in New York by adding a touch of
sugar to round out the citrus and potent spirits.

INGREDIENTS

1½ oz [45 ml] gin

½ oz [15 ml] yellow Chartreuse

½ oz [15 ml] grapefruit juice

¼ oz [7.5 ml] lemon juice

1 barspoon (⅙ oz [5 ml]) Rich Simple Syrup (page 33)

Grapefruit twist, for garnish

DIRECTIONS

*To a shaker, add the gin, yellow Chartreuse,
grapefruit and lemon juices, syrup, and ice.
Shake and strain into a chilled coupe glass.
Garnish with a grapefruit twist and serve.*

FINAL WARD

WE NOTED THAT THE LAST WORD (PAGE 181) HAS SPAWNED NUMEROUS VARIATIONS,
and one of our favorites comes from New York City bartender Phil Ward (hence the "Final
Ward," one of the most enviable cocktail puns in mixology history). Phil swapped out
the gin for rye. Then, since whiskey is generally a better friend to lemon than to lime, he
changed up the citrus too. The result is a drink with the recognizable DNA of the Last Word
but a wholly different flavor profile.

INGREDIENTS

¾ oz [22.5 ml] green Chartreuse

¾ oz [22.5 ml] rye

¾ oz [22.5 ml] maraschino liqueur

¾ oz [22.5 ml] fresh lemon juice

DIRECTIONS

*To a shaker, add the Chartreuse, rye,
maraschino liqueur, lemon juice, and ice.
Shake, strain into a chilled coupe glass, and
serve.*

COAST CITY SWIZZLE

AS WE MENTIONED IN THE VODKA CHAPTER, THAT SPIRIT'S NEUTRAL CHARACTER MAKES IT IDEAL FOR MIXING WHEN YOU WANT TO HIGHLIGHT THE FLAVORS OF OTHER INGREDIENTS YOU'RE MIXING WITH. That's why we reach for vodka to make this light, refreshing drink with Chartreuse. We adore Chartreuse, but its high proof and intense herbaceousness bring a lot of oomph when you employ it as a base spirit. Mixing it with vodka, citrus, and soda softens and stretches out those flavors, resulting in a very approachable cocktail with subtle complexity.

Swizzle refers to a specific way of mixing cocktails. Neither shaken nor stirred, swizzles are made by plunging a stick or rod into the drink and rotating, or "swizzling," it by hand. In the Caribbean, this might be a literal stick from the swizzlestick tree. Elsewhere you're more likely to use a plastic swizzle stick or just your standard barspoon. Whatever tool you use, the goal is to swizzle it up and down and round and round through the ice, thoroughly mixing the ingredients. In cocktails like this one that use fresh mint, the act of swizzling also helps extract the flavor of the herb by pressing it against the glass. Shall we swizzle?

INGREDIENTS

Crushed ice

1 oz [30 ml] vodka

½ oz [15 ml] green Chartreuse

½ oz [15 ml] fresh lime juice

¼ oz [7.5 ml] Rich Simple Syrup (page 33)

5 or 6 mint leaves

2 to 3 oz [60 to 90 ml] soda water

Mint sprig, for garnish

DIRECTIONS

In a tall glass filled with crushed ice, add the vodka, Chartreuse, lime juice, syrup, mint leaves, and soda. Swizzle to combine and top with additional crushed ice. Garnish with a sprig of fresh mint and serve.

BIJOU

THOUGH SOMETIMES THOUGHT OF AS A NEGRONI WITH CHARTREUSE IN PLACE OF CAMPARI, THE BIJOU ACTUALLY PREDATES ITS MORE POPULAR COLLEAGUE BY NEARLY TWO DECADES. This version was first published in the 1900 edition of Harry Johnson's *Bartenders' Manual*. The name, meaning jewel, is said to reflect the colors of its three ingredients (diamond, emerald, and ruby).

The Bijou is a potent balance of gin, sweet vermouth, and green Chartreuse. Unlike the Negroni, which is a harmonious blending of three spirits, the Bijou is more about showcasing the liqueur. While modern bartenders have been known to tweak the proportions to tame its potent herbaceousness, we recommend you start with the original specs to get a sense of what made this drink so appealing to begin with.

INGREDIENTS

1 oz [30 ml] green Chartreuse

1 oz [30 ml] gin

1 oz [30 ml] sweet vermouth

1 dash orange bitters

Lemon peel, for garnish

DIRECTIONS

To a mixing glass, add the Chartreuse, gin, vermouth, bitters, and ice. Stir and strain into a rocks glass filled with ice or a single large cube. Garnish with a lemon peel and serve.

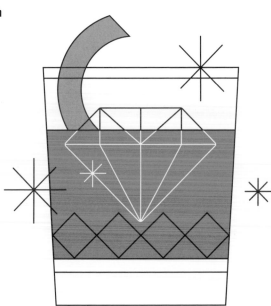

CHAMPS-ELYSÉES

FIRST APPEARING IN 1925'S *DRINKS LONG & SHORT* BY NINA TOYE AND A. H. ADAIR, THE CHAMPS-ELYSÉES IS FOR ANYONE WHO HAS EVER SIPPED A SIDECAR (PAGE 107) AND THOUGHT, *THIS IS GOOD, BUT IT NEEDS CHARTREUSE.* Gentle cognac provides a wonderful foundation to support the complex herbal liqueur. A lot of modern takes on this drink dial back the cognac, but the following version is closer to the original and we feel it does a better job keeping the drink's myriad flavors in line.

INGREDIENTS

2 oz [60 ml] cognac

½ oz [15 ml] green Chartreuse

¾ oz [22.5 ml] fresh lemon juice

¼ oz [7.5 ml] Rich Simple Syrup (page 33)

1 dash Angostura bitters

Lemon peel, for garnish

DIRECTIONS

To a shaker, add the cognac, Chartreuse, lemon juice, syrup, bitters, and ice. Shake and strain into a chilled coupe glass. Garnish with a lemon peel and serve.

PURITAN

WHEN YOU START DELVING INTO CHARTREUSE COCKTAILS, YOU'LL SOON COME ACROSS ONE KNOWN AS THE ALASKA. It's a straightforward mix of gin, yellow Chartreuse, and orange bitters. That's an appealing combination of ingredients, but it's also an exceedingly strong drink (even for us!). We gravitate instead toward a lesser-known cocktail from the turn of the twentieth century called the Puritan. It's martini-like in structure, with a substantial pour of dry vermouth taming the more spirituous elements to achieve a beguiling balance.

INGREDIENTS

2 oz [60 ml] gin

1 oz [30 ml] dry vermouth

2 barspoons (⅓ oz [10 ml]) yellow Chartreuse

1 dash orange bitters

Lemon peel, for garnish

DIRECTIONS

To a mixing glass, add the gin, vermouth, Chartreuse, bitters, and ice. Stir and strain into a chilled coupe glass. Garnish with a lemon peel and serve.

GREENPOINT

CREATED IN 2007 AT MILK & HONEY IN NEW YORK CITY, THE GREENPOINT WAS BAR-TENDER MICHAEL McILROY'S CONTRIBUTION TO THE GENRE OF MANHATTAN VARI-ATIONS NAMED AFTER NEW YORK NEIGHBORHOODS. He followed the template of the Red Hook (page 164) by subbing out half the sweet vermouth in a classic Manhattan for a liqueur, reaching in this instance for yellow Chartreuse. It was an outstanding decision. Easily one of the best Manhattan variations created and not known nearly as widely as it should be, the Greenpoint takes everything delicious about a Vieux Carré (page 159) and cranks up the herbal notes while managing to maintain balance. After mixing up this drink, you might be tempted to live like the residents of Greenpoint and rarely venture back to Manhattan.

INGREDIENTS

2 oz [60 ml] rye

½ oz [15 ml] sweet vermouth

½ oz [15 ml] yellow Chartreuse

1 dash Angostura bitters

1 dash orange bitters

Lemon peel, for garnish

DIRECTIONS

To a mixing glass, add the rye, vermouth, Chartreuse, both bitters, and ice. Stir and strain into a chilled coupe glass. Garnish with a lemon peel and serve.

DAISY DE SANTIAGO

THE EARLY-TWENTIETH-CENTURY DRINKS WRITER CHARLES H. BAKER WAS A FREQUENT VISITOR TO THE ORIGINAL BACARDI DISTILLERY IN HAVANA, AND HE PROCLAIMED THE DAISY DE SANTIAGO TO BE, "ALONG WITH THE IMMORTAL DAIQUIRI . . . THE BEST BACARDI DRINK ON RECORD." The formula is sort of a mash-up between the daiquiri (page 98) and a julep (page 52), with the sweetness coming partially from yellow Chartreuse and seasonal fruit garnish. Baker's judgment was questionable on a number of matters, but we agree with his assessment of this cocktail. It's fantastic.

INGREDIENTS
2 oz [60 ml] light rum

½ oz [15 ml] yellow Chartreuse, plus more (optional), for floating

1 oz [30 ml] fresh lime juice

¼ oz [7.5 ml] Rich Simple Syrup (page 33)

Mint and seasonal fruit, for garnish

DIRECTIONS
To a shaker, add the rum, Chartreuse, lime juice, syrup, and ice. Shake and strain into a rocks glass filled with crushed ice. Garnish with mint, seasonal fruit, and an optional float of even more yellow Chartreuse and serve.

LAST RITES

OUR FRIEND ADAM ROBINSON, OWNER OF THE PORTLAND BAR DEADSHOT, IS KNOWN for drawing on ingredients like red cabbage–infused aquavit, sesame, and mustard to create startlingly unique and delicious drinks. His Last Rites, however, shows that you don't have to go wild with esoteric additions to get tasty results. It's a tequila drinker's Last Word (page 181), softer and rounder than the original formula, and easy to mix up at home.

INGREDIENTS
¾ oz [22.5 ml] tequila

¾ oz [22.5 ml] yellow Chartreuse

¾ oz [22.5 ml] maraschino liqueur

¾ oz [22.5 ml] fresh lemon juice

DIRECTIONS
To a shaker, add the tequila, Chartreuse, maraschino liqueur, lemon juice, and ice. Shake, strain into a chilled coupe glass, and serve.

PARTY LINE

JACOB CAME UP WITH THIS COCKTAIL FOR A GUEST BARTENDING EVENT AT BARRA MEXICO, A LATIN AMERICAN BARTENDING CONVENTION HELD IN MEXICO CITY THAT'S EVERY BIT AS FUN AS IT SOUNDS. With the interplay of agave, Campari, and Chartreuse, there's a lot going on in this glass, but it's also an easy-to-enjoy party drink.

INGREDIENTS
1½ oz [45 ml] tequila

1 oz [30 ml] fresh lime juice

½ oz [15 ml] Campari

½ oz [15 ml] Honey Syrup (page 33)

¼ oz [7.5 ml] yellow Chartreuse

DIRECTIONS
To a shaker, add the tequila, lime juice, Campari, syrup, Chartreuse, and ice. Shake, strain into a chilled coupe glass, and serve.

MONTE CASSINO

THIS WAS THE WINNING RECIPE OF A 2010 COMPETITION PUT ON BY BENEDICTINE, bringing our count of cocktails winning Benedictine competitions to two. Like the Final Ward (page 182), Damon Dyer's Monte Cassino is a rye-based take on the Last Word (page 181). Yet his version takes things further, swapping every single ingredient while retaining the equal proportions and the essential structure of the original. The perception of sugar is a bit higher in this cocktail than in the Last Word, making it a fantastic introduction to these assertive flavors.

INGREDIENTS
¾ oz [22.5 ml] rye

¾ oz [22.5 ml] yellow Chartreuse

¾ oz [22.5 ml] Benedictine

¾ oz [22.5 ml] fresh lemon juice

DIRECTIONS
To a shaker, add the rye, Chartreuse, Benedictine, lemon juice, and ice. Shake, strain into a chilled coupe glass, and serve.

COLLEEN BAWN

A TERM USED OFTEN AMONG BARTENDERS IS THAT A COCKTAIL *READS WELL*. This isn't to say that the cocktail itself is making its way through *Gravity's Rainbow*, but rather that by simply looking at the recipe an experienced bartender can predict that a drink will taste good. Does the Colleen Bawn read well? Absolutely not. It seems like it would be too sweet, and it throws an entire egg into the mix. From reading the recipe, it simply doesn't seem possible that this would be a good cocktail. It dates back to 1903, and by the looks of it, you'd probably think it's a relic from times when people simply had different opinions about what is appealing in a drink. All of this is true until—and this is important—you actually make a Colleen Bawn. It turns out it's delicious.

INGREDIENTS

¾ oz [22.5 ml] rye

¾ oz [22.5 ml] Benedictine

¾ oz [22.5 ml] yellow Chartreuse

1 barspoon (⅙ oz [5 ml]) Rich Simple Syrup (page 33)

1 whole egg

Freshly grated nutmeg, for garnish

Freshly grated cinnamon, for garnish

DIRECTIONS

To a shaker without ice, add the rye, Benedictine, yellow Chartreuse, syrup, and egg. Dry shake for a few seconds to aerate the egg. Add ice and shake again, then strain into a chilled coupe glass. Top with grated nutmeg and cinnamon and serve.

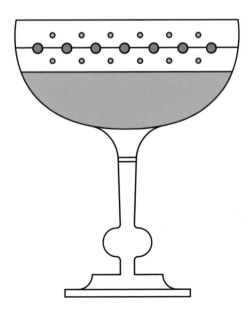

1
2
3

INTERLUDE

PUNCH BREAK

IF YOU'VE MADE IT THIS FAR, CONGRATULATIONS! You now have an enviable home bar and well over a hundred cocktails in your repertoire. So, perhaps you're thinking about hosting a cocktail party. We strongly encourage this idea. As nice as it is to stir up a cocktail for yourself after a long day, it's even better to be social and make them for your friends.

Making cocktails for a group isn't exactly the same as working behind a bar, but following some of the practices used in professional settings can help make your evening as a host fun and easy. After all, bartending is work, and you don't want to spend all the time at your party working. Here are some tips culled from our own experience that will help the night go smoothly.

PLAN YOUR MENU. If you're making drinks for just a few people, you can probably wing it. For a larger party, however, it can help a lot to offer a set menu. It will simplify your preparation and encourage your guests to be adventurous and try something they've never had before. Pick out a few drinks made in a variety of styles and with different base spirits, and you'll be sure to have something for everyone. (Don't forget to include a few nonalcoholic options too, for nondrinkers or anyone who just wants a break from alcohol.)

PREPARE YOUR JUICES AND OTHER INGREDIENTS. You can juice citrus as you need it when making drinks for yourself, but when you're serving a party, trying to do that would slow you down substantially. Juice your lemons, limes, and any other fruit you need before your guests arrive and keep them in glass bottles, preferably refrigerated or on ice. Similarly, make sure you have enough of your garnishes, syrups, and other ingredients prepared.

SET UP A STATION. Professional bartenders work out of what's called a well, a station that has all their bottles, tools, ice, glassware, and garnishes within easy reach. A smartly set-up well makes all the difference for speed and efficiency when serving a crowd. You probably won't have a professional well at home, but setting up a station where you can make your drinks with convenient access to anything you need will help a lot.

HAVE PLENTY OF ICE. This one seems pretty obvious, but if there's one pitfall of cocktail parties we encounter more than any other, it's not having enough ice. You go through a lot of ice making cocktails.

It's better to have too much than to have to send someone out in the middle of the party to replenish the supply.

CHILL YOUR GLASSWARE. This is a good tip for anytime, but chilling your coupes and other glasses for drinks served without ice is a simple touch that takes your hospitality to the next level.

OFFER SNACKS. Alcohol hits harder on an empty stomach. Everyone will have a better time and be able to enjoy your party longer if there's some food on hand. You don't have to cook a three-course dinner, but offering a few things to snack on will help ensure no one's falling asleep under the table.

MAKE A PUNCH. This last idea will do more than almost anything else to take the stress out of hosting a cocktail party. Cocktails are all about individual preference, a single drink for a solo person. For parties, you should also provide a punch. Punch is a communal drinking experience. By having a bowl or pitcher of punch ready to go when your party begins, you make things easier for yourself and your guests. We think of this as the "welcome punch" and we prepare one pretty much anytime we host a party. For the host, it means that the first drink you serve requires nothing more than pouring some punch into a glass, allowing you to devote more attention to greeting your guests and avoiding a rush at the bar. For the guests, it means being welcomed with a glass of a light drink as soon as they arrive and not having to think about what they want. We highly recommend it, and the next section is about how to make a punch with the bottles you have in your home bar.

THE ART OF MAKING PUNCH

IF YOU KNOW HOW TO MAKE A COCKTAIL, YOU ALREADY SORT OF KNOW HOW TO MAKE A PUNCH. Both are all about achieving balance. Yet it's not quite as simple as taking a cocktail recipe and making it bigger. A cocktail is meant to be strong stuff; you have one and then move on to something else, even if that something else is another cocktail. Punch, in contrast, is meant to be light, easy, and drinkable all night long, should one be so inclined.

As when making a cocktail, with a punch you'll be balancing spirituous, sour, sweet, and bitter elements. Punch also tends to benefit from a spice element, such as a fresh grating of nutmeg. And just as dilution is an essential factor in cocktails, it comes into play in punches too. A low-proof or zero-proof ingredient to stretch out flavors and lighten intensity is key to making a good punch.

We've included a few recipes for punches to get you started, but we rarely follow recipes precisely when making them at home. A punch is something you can improvise and tinker with until you get it right. We'll often make ours by taking a look at what bottles we have in stock and going from there. If we find half a bottle of gin, whiskey, or brandy, and a few ounces of a flavorful liqueur like Chartreuse, Benedictine, or maraschino, we're well on our way to making a tasty bowl of punch. Unlike a cocktail, with a punch you can always add a dash of this or a splash of that until the taste is where you want it to be.

ANATOMY OF A PERFECT PUNCH

A BASE SPIRIT
+
A LIQUEUR
=
A GREAT BEGINNING

AFTER THAT, YOU'LL PROBABLY WANT TO ADD SOME CITRUS.
Lemons, limes, grapefruits, and oranges can all work great, and
with a punch you can blend them as you please. You'll also need
a sweetener, such as sugar or Honey Syrup (page 33). Then you
need a light element to add volume; this could be as simple as
chilled soda water, or something more complex like sparkling
wine or tea. Finally, once everything is chilled and mixed in the
bowl, we'll often add our spice. You can get as fancy as you like
with the presentation of punch, perhaps by making a large ice
block with frozen fruit inside.

There's one other trick to making a great punch, and that's to
start with an "oleo-saccharum." It sounds fancy, but it just means
"oil-sugar." You know how a spritz of oil from a citrus zest can
be the finishing touch that elevates a cocktail? It's the same with
punches, except we extract the oil at the beginning rather than at
the end. We do that by muddling the citrus peels in the sugar and
then allowing them to sit for thirty minutes to an hour. Doing
so saturates the sugar with citrus oil, producing a more flavorful
and aromatic punch. It takes some elbow grease, but it's worth
the effort. (As a bonus, you can leave the peels in the mixture to
serve as garnishes in the finished punch.)

GIN PUNCH
À LA TERRINGTON

THIS VINTAGE RECIPE FROM WILLIAM TERRINGTON'S 1868 BOOK *COOLING CUPS AND DAINTY DRINKS* IS ONE OF OUR GO-TOS WHEN HOSTING PARTIES OR EVENTS. It's light and refreshing, a cinch to make, and wonderfully complex thanks to the addition of herbaceous Chartreuse.

INGREDIENTS
Peel of 1 lemon
¼ cup [50 g] granulated sugar
2 oz [60 ml] fresh lemon juice
8 oz [240 ml] gin
3 oz [90 ml] green Chartreuse
20 oz [600 ml] soda water

SERVES 6 TO 8

DIRECTIONS
In a punch bowl, gently muddle the lemon peel and sugar, pressing to extract juice from the lemon, and let rest for about an hour. Add the lemon juice and stir to dissolve the sugar. Add the gin and Chartreuse and stir to combine. Immediately before serving, add the soda and stir one more time. Slip a large ice block or large ice cubes into the bowl and ladle into individual glasses to serve.

TRY SOME OF THESE RECIPES

to see how making punch works in practice. Once you get a feel for how the punches come together, you'll be able to improvise your own with all kinds of different ingredients.

POTENT POTION

ALMOST ALL THE TIME WHEN WE MAKE PUNCHES, WE INCLUDE AT LEAST ONE KIND OF CITRUS JUICE. That makes our punches somewhat like a cocktail in the sour family. However, it's also possible to take a more spirit-forward cocktail and adapt it to the punch format by opening it up and extending it with dilution. As the name implies, this "Potent Potion" has a little more kick than your average punch. It's essentially a Manhattan (page 68), just bigger and a little lighter. Although there's no juice in this punch, the lemon peel in the oleo-saccharum does help make it brighter and more aromatic.

INGREDIENTS

Peel of ½ lemon

5 tsp [25 g] demerara sugar

8 oz [240 ml] water

16 oz [480 ml] rye

8 oz [240 ml] sweet vermouth

1 tsp [5 ml] Angostura bitters

SERVES 6 TO 8

DIRECTIONS

In a punch bowl, gently muddle the lemon peel and sugar, pressing to extract juice from the lemon peel, and let rest for up to an hour. Add the water and stir to dissolve the sugar. Add the rye, vermouth, and bitters and stir. Slip in a block of ice or large ice cubes and ladle into individual glasses to serve.

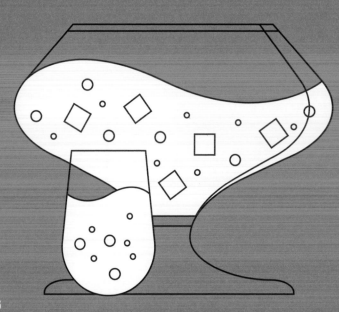

BRANDY PUNCH
À LA GOLDIE

AS AN EXAMPLE OF HOW TO ADAPT RECIPES TO MAKE PUNCH WITH WHATEVER YOU HAPPEN TO HAVE ON HAND, THIS IS ONE BASED ON TERRINGTON'S GIN PUNCH (PAGE 195) THAT WE CREATED WITH A FEW OTHER BOTTLES FROM THE FIRST PART OF THE BOOK. As you can tell by comparing the recipes, the ingredients differ, but the basic structure is the same. We use cognac in place of gin and Benedictine in place of Chartreuse. Sparkling wine replaces the soda. Lemon is complemented by a bit of orange. Lastly, we bring in spice notes with Angostura bitters and nutmeg. If the gin punch is ideal for a summer garden party, this one is a little more autumnal. (And who is Goldie? She is Brett's cat, who looked on with what we interpret as interest and approval when we were putting this together.)

INGREDIENTS

Peel of 1 lemon

Peel of ½ orange

¼ cup [50 g] demerara sugar

2 oz [60 ml] fresh lemon juice

1 oz [30 ml] fresh orange juice

8 oz [240 ml] cognac

3 oz [90 ml] Benedictine

1 tsp [5 ml] Angostura bitters

1 bottle [750 ml] sparkling wine

Freshly grated nutmeg, for garnish

SERVES 8 TO 10

DIRECTIONS

In a punch bowl, muddle the citrus peels and sugar, pressing to extract juice from the citrus, and let rest for about an hour. Add the lemon and orange juices and stir to dissolve the sugar. Add the cognac, Benedictine, and bitters and stir to combine. Immediately before serving, add the bottle of sparkling wine. Slip in a block of ice or large ice cubes and grate nutmeg over the surface of the punch. Ladle into individual glasses.

PART TWO

THE ADVANCED BAR

THE FIRST HALF OF THE BOOK WAS ALL ABOUT LEARNING THE FUNDAMENTALS OF MAKING COCKTAILS AND STOCKING YOUR BAR TO FORM A STEADY FOUNDATION. The order of the bottles was determined largely by their importance in the classic canon and how they mixed with the spirits already in your collection. The second half of the book is about getting more adventurous. Here we'll delve into spirits that are a little more niche, including some that arrived relatively recently in the history of mixology but that have developed a strong following in contemporary bars. We've still given the bottles in order such that if you follow along, you'll always have what you need to make the drinks in each chapter. That said, the ordering of this half of the book is a little more arbitrary. If you feel like skipping a chapter or jumping ahead to a spirit that excites you, feel free to do so! On the other hand, if you've trusted us so far, we encourage you to take a chance on the less familiar bottles we feature here. It was difficult for us to limit ourselves to the handful of spirits we included, so the ones that made the cut are the ones we feel make the most valuable additions to a versatile home bar.

CHAPTER 15

APPLE BRANDY

WE WOULDN'T BE SURPRISED IF YOU HAVEN'T GIVEN MUCH THOUGHT TO APPLE BRANDY. Despite a lengthy history, apple brandy hasn't captured the kind of loyal following that spirits like whiskey, rum, or cognac have won over. It's not for lack of flavor or versatility; apple brandy is delicious and particularly well suited for use in cocktails. One might argue that the reason it doesn't get more attention is that it's almost *too* easy to use. Unlike spirits whose big, bold flavors dominate drinks, apple brandy is great at rounding out the rough edges of other spirits, and as a result it's commonly used in collaboration with another type of booze. In the world of cocktails, apple brandy is the ultimate wingman—an essential component that never quite gets the recognition it deserves.

Brandy is the broad term given to any fruit that's been fermented and distilled, and so it follows that apple brandy is distilled from fermented apple juice, a.k.a. cider. It's worth pointing out right at the start that because apple brandy is distilled, and because sugar doesn't make it through distillation, apple brandy is as dry as any other base spirit. There may be some sweetness in the final product due to the influence of the barrels it's aged in, but no more than you'd find in a similarly aged whiskey.

Although apple cider and brandy are made just about everywhere in the world where apples grow, the traditions of production in the northern French region of Calvados and across the United States have had the biggest impact on the world of cocktails, so we will narrow our focus on those two areas. Calvados, located in Normandy, is to apple brandy what Cognac is to grape brandy: a protected place of origin with strict rules of production and acclaim for its spirits. The brandy from there is synonymous with the region and labeled as *Calvados* on the bottle. Often made from a combination of bitter, tart, and sweet apples (and with pears often added to the mix as well), it typically undergoes a long fermentation followed by an even longer resting period before being distilled. It's then aged in oak for a minimum of two years. Calvados tends to emphasize fruit over barrel. In the younger expressions best suited for cocktails, the apple flavors shine bright, while the spice of French oak provides an understated foundation.

American apple brandy is less strictly regulated: It simply needs to be made in the United States and produced entirely from apples. Typically made with sweet apples, fermentation and distillation of American apple brandy operates on a similar timeline as bourbon and rye, and it is often aged in ex–bourbon barrels. Compared with its French counterpart, it tends to feature more vanilla and overall oak influence.

The United States is also home to a spirit known as applejack. This word has its origins in the colonial era. In a process known as jacking, they would leave fermented apple cider outside in the winter, allowing the water to freeze off and concentrating the alcohol. In modern terminology, *blended applejack* refers to a blend of distilled apple brandy and neutral grain spirits. For obvious reasons, these tend to be less fruit forward than a brandy made entirely from apples, although they can still be quite good in cocktails.

Despite presenting different expressions of apple and oak, Calvados and American apple brandies can be used similarly for mixing. Calvados adds a brighter note to drinks, while the more bourbon-influenced American bottlings do more to round out and soften the drinks they're in. Apple brandy works especially well with gin, cognac, and many types of whiskey. It also turns up as a frequent partner to grenadine, and through very extensive and highly professional testing we can confirm that this is indeed a great combination. Use the cocktails that follow as a jumping-off point to learn about this incredible spirit, and hopefully it will inspire you to make apple brandy a staple in your home bar.

APPLE BRANDY 101

THERE ARE THREE MAIN TYPES OF APPLE BRANDY YOU ARE LIKELY TO COME ACROSS.

APPLE BRANDY: As the name suggests, this is brandy distilled from apples. American apple brandies will typically be distilled from sweet apples and aged in ex-bourbon barrels.

CALVADOS: An apple brandy from the Normandy region of France, Calvados is made from a variety of cider apples (and sometimes pears) and aged for at least two years in oak. Regulations and production methods vary among different appellations within Normandy.

BLENDED APPLEJACK: In the United States, this refers to a blend of apple brandy and neutral grain spirits.

BOTTLES WE REACH FOR

CLEAR CREEK 2 YEAR APPLE BRANDY
Aged in Limousin oak and distilled in Oregon, Clear Creek marries American and French distilling traditions. Restrained in flavor, with some heat up front and lingering notes of apple, it's a team player in cocktails. We also enjoy the Old Delicious apple brandy from the same distillery, which spends some additional time in former bourbon barrels.

BOULARD CALVADOS VSOP
For a luxurious option at a reasonable price, we greatly enjoy this calvados from Boulard. From the Pay d'Auge appellation in Normandy, it's a blend of distillates from 4 to 10 years old. Sweet and rich with notes of cinnamon and vanilla, it's practically made for autumnal imbibing.

LAIRD'S BOTTLED-IN-BOND APPLE BRANDY
For a more whiskey-like experience, try the bottled-in-bond bottling from Laird's. Four years of aging in charred oak barrels provide strong vanilla and spice notes, with fruit coming through on the finish.

PERE MAGLOIRE FINE VS
Aged in very old oak, Pere Magloire Fine VS has a fresh, apple-forward flavor that mixes wonderfully.

JACK ROSE

THE FIRST PUBLISHED RECIPE FOR THE JACK ROSE WAS AN OVERLY COMPLICATED CONCOCTION CALLING FOR APPLE BRANDY, THREE TYPES OF JUICE, TWO SYRUPS, AND SODA WATER. A few years later, in Jacques Straub's 1913 *Straub's Manual of Mixed Drinks*, the recipe was pared down to its essentials. Unsurprisingly, it's Straub's take that has stood the test of time. We've given the recipe with lime, but we recommend you try it with lemon, too.

INGREDIENTS

1½ oz [45 ml] apple brandy

¾ oz [22.5 ml] fresh lime juice

¾ oz [22.5 ml] grenadine

DIRECTIONS

To a shaker, add the brandy, lime juice, grenadine, and ice. Shake, strain into a chilled coupe glass, and serve.

VARIATION

Follow the recipe above and add a dash or two of absinthe to taste to make a Pan American Clipper, a cocktail recounted in Charles H. Baker's The Gentleman's Companion.

HARVEST SOUR

A MODERN RIFF ON THE CLASSIC SOUR FORMAT BY NEW YORK BARTENDER SAM ROSS, the Harvest Sour layers apple brandy and a grating of cinnamon atop the standard whiskey version of the drink (see page 47) for an autumnal go-to that is good enough to enjoy year-round.

INGREDIENTS

1 oz [30 ml] apple brandy

1 oz [30 ml] rye

¾ oz [22.5 ml] fresh lemon juice

½ oz [15 ml] Rich Simple Syrup (page 33)

Egg white

Freshly grated cinnamon, for garnish

DIRECTIONS

To a shaker without ice, add the apple brandy, rye, lemon juice, syrup, and egg white. Dry shake to aerate the egg white. Add ice and shake again, then strain into a chilled coupe glass. Grate cinnamon on top and serve.

PINK LADY

WHEN YOU LOOK INTO THE HISTORY OF THE PINK LADY, IT BECOMES CLEAR THAT THE ONLY THING COCKTAIL BOOK WRITERS COULD AGREE ON FOR THE LAST CENTURY IS THAT PINK LADY IS A GREAT NAME FOR A COCKTAIL. Jacques Straub made his with gin, apple brandy, lime, and grenadine. Simple enough, but other recipes are all over the place. The apple brandy was either replaced with regular brandy or outright abandoned. Sometimes there was lime juice, but sometimes it was lemon, orange, or no juice at all. A few writers included egg white, while others added a measure of cream. Our take on the Pink Lady looks to Straub's original for ingredients, adds egg white from later versions, and then measures out everything in more modern proportions. It's a nod to different aspects of the drink's history, but most important, it's delicious.

INGREDIENTS
1½ oz [45 ml] gin
¾ oz [22.5 ml] apple brandy
¾ oz [22.5 ml] fresh lime juice
½ oz [15 ml] grenadine
1 egg white
Cocktail cherry, for garnish

DIRECTIONS

To a shaker without ice, add the gin, brandy, lime juice, grenadine, and egg white. Dry shake to aerate the egg white. Add ice and shake again, then strain into a chilled coupe glass. Garnish with a cherry and serve.

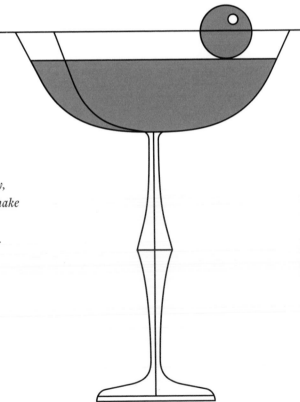

DEMPSEY

PROVING THAT THE COMBINATION OF APPLE BRANDY AND GIN REALLY DOES HAVE MILEAGE, THE DEMPSEY PAIRS THEM IN A MORE SPIRIT-FORWARD WAY THAN THE PINK LADY. The drink is remarkably sharp, and it's a reminder that it's not just acid and bitters that balance out sweetness. Gin and absinthe provide enough bright botanical ingredients to punch through the grenadine while apple brandy adds a soft, fruity note that keeps the cocktail anchored. It's a strong drink, and the high proportion of spirits keeps it vibrant on the palate.

INGREDIENTS
1½ oz [45 ml] apple brandy
1½ oz [45 ml] gin
½ oz [15 ml] grenadine
¼ oz [7.5 ml] absinthe

DIRECTIONS
To a mixing glass, add the brandy, gin, grenadine, absinthe, and ice. Stir, strain into a chilled coupe glass, and serve.

DIAMONDBACK

THE DIAMONDBACK LOUNGE COCKTAIL HAILS FROM BALTIMORE AND, LIKE ITS CITY OF ORIGIN, PULLS ABSOLUTELY NO PUNCHES. It's a strong one. Made from rye whiskey, yellow Chartreuse, and apple brandy, it's 3 oz [90 ml] of full-proof spirits. It's a good thing this is a home bartending book, because this is exactly the kind of cocktail that's best enjoyed when you're already safely home and have nowhere else to be for a while. Yet despite being worryingly high-proof, it's easy to love. If you like the way that Benedictine and rye worked together in the Monte Carlo (page 158), consider this as a more intense cocktail in the same mold. The Chartreuse adds sweetness and an intense herbal complexity to the rye, while the apple brandy comes in and does what it does so well: making a palatable and pleasurable drink from potent ingredients.

INGREDIENTS
1½ oz [45 ml] rye
¾ oz [22.5 ml] yellow Chartreuse
¾ oz [22.5 ml] apple brandy

DIRECTIONS
To a mixing glass, add the rye, Chartreuse, brandy, and ice. Stir, strain into a chilled coupe glass, and serve.

HONEYMOON

FIRST APPEARING IN HUGO ENSSLIN'S PRE-PROHIBITION *RECIPES FOR MIXED DRINKS,* the Honeymoon is a drink that, to the eyes of a modern bartender, looks all wrong. Listed as equal parts apple brandy and Benedictine, with the juice of a half a lemon and dash of curaçao, the drink screams, "Too sweet!" to the modern eye. Most modern takes on the Honeymoon convert the drink into something closer to standard ratios for a sour. We almost included one of these ourselves, but just for fun, we decided to shake up something closer to the original specs. And guess what? It was good. In fact, it was better. The Honeymoon is a reminder that sweetness isn't always something to be avoided. We like ice cream, we think candy bars are great, and we dig the richness of this cocktail. It's called a Honeymoon after all, named for that fleetingly brief spell of joy and ease that we all know, despite our best intentions, will not reflect day-to-day life. Is the Honeymoon an everyday cocktail? Absolutely not. Enjoy!

INGREDIENTS

1¼ oz [37.5 ml] apple brandy

1 oz [30 ml] Benedictine

1 barspoon (⅙ oz [5 ml]) orange liqueur

½ oz [15 ml] fresh lemon juice

1 dash orange bitters

Orange peel, for granish

DIRECTIONS

To a shaker, add the apple brandy, Benedictine, orange liqueur, lemon juice, bitters, and ice. Shake and strain into a rocks glass filled with ice. Garnish with an orange peel and serve.

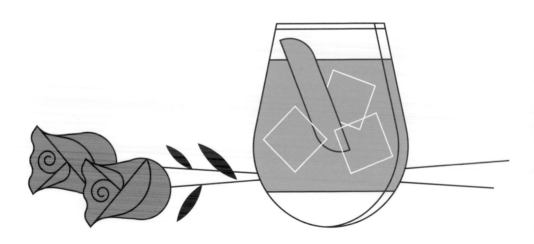

SO SO COCKTAIL

IF YOU'RE LOOKING FOR A HUMBLER ALTERNATIVE TO THE BRAVADO OF THE PERFECT MANHATTAN (see page 68), may we suggest a So So Cocktail? This meekly monikered beverage appeared in the 1923 Harry MacElhone's *ABC of Mixing Cocktails*. At the risk of ruining the fun, the book reveals that the drink was actually named after a club manager, Mr. P. Soso. Regardless, the cocktail itself drinks with impressive swagger. The earthiness of sweet vermouth wonderfully balances the floral notes of gin, with apple brandy providing a touch of brightness. We think it's time the So So puffs its chest out and claims some space in the spotlight.

INGREDIENTS

1 oz [30 ml] gin

1 oz [30 ml] sweet vermouth

½ oz [15 ml] apple brandy

½ oz [15 ml] grenadine

Cocktail cherry, for garnish

DIRECTIONS

To a mixing glass, add the gin, vermouth, apple brandy, grenadine, and ice. Stir and strain into a chilled coupe glass. Garnish with a cherry and serve.

VARIATION

We mistakenly made this with dry vermouth the first time out, and it was the kind of moment that inspires the lazy cliché, "if something this good is wrong, then I don't want to be right." Try the So So with dry vermouth for a lighter, predinner drink.

CORPSE REVIVER NO.1

FOR MORE THAN 150 YEARS, BARTENDERS HAVE AGREED THAT *CORPSE REVIVER* IS AN EXCELLENT NAME FOR A COCKTAIL. What they couldn't quite find consensus on is what exactly this cocktail should be composed of. The most famous and enduring version is the Corpse Reviver #2 from *The Savoy Cocktail Book*. That cocktail has nothing at all in common with the Corpse Reviver #1, which, conveniently for this chapter, features apple brandy. A blend of said apple spirit, cognac, and sweet vermouth, it's the perfect drink for those nights when you're in the mood for a Manhattan (page 68) but want something a bit softer. It's the cocktail version of picking up a Vonnegut novel instead of, say, Dostoyevsky: very respectable, but with an approachable levity.

INGREDIENTS

1½ oz [45 ml] cognac

¾ oz [22.5 ml] apple brandy

¾ oz [22.5 ml] sweet vermouth

Cocktail cherry, for garnish

DIRECTIONS

To a mixing glass, add the cognac, apple brandy, vermouth, and ice. Stir and strain into a chilled coupe glass. Garnish with a cherry and serve.

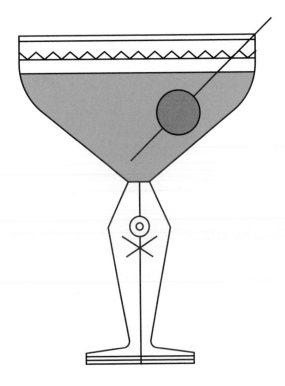

CHAPTER 16

CYNAR

OUR FEATURED SPIRIT FOR THIS CHAPTER IS MADE FROM ARTICHOKES, BUT WORRY NOT, IT DOESN'T TASTE LIKE ARTICHOKES—AT LEAST, NOT IN AN OBVIOUS WAY. Made from a combination of thirteen botanicals, of which artichoke leaves are one, Cynar (pronounced "chee-nar") is the second truly bitter spirit you'll be adding to your bar.

Like Campari, Cynar is a bitter Italian amaro. Unlike Campari, Cynar functions more as a digestivo than an aperitivo; its herbaceousness is richer and earthier, making it more customary to consume after a meal than before. And while the lines between the categories are rather blurry, knowing which camp an amaro fits in is useful in predicting how it will function in a cocktail. Aperitivi are often brighter, with stronger citrus influences, and as a result they tend to provide lift to cocktails. In contrast, the more brooding bitterness in digestivi is an anchoring component to a drink, tethering any sweetness and acidity to its metaphorical, and literal, herbal roots.

The signature ingredient in Cynar is artichoke, which inspires both the artwork on the bottle as well as the name of the amaro itself (the scientific name for artichoke is *Cynara scolymus*). Despite the branding, you likely won't identify artichoke simply by taking a sip, because its contribution is a unique bitterness instead of the buttery vegetal flavors you'd normally associate with the plant. Though there is a slight vegetal quality to the amaro, it's defined mostly by earthiness, cola flavors, some citrus pith, and a bitterness that builds as you drink.

The world of amari is vast, but we recommend Cynar as an excellent introduction to the darker, richer end of the spectrum. It's bitter but not too bitter, and it works wonderfully in cocktails. Its flavor profile is relatively direct, and this makes it easy to combine with other spirits. In small amounts it functions almost like a cocktail bitter, lending its spice profile to the drink, while in larger doses it acts as a very solid team player.

Unlike some amari, Cynar doesn't boast a storied, century-spanning history. It was introduced in 1949 by an Italian entrepreneur, and while it managed to quickly gain traction, it missed the critical early eras of cocktail development. We won't be digging into pre-Prohibition bar manuals to find Cynar cocktails—these are all modern creations, with most coming from just the past two decades.

We'll be providing more uses for Cynar as your bar expands, but even with what you have now, you'll find it to be a very functional addition. On days when you don't feel like making a complicated drink, it's the perfect low-ABV amaro to sip on the rocks or to top with soda and an orange twist. When you want something a bit more involved, mix up the drinks in this chapter.

IF YOU LIKE CYNAR, TRY...

AVERNA
This Sicilian amaro is one of our favorites to reach for when we want to add approachable bitterness to drinks, offering notes of bitter orange peel and baking spices. Soda brings out its cola qualities and we'll never say no to a black Manhattan, which swaps out Averna for sweet vermouth in the standard recipe.

RAMAZZOTTI AMARO
Rhubarb, gentian, orange peel, rosemary, hyssop, and myrrh are among the botanicals in this rich, complex amaro. It brings depth to cocktails and is a great way to end a night.

AMARO MONTENEGRO
As sweet as it is bitter, Montenegro is a great entry point for those skeptical of the amaro category. It's the kind of amaro you could sip absentmindedly by the fire, or tip into a Daiquiri (page 98) to add pleasant notes of spice.

SFUMATO
If you found yourself drawn to Cynar's more bitter elements, you may love Sfumato. It adds an earthy bitterness to drinks with distinctive notes of iron and smoke to challenge the palate. A little goes a long way, so you'll get an enduring use out of your bottle.

LITTLE ITALY

A FORMULA FOR MAKING A MODERN CLASSIC: TAKE THE MANHATTAN COMBINATION
OF WHISKEY AND VERMOUTH, ADD A COMPLEX, FLAVORFUL LIQUEUR, AND NAME IT
AFTER A NEW YORK NEIGHBORHOOD. Audrey Saunders was one of the first to mine this
vein with her Little Italy, an absolutely delicious drink. Audrey recommends a spicy 100-
proof rye, such as Rittenhouse bottled-in-bond, to cut through the other rich ingredients.
The earthy bitterness of Cynar works wonderfully with whiskey and rye, building on the
elements that make the Manhattan (page 68) such an excellent cocktail. If a Manhattan is
the perfect cold-weather cocktail, the Little Italy is the perfect colder-weather cocktail.

INGREDIENTS

2 oz [60 ml] rye

¾ oz [22.5 ml] sweet vermouth

½ oz [15 ml] Cynar

Cocktail cherry, for garnish

DIRECTIONS

*To a mixing glass, add the rye, vermouth,
Cynar, and ice. Stir and strain into a chilled
coupe glass. Garnish with a cherry and serve.*

CE SOIR

THIS CONTEMPORARY RECIPE WAS CREATED BY NICOLE LEBEDEVITCH AT A BOSTON
COCKTAIL LOUNGE, THE HAWTHORNE. With a formula that's 100 percent spirits-based
and boasting rich notes of cognac, amaro, and Chartreuse, this is a true settle-in-by-the-fire
kind of cocktail. Treat it as a nightcap—there's not much you can make to follow this.

INGREDIENTS

2 oz [60 ml] cognac

¾ oz [22.5 ml] Cynar

½ oz [15 ml] yellow Chartreuse

1 dash Angostura bitters

1 dash orange bitters

Lemon peel, for garnish

DIRECTIONS

*To a mixing glass, add the cognac, Cynar,
Chartreuse, both bitters, and ice. Stir and
strain into a chilled coupe glass. Garnish with
a lemon peel and serve.*

CIN-CYN

CIN-CIN, PRONOUNCED "CHIN-CHIN," IS AN INFORMAL ITALIAN TOAST. The Cin-Cyn cocktail is a variation on the Negroni with Cynar in place of Campari. The latter half of the name alludes to the liqueur, while the first Cin is said to be a reference to the Italian vermouth brand Cinzano. You can, however, make it with whatever vermouth brand you like; we think this works particularly well with richer sweet vermouths like Carpano Antica or Cocchi di Torino. Regardless, it's a very tasty play on the Negroni (page 129), with more weight than the classic Campari version.

INGREDIENTS

1 oz [30 ml] Cynar

1 oz [30 ml] gin

1 oz [30 ml] sweet vermouth

Orange peel, for garnish

DIRECTIONS

To a mixing glass, add the Cynar, gin, vermouth, and ice. Stir and strain into a rocks glass filled with ice or a single big cube. Garnish with an orange peel and serve.

PHYSICALLY FORGOTTEN

YOU CAN NEVER HAVE TOO MANY SIMPLE, STIRRED COCKTAILS IN YOUR REPERTOIRE. When you come home after a long day and you don't want to be bothered with squeezing citrus or making syrups, a cocktail that can be made with bottles taken right off the shelf is just what you need. The Physically Forgotten from Alise Moffat, former owner of Portland's much-missed Shift Drinks bar, fits that profile perfectly. It's dark, bitter, and quick to whip up, but rich and complex on the palate.

INGREDIENTS

1½ oz [45 ml] gin

¾ oz [22.5 ml] Cynar

½ oz [15 ml] maraschino liqueur

2 dashes orange bitters

Lemon peel, for garnish

DIRECTIONS

To a mixing glass, add the gin, Cynar, maraschino liqueur, bitters, and ice. Stir and strain into a chilled coupe glass. Garnish with a lemon peel and serve.

CYNAR-GARITA

WHEN YOU THINK OF MARGARITA VARIATIONS, IT'S LIKELY FRUITY CONCOCTIONS LIKE STRAWBERRY MARGARITAS THAT COME TO MIND. Adding fruit to a margarita is undeniably delicious, but we also love the complexity that bitterness brings. Cynar is particularly well suited to this task because its relatively uncomplicated flavor melds perfectly with the other elements, adding depth and earthiness that cut through the tart lime and sweet orange liqueur. If you sometimes find a classic margarita (page 87) a bit too bracing, we highly recommend the Cynar-garita as an alternative.

INGREDIENTS

1 lime

Salt, for garnish

1½ oz [45 ml] tequila

1 oz [30 ml] Cynar

½ oz [15 ml] orange liqueur

½ oz [15 ml] fresh lime juice

Orange peel, for garnish

DIRECTIONS

Using the cut side of a lime, wet half the exterior edge of a rocks glass and then dip it into a shallow dish filled with salt so that the salt sticks to the rim. To a shaker, add the tequila, Cynar, orange liqueur, lime juice, and ice. Shake and strain into the prepared rocks glass filled with ice. Garnish with an orange peel and serve.

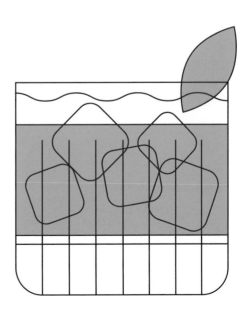

NASSAU STREET COCKTAIL

IN HIS NASSAU STREET COCKTAIL, HOUSTON BARTENDER CHRIS FRANKEL SWAPS OUT GIN AND CAMPARI FOR APPLE BRANDY AND CYNAR IN ANOTHER GREAT TAKE ON THE NEGRONI FORMAT (SEE PAGE 129). Naussau Street refers to the main thoroughfare in downtown Princeton, New Jersey, with the apple brandy tying in to the New Jersey theme. Chris makes this with Punt e Mes for the vermouth, a recommendation we wholeheartedly endorse. Other rich vermouths, such as the chocolatey Cocchi di Torino, will also do nicely here.

INGREDIENTS

1 oz [30 ml] Cynar

1 oz [30 ml] apple brandy

1 oz [30 ml] sweet vermouth

2 dashes Peychaud's bitters

Cocktail cherry, for garnish

DIRECTIONS

To a mixing glass, add the Cynar, apple brandy, vermouth, bitters and ice. Stir and strain into a glass filled with ice or a single large cube. Garnish with a cherry and serve.

CYNAR FLIP

FINALLY, A DRINK FOR THOSE MOMENTS WHEN YOU'RE IN THE MOOD FOR A BITTER, LOW-ABV COCKTAIL BUT ARE ALSO TRAINING TO DEFEAT APOLLO CREED. The Cynar Flip, created by bartender Ben Sandrof, first appeared in Jeffrey Morgenthaler's 2014 *The Bar Book*. It's deceptively simple, and Sandrof displayed impressive restraint when creating this drink. It's sometimes tempting to keep layering on additional ingredients instead of recognizing when a simple drink is good as is. This is an example of when less can be more.

INGREDIENTS

2 oz [60 ml] Cynar

2 barspoons (⅓ oz [10 ml]) Rich Simple Syrup (page 33)

1 whole egg

2 dashes Angostura bitters, for garnish

DIRECTIONS

To a shaker without ice, add the Cynar, syrup, and egg. Dry shake to aerate the egg. Add ice and shake again, then strain into a chilled coupe glass. Garnish with Angostura bitters atop the drink and serve.

TOO SOON

YET ANOTHER AUGHTS-ERA CREATION FROM SAM ROSS, THE TOO SOON LEANS INTO THE CITRUS PITH NOTES OF CYNAR BY ADDING SLICES OF ORANGE DIRECTLY TO THE SHAKER. This is a highly underrated and underutilized method of adding a more developed citrus note to drinks, particularly when it comes to orange and grapefruit. It gives a sensation of biting into a citrus wedge, with a pithy bitterness that lingers on the tongue. Here this marries perfectly with the bitterness of Cynar. The Too Soon is a great example of a moderate-alcohol drink that doesn't skimp on complexity.

INGREDIENTS

1 oz [30 ml] Cynar

1 oz [30 ml] gin

¾ oz [22.5 ml] fresh lemon juice

Generous ¼ oz [7.5 ml] Rich Simple Syrup (page 33)

2 thin orange slices

Orange wedge, for garnish

DIRECTIONS

To a shaker, add the Cynar, gin, lemon juice, syrup, orange slices, and ice. Shake and strain into a chilled coupe glass. Garnish with an orange wedge and serve.

TIGHT FIVE

STIRRED TEQUILA COCKTAILS AREN'T THE MOST COMMON OF DRINKS, AND WHEN THEY DO APPEAR, THEY TEND TO BE MADE WITH BARREL-AGED TEQUILA. While this makes sense from a drink development perspective, it's a bit inconvenient for our book, seeing as we told you to go out and buy a bottle of blanco tequila. In an effort to ensure you get the most bang for your buck, we stacked the deck a bit and came up with the Tight Five. To incorporate the vanilla notes of a barrel-aged spirit, we ring in a touch of apple brandy, proving once again its usefulness as a team player.

INGREDIENTS

1½ oz [45 ml] tequila

¾ oz [22.5 ml] sweet vermouth

½ oz [15 ml] apple brandy

¼ oz [7.5 ml] Cynar

1 barspoon (⅙ oz [5 ml]) Benedictine

Orange peel, for garnish

DIRECTIONS

To a mixing glass, add the tequila, vermouth, apple brandy, Cynar, Benedictine, and ice. Stir and strain into a rocks glass filled with ice or a single large cube. Garnish with an orange peel and serve.

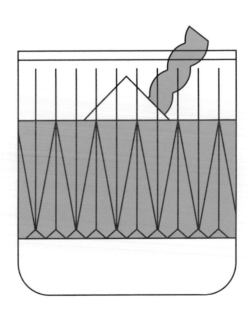

NEGRONI TREDICI

WITH THE INGREDIENTS OF A NEGRONI (PAGE 129) VARIATION AND THE PROPORTIONS OF A MARTINEZ (PAGE 151) RIFF, TOBY MALONEY'S NEGRONI TREDICI WALKS THE LINE BETWEEN BOTH COCKTAILS. Created at the pioneering Chicago cocktail bar The Violet Hour, it's perfect for when you want some bitterness in your drink, but not quite at the level of a traditional Negroni. Toby recommends a bold Italian sweet vermouth for use here. (As for the name? *Tredici* is Italian for thirteen, a reference to the thirteen botanicals in Cynar.)

INGREDIENTS

2 oz [60 ml] gin

1 oz [30 ml] sweet vermouth

¼ oz [7.5 ml] Campari

¼ oz [7.5 ml] Cynar

2 dashes orange bitters

Lemon peel, for garnish

DIRECTIONS

To a mixing glass, add the gin, vermouth, Campari, Cynar, bitters, and ice. Stir and strain into a chilled coupe glass. Garnish with a lemon peel and serve.

ART OF CHOKE

THE ART OF CHOKE IS A WEIRD DRINK IN ALL THE BEST WAYS. A split base of light rum and Cynar? Such a small amount of lime juice? Stirred instead of shaken? It's all unexpected but it works, and when Kyle Davidson created it at The Violet Hour in Chicago, it soon became a guest favorite due to its unique combination of bitterness and herbaceousness.

INGREDIENTS

1 oz [30 ml] light rum

1 oz [30 ml] Cynar

¼ oz [7.5 ml] green Chartreuse

⅛ oz [4 ml] lime juice

⅛ oz [4 ml] Rich Demerara Syrup (page 33)

2 dashes Angostura bitters

Three sprigs of mint

DIRECTIONS

To a mixing glass, add the light rum, Cynar, Chartreuse, lime juice, syrup, bitters, and two sprigs of mint. Lightly muddle the mint and let rest a few moments. Add ice, stir, and strain into a rocks glass filled with ice or a single large cube. Garnish with the remaining sprig of mint and serve.

CHAPTER 17

AGED RUM

THE DEFINITION OF *AGED RUM* SEEMS OBVIOUS. It's just rum that's been aged, right? Well, yes. But as we saw in the light rum chapter (page 95), things are rarely that simple when it comes to sugar cane spirits. Because rum can be made in so many different ways, with few hard-and-fast rules for particular styles, we have to unpack the concept a little bit to clarify what we mean when we call for an aged rum. Bear with us while we explain.

Perhaps we should start with what we *don't* mean by aged rum. We don't mean just any rum with an amber, brown, or golden hue. While these shades of color are meant to imply aging in a barrel, often very little of the character comes from wood. Producers may add sugar, color, and artificial flavors to simulate wood aging. We also don't mean "dark rum" or "black rum," which usually get almost all of their color from the addition of caramel. And we definitely don't mean light rum, even though it technically is often aged in barrels prior to being filtered to remove taste and color.

What we do mean is a rum whose characteristics are significantly influenced by aging in wooden barrels. That makes sense, but we still need to dial in our definition a little tighter, because that leaves open a wide range of rums that fit the description. Raw ingredients and methods of distillation have a profound influence on the character of rum. A rum that is distilled to a high degree of purity in column stills—the kind that's perfect for a light rum—can be dominated by oaky flavors when aged in barrels. It might be sweet and approachable with pleasant vanilla notes, but often not very interesting; you'll taste the wood and not much else.

At the other extreme, spirits that are distilled from fresh sugar cane juice instead of molasses, or produced in pot stills with wildly aromatic fermentations, can result in dramatically distinct flavors. We love these rums, but they're not what we're looking for in this chapter, even though they are also often aged in barrels. What we're looking for here are heavy-bodied, flavorful rums. That typically means a spirit made from molasses and distilled in ways that don't strip out too much of its character, then aged in oak barrels for at least a few years. The result is a rum that, much like a bourbon or a cognac, reflects its raw ingredients, its distillation style, and the influence of oak.

Unlike bourbon or cognac, however, you can't go just go to the liquor store and pick up a bottle labeled *aged rum* and know exactly what you're getting. So, what should you look for? Well, you can start with the brands we recommend on the next page, but in a more general sense you want to find rums with genuine aging. The meaning of an age statement varies from country to country, but a good rule of thumb is to make sure that if it has a number on the label, it's accompanied by the word "years." Barbados, Guyana, and Trinidad and Tobago are among the rum-producing countries we often look to for aged rum.

A related question is whether the aged rums you seek should allow any additions or manipulations beyond the basic techniques of distillation, aging, and blend-ing. We have great admiration for producers who take a purist approach, but we also acknowledge that there are rums we enjoy very much that have clearly been rounded out with a bit of sugar. You'll draw your own conclusions about this as you sample more rum, but we advise not worrying too much about it starting out; it's often hard to find specific information about this anyway.

As with other aged spirits we've discussed, your goal should be finding a mid-priced aged rum that you'd happily sip on its own but that's also suitable for the cocktails in this chapter and beyond. Aged rum cocktails have a strikingly different flavor profile than those we mixed with light rum, with more emphasis on richness and depth. Welcome to the dark side.

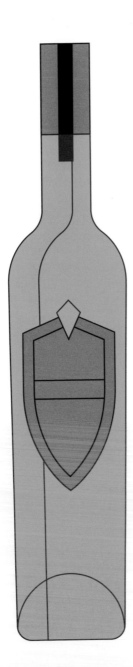

REAL MCCOY 5

Real McCoy 5 from Barbados does for aged rum what its younger sibling did for light rum. Straightforward rum flavor with a nice dose of oak and no added sugar, it's a rum that bourbon lovers can get behind.

MOUNT GAY BLACK BARREL

For another Bajan rum option, we are fans of Mount Gay Black Barrel. Finished in charred bourbon casks, it's rich with notes of brown sugar and molasses.

CHAIRMAN'S RESERVE ORIGINAL

This St. Lucian rum blends column and pot still spirits aged in ex-bourbon barrels. With a subtle fruitiness and plenty of vanilla, it's an excellent aged rum for cocktails.

ENGLISH HARBOUR 5

This rum from Antigua is well-balanced and approachable, offering hints of malted milk chocolate.

EL DORADO 12

While the 5- and 8-year-old rums from El Dorado are solid choices, we think their 12-year-old option is a worthwhile splurge. Blended from rums made on multiple stills in Guyana, it's rich, complex, and just on the right side of sweet.

WINTER DAIQUIRI

YOU ALREADY KNOW, AND HOPEFULLY LOVE, THE DAIQUIRI (PAGE 98). SO WHY BRING IT UP AGAIN? BECAUSE SWAPPING LIGHT RUM FOR AN AGED RUM IS AN OPPORTUNITY TO THINK ABOUT HOW YOU CAN HAVE FUN ADAPTING A CLASSIC COCKTAIL TEMPLATE. You could keep everything else in the recipe exactly the same, but the different flavor profile of an aged rum opens up other possibilities. It offers sweet vanilla notes contributed by the barrel. We can enhance those by sweetening the cocktail with demerara sugar instead of a plain simple syrup. And as you know from mixing whiskey cocktails, barrel-aged spirits also pair wonderfully with Angostura bitters. By making a Daiquiri with aged rum, more complex sugar, and aromatic bitters, you can transform a quintessential warm-weather cocktail into something you might cozy up with on a frosty night. That's why we call this a Winter Daiquiri. Though if we're being honest, we'll take any kind of Daiquiri in any kind of weather.

INGREDIENTS

2 oz [60 ml] aged rum

1 oz [30 ml] fresh lime juice

½ oz [15 ml] Rich Demerara Syrup (page 33)

2 dashes Angostura bitters

DIRECTIONS

To a shaker, add the rum, lime juice, syrup, bitters, and ice. Shake, strain into a chilled coupe, and serve.

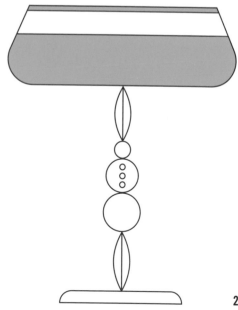

AIR MAIL

NOW THAT WE'VE MADE A DAIQUIRI WITH AGED RUM, LET'S TAKE THAT COCKTAIL IN A MORE INTERESTING DIRECTION. The likely origins of the Air Mail trace back to Cuba, and it's essentially an evolved version of a traditional Daiquiri (page 98). It calls for aged rum in place of light rum and honey in place of sugar, it's served tall with ice instead of in a compact coupe, and the whole thing is topped with champagne. Think of it as a Daiquiri that grew up with a trust fund.

INGREDIENTS

1½ oz [45 ml] aged rum

¾ oz [22.5 ml] fresh lime juice

¾ oz [22.5 ml] Honey Syrup (page 33)

2 oz [60 ml] sparkling wine

DIRECTIONS

To a shaker, add the rum, lime juice, syrup, and ice. Shake and strain into a rocks or highball glass filled with ice. Top with sparkling wine, stir gently to combine, and serve.

RUM OLD-FASHIONED

AS WE'VE SEEN THROUGHOUT THE BOOK, OLD-FASHIONEDS AREN'T JUST FOR WHISKEY. You can make the drink with just about anything. That said, aged rums have the potential to be particularly delicious when served this way. Since this is such a spirit-forward cocktail, the quality of the rum makes a great difference on how it comes out. A boring rum will taste, well, boring, and a flawed rum won't have much to cover it up. But if you take a good rum and accent it with just a little sugar, some spice from bitters, and aromatics from an orange peel, you can end up with a wonderfully complex Rum Old-Fashioned. (Given that rums vary considerably in sweetness, you may need to adjust the amount of sugar called for here. Feel free to cut back if your rum is already a little sweet.)

INGREDIENTS

2 oz [60 ml] aged rum

1 barspoon (⅙ oz [5 ml]) Rich Demerara Syrup

2 dashes Angostura bitters

1 dash orange bitters

Orange peel, for garnish

DIRECTIONS

To a mixing glass, add the rum, syrup, both bitters, and ice. Stir and strain into a rocks glass filled with ice or a large ice cube. Garnish with an orange peel and serve.

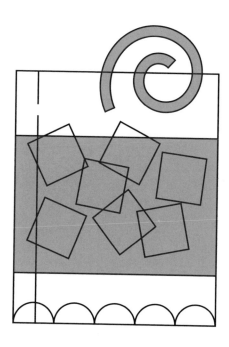

PEDRO MARTINEZ

RUM CLUB ISN'T JUST ONE OF OUR FAVORITE BARS IN PORTLAND, IT'S ONE OF OUR FAVORITE BARS ANYWHERE. The Pedro Martinez, their rum-based take on the classic Martinez (page 151), is one of the bar's longest-running cocktails and a drink that we've enjoyed on many nights on the Rum Club patio. Their house recipe is difficult to replicate, involving their own custom rum blend and bitters, but owner Michael Shea has kindly offered an adaptation for home bars. He recommends using aged rums from Guyana or Barbados and a flavorful vermouth such as Cocchi di Torino. This is a precision recipe that's worth the effort, and while it's not quite the same experience as being up in da Club, it's the next best thing.

INGREDIENTS

2 oz [60 ml] aged rum

1 oz [30 ml] sweet vermouth

¼ oz [7.5 ml] maraschino liqueur

3 dashes orange bitters

10 drops Angostura bitters

4 drops absinthe

1 strip lime peel

2 lemon peels

DIRECTIONS

In a mixing glass, add the rum, vermouth, maraschino liqueur, both bitters, absinthe, lime peel, and ice. Stir and strain into a rocks glass filled with ice or a single large cube. Express both lemon peels over the drink, discard the peels, and serve.

BRASS RAIL

ALL-STAR BARMAN TONY ABOU-GANIM CREATED THE BRASS RAIL IN HONOR OF HIS LATE AUNT HELEN DAVID, PROPRIETOR OF THE BRASS RAIL BAR IN PORT HURON, MICHIGAN. Benedictine was her favorite nightcap, inspiring its use in this deliciously rich rum sour. According to Tony, Helen's frequent toast when raising a glass to friends was just one word, "Happiness!" We predict that's what you'll feel when you mix up one of these too.

INGREDIENTS

1½ oz [45 ml] aged rum

½ oz [15 ml] Benedictine

1 oz [30 ml] fresh lemon juice

Scant ½ oz [15 ml] Rich Simple Syrup (page 33)

2 dashes orange bitters

1 egg white

3 drops Angostura bitters, for garnish

DIRECTIONS

To a shaker without ice, add the rum, Benedictine, lemon juice, syrup, bitters, and egg white. Dry shake to aerate the egg white. Add ice and shake again, then strain into a chilled coupe glass. Garnish with Angostura bitters atop the drink and serve.

COTILLION

RUM PROBABLY ISN'T THE FIRST SPIRIT THAT COMES TO MIND WHEN YOU HEAR THE WORD *COTILLION*, AND INDEED THIS IS SLIGHTLY MORE OF A BOURBON COCKTAIL. Appearing in the 1946 *Stork Club Bar Book*, the original proportions were a bit weird, calling for just ¼ oz [7.5 ml] of rum. We prefer this modernized version from Chicago bartender Scott Kennedy.

INGREDIENTS

1 oz [30 ml] bourbon

¾ oz [22.5 ml] aged rum

½ oz [15 ml] orange liqueur

¾ oz [22.5 ml] fresh lemon juice

½ oz [15 ml] fresh orange juice

Flamed orange peel, for garnish (page 26)

DIRECTIONS

To a shaker, add the bourbon, rum, orange liqueur, lemon and orange juices, and ice. Shake and strain into a chilled coupe glass. Garnish with a flamed orange peel and serve.

CREAM PUFF

DON'T LET THE NAME FOOL YOU. The Cream Puff is a serious cocktail, and it's seriously delicious. An original from *The Old Waldorf-Astoria Bar Book*, it's a fine example of an old-school fizz. It's served short, with no ice, and the soda cuts through the cream to make it deceptively easy-drinking. We've adapted the recipe just a little bit, bringing in Rich Demerara Syrup instead of simple syrup and adding a finishing touch of freshly grated nutmeg for aromatics.

The method of making this type of drink is a bit unusual. You start with the soda in the glass, then shake everything else with ice and strain it into the soda. This causes it to "puff" up, forming a creamy head on top of the cocktail. Since there's no ice in the drink itself, it's imperative to use chilled soda.

INGREDIENTS

3 oz [90 ml] chilled soda water

2 oz [60 ml] aged rum

1 oz [30 ml] cream

½ oz [15 ml] Rich Demerara Syrup (page 33)

Freshly grated nutmeg, for garnish

DIRECTIONS

Pour the soda into a chilled glass, such as a rocks glass or short fizz glass. To a shaker, add the rum, cream, syrup, and ice. Shake and strain into the soda. Grate nutmeg over the top and serve.

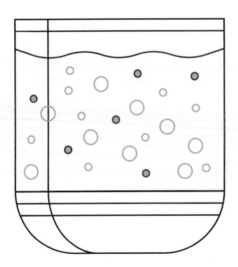

PARISIAN BLONDE

THE ORIGINAL RECIPE FOR THIS COCKTAIL WASN'T ANYTHING TO WRITE HOME ABOUT.
Made with Jamaican rum, orange curaçao, and cream, it was all shaken together into a sweet, milky concoction. In 2009, cocktail writer Erik Ellestad published an idea that we believe makes it much better: stirring the rum and orange liqueur separately, then floating cream in a layer atop the drink. This is visually much more appealing, and it also allows every ingredient in the drink to stand out. You taste the richness of the rum and orange liqueur, complemented by the sweet finish of the cream. We've also followed the lead of Smuggler's Cove in San Francisco in making the Parisian Blonde with a straightforward aged rum. Jamaican rum often has a very different flavor profile that doesn't work quite as well here. Definitely do try this updated version of the cocktail; it's a great dessert drink or nightcap.

INGREDIENTS

1 oz [30 ml] aged rum

1 oz [30 ml] orange liqueur

Cream, lightly aerated (see Note)

Freshly grated cinnamon or nutmeg, for garnish

DIRECTIONS

To a mixing glass, add the rum, orange liqueur, and ice. Stir and strain into a chilled coupe glass. Gently pour the cream on top to form a layer (see Note). Garnish with freshly grated cinnamon or nutmeg and serve.

NOTE ON TECHNIQUE

To float the cream, it helps to lighten it with a little air. An easy way to do this is to pour it in a jar with some headspace, seal it, and shake for a minute or so. Then, when you're ready to pour, do so as close to the surface of the drink as possible, pouring down the side of the glass to float a thin layer on top.

CHAPTER 18

SCOTCH

FIRE UP YOUR BEST RON BURGUNDY IMPRESSION, BECAUSE IT'S TIME FOR SCOTCH! Choosing your first bottle can be a bit overwhelming because while popular perception tends to focus solely on its supposedly smoky character, scotch is an incredibly diverse category of whiskies ranging from robust and peaty to light and ethereal. With that in mind, we'll give you a quick overview of what scotch is, explain why it's so diverse, and give you some guidelines to help you buy a bottle. After all that, we will, of course, provide some of our favorite scotch cocktails.

There are technical rules that define scotch: It must be made and aged in Scotland, can't be bottled below 40 percent ABV, must contain a portion of malted barley, and can be distilled to a wide range of strengths. What makes scotch truly unique, however, has less to do with regulations and more to do with traditions. The two traditions to focus on are the use (or lack thereof) of peat and the process of aging in used barrels.

Let's start with peat. Think of peat as the coal of wet climates. Naturally formed from centuries of decaying vegetation, it can be dug up, dried, and burned as fuel. When early scotch distillers needed to kiln their barley, they burned peat. The vegetal smoke from those fires was infused into the grain and therefore into the whisky itself. As scotch expanded in popularity and fuel sources diversified, many distillers chose to eliminate peat smoke from their process. In fact, most contemporary scotch whiskies are unpeated. Peaty scotch takes time to appreciate, and as much as we love it, it's not where we suggest you begin your exploration of the category. Unpeated scotch is eminently enjoyable and often preferable for mixing in cocktails.

The other reason we suggest starting with an unpeated scotch has everything to do with tradition number two: aging in used barrels. You've already added bourbon and rye to your bar, and both of those styles of whiskey are aged in brand new barrels. New American oak is loaded with wood sugars and notes of caramel and vanilla, so it's no surprise that those flavors are abundant in whiskeys aged in them. In contrast, scotch is traditionally aged in used barrels. This makes sense because, while the Scotch countryside is gorgeous and verdant, deforestation reduced the availability of oak. Unable to make their own barrels, scotch whisky makers simply refilled barrels that had previously been used to ship sherry, wine, or port; these days the majority of scotch whisky is aged in used bourbon barrels sent from the United States.

Whisky aging in used oak matures more slowly than whiskey aged in new oak, especially in a cool climate like Scotland's. The impact of the barrel is also more subtle, and so the character of scotch tends to be drier and more grain-forward. We suggest focusing first on appreciating the influence of different types of barrels before adding the complexity of peat to the mix.

Much, much more can be said about the glorious diversity of scotch, and we urge you to experience it for yourself, in time. First, though, pick up a bottle of unpeated scotch, enjoy it neat, and then make some cocktails. We recommend you stir up a classic Rob Roy (page 231), the scotch counterpart to the Manhattan (page 68), and notice how the differences in grain and oak can make two similar whiskey cocktails taste entirely unique. Following that, there's a vast world of scotch and scotch cocktails to explore.

SCOTCH 101

THE WORLD OF SCOTCH CAN SEEM INTIMIDATING, BUT THANKFULLY THE BASIC RULES GOVERNING THE SPIRIT ARE PRETTY STRAIGHTFORWARD. It's a whisky (Scotland spells it without the *e*) distilled and produced in Scotland, aged in oak for at least three years, made without additives other than water and optional caramel coloring, and bottled at no less than 40 percent ABV. The legal classifications of scotch depend on the type of grains and stills used and whether the whisky comes from a single distillery or is blended from more than one source.

The three classifications you'll see most often are:

SINGLE MALT: Made entirely from malted barley and distilled in pot stills at a single distillery.

BLENDED MALT: A blend comprised of malt whiskies from more than one distillery.

BLENDED SCOTCH: A blend that incorporates both malt whisky and grain whisky, the latter of which tends to be lighter in flavor and can be made with column stills.

It's less common to come across grain whiskey bottled on its own, but "single grain" (from one distillery) and "blended grain" (from more than one distillery) are also permitted categories.

A common myth about scotch is that it's inherently smoky. While some excellent scotches do take on a strong character imparted by peat smoke, most scotch does not use this process and develops its flavor from the interaction of the distillate and the barrels in which it ages.

BOTTLES WE REACH FOR

MONKEY SHOULDER
As a blended malt, Monkey Shoulder has the oomph to not get lost in cocktails while also serving as a perfectly fine scotch for sipping. Blended from Speyside whiskeys aged in ex-bourbon casks, it offers a classic profile at a price that's really hard to beat.

COMPASS BOX ARTIST BLEND
Compass Box is consistently one of our favorite blenders and their Artist Blend is proof that affordable blended scotch can still be plenty interesting. With a distinctly fruity profile, it's a pleasure to drink and to mix.

BENRIACH 10
Matured in ex-bourbon, sherry, and, uncommonly, virgin oak barrels, Benriach 10 has a honeyed, orchard fruit note that works as well in a drink as it does neat in a glass.

BRUICHLADDICH CLASSIC LADDIE
Aged in ex-bourbon barrels, the Classic Laddie has a light honeyed hay flavor that, with its bracing 50 percent ABV, makes it perfect for stirred drinks like Scotch Old-Fashioneds (page 232).

ABERLOUR 12
Aberlour is shockingly affordable for how nutty and rich it tastes. It's an excellent single malt, and a fantastic option if you'd like to add a scotch with sherry cask influence to your home bar.

ROB ROY

CREATED IN 1894 AT THE OLD WALDORF-ASTORIA BAR IN NEW YORK CITY, THE ROB ROY WAS NAMED IN CELEBRATION OF AN OPERETTA BASED ON THE LIFE OF SCOTTISH OUTLAW ROB ROY MACGREGOR. The drink is a straightforward combination of scotch, sweet vermouth, and bitters; in other words, it's a Manhattan (page 68) made with Scottish whisky instead of American rye or bourbon. It's a study in just how differently these styles of whisky work in cocktails, and it's one of the handful of vintage scotch drinks that have stood the test of time. Unlike the Manhattan, which is almost always made with Angostura bitters, the selection of bitters for the Rob Roy varies considerably. We've given it with orange bitters, but you could also try it with Peychaud's, a dash of each, or Angostura for a flavor profile closer to the more familiar Manhattan.

INGREDIENTS

2 oz [60 ml] scotch

1 oz [30 ml] sweet vermouth

2 dashes orange bitters

Lemon peel

Cocktail cherry, for garnish

DIRECTIONS

To a mixing glass, add the scotch, vermouth, bitters, and ice. Stir and strain into a chilled coupe glass. Express the lemon peel over the drink and discard the peel. Garnish with a cherry, and serve.

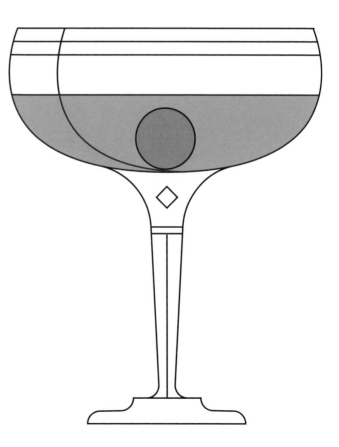

SCOTCH OLD-FASHIONED

IT SHOULD GO WITHOUT SAYING THAT IF YOU CAN MAKE A MANHATTAN-LIKE COCKTAIL WITH SCOTCH, YOU CAN MAKE AN OLD-FASHIONED WITH IT TOO. Because scotch tends to have less oak influence than bourbon, we typically make our scotch Old-Fashioneds with a slightly different recipe. We use Rich Simple Syrup (page 33) instead of the more dominating Demerara, one fewer dash of bitters, and a zesty strip of lemon peel in place of orange.

INGREDIENTS

2 oz [60 ml] scotch

1 barspoon (⅙ oz [5 ml]) Rich Simple Syrup (page 33)

1 dash Angostura bitters

1 dash orange bitters

Lemon twist, for garnish

DIRECTIONS

To a mixing glass, add the scotch, syrup, both bitters, and ice. Stir and strain into a rocks glass filled with ice or a large ice cube. Garnish with a lemon peel and serve.

AFFINITY

THE FIRST REFERENCE WE COULD FIND TO THE AFFINITY WAS THE 1916 *COCKTAIL-OLOGY* BY THE AMAZINGLY NAMED COUNT BENVENITO MARTINI, A SELF-DESCRIBED "CONNOISSEUR EXTRAORDINAIRE." And who are we to doubt his claim? We trust him completely because he gave us the Affinity, and the Affinity is fantastic. It's a simple variation on the Rob Roy (page 231) that invites dry vermouth to the party. At first glance it doesn't seem like this would accomplish much, but the addition of dry vermouth allows the maltiness of the scotch to come through more cleanly.

INGREDIENTS

1½ oz [45 ml] scotch

¾ oz [22.5 ml] sweet vermouth

¾ oz [22.5 ml] dry vermouth

2 dashes Angostura bitters

Lemon peel and cocktail cherry, for garnish

DIRECTIONS

To a mixing glass, add the scotch, sweet and dry vermouths, bitters, and ice. Stir and strain into a chilled coupe glass. Garnish with a lemon peel and cherry and serve.

BOBBY BURNS

THIS DRINK FIRST APPEARED IN PRINT IN THE 1895 *BARTENDER'S GUIDE* DISTRIB-
UTED BY THE BERNER-MAYER BARWARE COMPANY. THE BOOK INCLUDED A HANDFUL
OF COCKTAIL RECIPES, RULES FOR POKER AND BILLIARDS, AND ADVERTISEMENTS
FOR THE COMPANY'S JIGGERS, SHAKERS, AND OTHER PARAPHERNALIA. The cocktail
was first known as the "Baby Burns" but renamed "Bobby Burns" in Hugo Ensslin's *Recipes for
Mixed Drinks*. Unsurprisingly, it's the latter name that stuck, and because of this, the cocktail
is now drunk in celebration of Scottish poet Robert Burns on the anniversary of his birth.

But wait. Was the cocktail actually named for the poet? Probably not, unless Robert Burns
was nicknamed "Baby" at some point, which we find unlikely. Nevertheless, the Bobby
Burns is a really good cocktail. The Benedictine and scotch work together in a way that
recalls honeyed hay. Mix up a Bobby Burns and toast your favorite Scottish poet and/or
late-nineteenth-century mystery baby.

INGREDIENTS

1½ oz [45 ml] scotch

1 oz [30 ml] sweet vermouth

½ oz [15 ml] Benedictine

Lemon peel, for garnish

DIRECTIONS

*To a mixing glass, add the scotch, vermouth,
Benedictine, and ice. Stir and strain into a
chilled coupe glass. Garnish with a lemon peel
and serve.*

VARIATIONS

*You'll sometimes see this drink made with the
liqueur Drambuie, which has the advantage of
being rather more Scottish than Benedictine.
There's also a cocktail called the Robert Burns,
which, it turns out, also may not be named
after the Scottish bard. (The poet just can't
catch a break!) To make the Robert Burns,
omit the Benedictine and add a barspoon (⅙ oz
[5 ml]) of absinthe and a dash of orange bitters.*

MICKIE WALKER

THOUGH WE PRESUME THIS DRINK WAS NAMED AFTER CHAMPION BOXER MICKEY WALKER, IT DOESN'T PACK MUCH OF A PUNCH. In fact, it's so delicious and easy to drink, it might even lead you to forgive us for that cheesy opening line. Another contribution from *The Savoy Cocktail Book*, the Mickie Walker is a complex sour that benefits from a lighter style of scotch, allowing the grenadine and sweet vermouth a bit more space to breathe. The end result is a cocktail with a lot going on but every ingredient clearly defined and nicely layered.

INGREDIENTS

1½ oz [45 ml] scotch

½ oz [15 ml] sweet vermouth

½ oz [15 ml] grenadine

½ oz [15 ml] fresh lemon juice

Cocktail cherry, for garnish

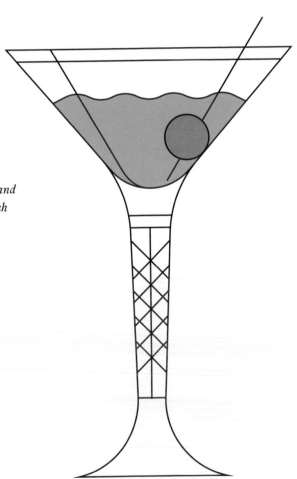

DIRECTIONS

To a shaker, add the scotch, vermouth, grenadine, lemon juice, and ice. Shake and strain into a chilled coupe glass. Garnish with a cherry and serve.

MORNING GLORY FIZZ

IN O.H. BYRON'S 1884 BOOK *THE MODERN BARTENDER'S GUIDE,* his recommendations for imbibing the Morning Glory Fizz are as follows: "To be drank immediately, or the effect will be lost. It is a morning beverage, a tonic and a nerve quieter." Only you know the volume of your nerves, so it's up to you if they need quieting with 2 oz [60 ml] of scotch first thing in the morning. Regardless of whether you follow Byron's specific guidance, we do think you should mix up a Morning Glory Fizz at some point in your life. It calls for both lemon and lime, which is mildly inconvenient, but as demonstrated by the success of Sprite and 7UP, sometimes two juices are better than one. Despite its potent combination of scotch and absinthe, the Morning Glory Fizz does have the makings of a decent brunch cocktail. To quote the great Mitch Hedberg, it is "saved by the buoyancy of citrus."

INGREDIENTS

2 oz [60 ml] scotch

½ oz [15 ml] fresh lemon juice

¼ oz [7.5 ml] fresh lime juice

½ oz [15 ml] Rich Simple Syrup (page 33)

1 egg white

Soda water, for topping

Absinthe, for garnish (optional)

DIRECTIONS

To a shaker without ice, add the scotch, juices, syrup, and egg white. Dry shake to aerate the egg white. Add ice and shake again, then strain into a highball glass filled with ice. Top with soda, spritz with absinthe (if desired), and serve.

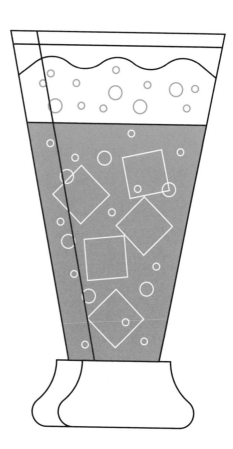

KICK DRUM

THERE'S A VINTAGE COCKTAIL THAT ENJOYED A MODERN REVIVAL CALLED THE CAMERON'S KICK, AN APPEALING MIX OF LEMON, ORGEAT, SCOTCH, AND IRISH WHISKEY. It's a great drink, but that last ingredient takes it just outside the scope of this book. Should that stop you from making it? Absolutely not. Because honestly, the two styles of whiskey are similar enough that you can get by with only scotch and still get very tasty results. We've changed the name out of deference to the original, but this simplified version is well worth making in a pinch.

INGREDIENTS
2 oz [60 ml] scotch
½ oz [15 ml] fresh lemon juice
½ oz [15 ml] orgeat

DIRECTIONS
To a shaker, add the scotch, lemon juice, orgeat, and ice. Shake, strain into a chilled coupe glass, and serve.

VARIATION
To make the original Cameron's Kick, use 1 oz [30 ml] each of scotch and Irish whiskey and proceed as above.

AUTOMOBILE

THE AUTOMOBILE WAS CREATED AT THE HOFFMAN HOUSE IN NEW YORK IN 1905, AND ITS COMBINATION OF SCOTCH, GIN, AND SWEET VERMOUTH INTO ONE ROB ROY-INSPIRED COCKTAIL DOESN'T SEEM LIKE IT SHOULD WORK. Both versions of the Automobile are testaments to American inventiveness. Give this one a try; it's unexpectedly good.

INGREDIENTS
¾ oz [22.5 ml] scotch
¾ oz [22.5 ml] gin
¾ oz [22.5 ml] sweet vermouth
2 dashes orange bitters
Olive or cocktail cherry, for garnish

DIRECTIONS
To a mixing glass, add the scotch, gin, vermouth, bitters, and ice. Stir and strain into a chilled coupe glass. Garnish with an olive or cherry and serve.

WHISKY HIGHBALL

YOU MIGHT GLANCE AT THIS RECIPE AND WONDER WHY WE'RE DEVOTING SPACE TO SUCH A BASIC DRINK. We didn't bother with other two-ingredient cocktails like the rum and Coke, and the Whisky Highball could just as easily be called a scotch and soda if you don't want to be fancy about it. Yet if you do get fancy about it, you'll find that this drink is more rewarding than its simple nature suggests. Take the time to make sure your soda is thoroughly chilled so that the bubbles are as sharp as can be. Pick out a good, but not extravagantly good, scotch. Use fresh ice cubes, and maybe even chill a tall glass in the freezer to make it extra cold. Garnish it with a light twist of lemon, if you like. When it all comes together perfectly, you've got a drink that can be truly enlightening, opening up the subtleties of the whisky for enjoyment.

That paean to the highball aside, this is also one of our go-to drinks when we find ourselves in a subpar cocktail situation, like a catered banquet or business reception. When the selection of spirits is as limited as the attention to detail of the bartender, you can do far worse than cheap scotch on ice with soda.

INGREDIENTS

1½ oz [45 ml] scotch

3 to 4 oz [90 to 120 ml] chilled soda water

Lemon peel, for garnish (optional)

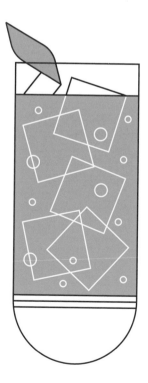

DIRECTIONS

In a tall highball glass filled with ice, add the scotch and soda. Stir gently to combine, garnish with a lemon peel, if desired, and serve.

MAMIE TAYLOR

THE MAMIE TAYLOR WAS A SENSATION FOR A BRIEF PERIOD AT THE DAWN OF THE TWENTIETH CENTURY, CREATED FOR A POPULAR THEATER ACTRESS OF THE SAME NAME. Well, she had almost the same name. She actually spelled hers *Mayme Taylor*, but the drink took on a life of its own. The drink was nearly forgotten until the modern cocktail revival, but now it's come back into fashion. It's more flavorful than the Moscow mule (page 137) and subtler than the Kentucky rendition (see page 51). Scotch and ginger make an ideal match.

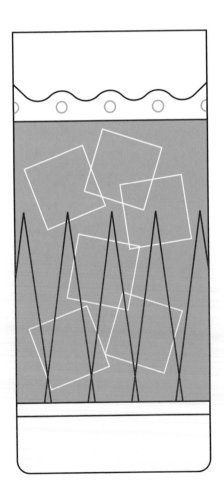

INGREDIENTS

2 oz [60 ml] scotch

½ oz [15 ml] fresh lime juice

4 to 5 oz [120 to 150 ml] ginger beer

DIRECTIONS

In a highball or rocks glass filled with ice, add the scotch and lime juice. Top with ginger beer, stir gently, and serve.

CHAPTER 19

APRICOT LIQUEUR

YOU'VE BEEN ADDING A LOT OF BITTER AND HERBAL LIQUEURS TO YOUR BAR, and while we hope you've learned to appreciate their complex and sometimes challenging flavors, fruit liqueurs are straightforward, simple, and, most important, unapologetically delicious.

Technically, you already have a couple fruit liqueurs—orange liqueur and maraschino—although we don't always think of them that way. Orange liqueur has an edge to it thanks to its relatively high proof. And because it's distilled after the fruit is infused, maraschino carries more of the aura of fruit rather than its essence. What your bar needs now is a no-nonsense fruit liqueur that tastes like, well, the fruit on the label, and we think you should start with a bottle of apricot liqueur.

There are three good reasons for this. First off, it's classic. Apricot liqueur started appearing in cocktail books around the turn of the twentieth century and was quickly embraced in the bar world. Second: It's versatile. It works well in warm-weather cocktails, but mixed with apple brandy it feels autumnal, and when used with whiskey and nutmeg it takes on wintry characteristics.

Lastly, apricot liqueur doesn't dominate drinks the way that many fruit liqueurs often do. Peach, banana, or blackberry can hog the spotlight. Apricot is less broad-shouldered. It shares space and can be used effectively in drinks that aren't necessarily fruity. It can play a role in more styles of cocktails, and that's why we think it's a great starter fruit liqueur.

The production of fruit liqueurs is generally as straightforward as their flavor. High-quality apricot liqueur is made by first infusing apricots in alcohol. Neutral spirit is most commonly used, although some brands infuse in an eau de vie (unaged distillate) made from fermented apricot juice. The maceration period can be relatively short or extend many months, after which it will be filtered, sweetened, and reduced to its final proof. Some brands exclusively use fresh fruit, others use dried, and some a blend of both. There are enough variables in the process that no two brands are identical, and we've found excellent bottlings that embrace fresh apricot flavors as well as others that emphasize the richer, more concentrated notes of preserved apricot.

BOTTLES WE REACH FOR

BAILONI GOLD APRICOT LIQUEUR
Made in the Wachau region of Austria, this liqueur is especially luscious, rich, and fruity with a great depth of flavor.

GIFFARD ABRICOT DU ROUSSILLON
The unmistakable fruit flavor of this liqueur comes from *abricots rouges du roussillon,* a variety from southern France. With exceptionally well-balanced fruit and acidity, it's a wonderful all-purpose apricot liqueur.

BITTER TRUTH APRICOT LIQUEUR
Rich but slightly more restrained, this liqueur accents the fruity notes of apricot with a hint of nuttiness.

COMBIER LIQUEUR ABRICOT
Made by infusing fresh apricots in a neutral spirit, Combier Abricot is a clean, distinct expression of its namesake fruit. We love it in simpler cocktails, but find it can get a little lost as the ingredient list grows.

ROTHMAN AND WINTER ORCHARD APRICOT
There's a touch of a cooked apricot bitterness that helps this liqueur to stand out well in cocktails, offering a fruity counterpoint to sharper spirits.

KATINKA

THE EARLIEST REFERENCE TO THE KATINKA WE COULD FIND WAS IN DAVID EMBURY'S 1948 *THE FINE ART OF MIXING DRINKS*. With only three ingredients, one of which is the blank slate of vodka, it's an ideal drink for demonstrating how a fruit liqueur brings layers of flavor to the simple sour template. You'll taste apricot, lime, and, well, that's about it. But it's a delicious combination and also an offbeat cocktail to have on hand for your vodka-drinking guests. (Because of its simplicity, this is one cocktail that depends greatly on the brand of apricot liqueur you use. Should you find yourself craving a little extra depth, a barspoon [⅙ oz (5 ml)] of Honey Syrup [page 33] will set it right.)

INGREDIENTS
1½ oz [45 ml] vodka
¾ oz [22.5 ml] apricot liqueur
½ oz [15 ml] fresh lime juice

DIRECTIONS

To a shaker, add the vodka, apricot liqueur, lime juice, and ice. Shake, strain into a chilled coupe glass, and serve.

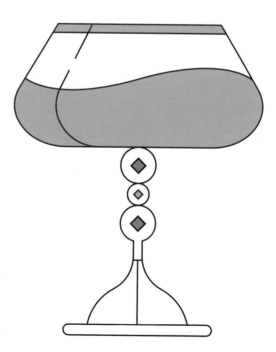

CLARIDGE

FRUIT LIQUEURS AREN'T JUST FOR SOURS. They're also extremely useful in spirit-forward stirred cocktails, where they contribute body, sweetness, and flavor. Take, as an example, the Claridge. The official drink of the Hotel Claridge in Paris (at least when it was published in 1927), this is an excellent apricot martini. While a lot of old recipes need to be adapted to suit a modern palate, the Claridge still hits the right notes almost a century later.

INGREDIENTS

1 oz [30 ml] gin

1 oz [30 ml] dry vermouth

½ oz [15 ml] apricot liqueur

½ oz [15 ml] orange liqueur

DIRECTIONS

To a mixing glass, add the gin, vermouth, apricot and orange liqueurs, and ice. Stir, strain into a chilled coupe glass, and serve.

THE SLOPE

WE TRIED A MARTINI WITH APRICOT LIQUEUR (SEE ABOVE). NOW HOW ABOUT A MAN-HATTAN? Created by Julie Reiner at the Clover Club, the Slope is a boozy drink, but the splash of liqueur takes away the bite without stealing the show. If you didn't know there was apricot in here, you might not be able to guess. What you would know is that you'll probably want another and that you're really glad you're making these at home, stumbling distance from bed.

INGREDIENTS

2½ oz [15 ml] rye

¾ oz [22.5 ml] sweet vermouth

¼ oz [7.5 ml] apricot liqueur

1 dash Angostura bitters

Cocktail cherry, for garnish

DIRECTIONS

To a mixing glass, add the rye, vermouth, apricot liqueur, bitters, and ice. Stir and strain into a chilled coupe glass. Garnish with a cherry and serve.

YACHT CLUB

POP YOUR COLLAR AND LEAVE YOUR SOCKS AT HOME BECAUSE THIS SIMPLE DRINK FROM *THE OLD WALDORF-ASTORIA BAR BOOK* IS JUST THE THING TO MIX UP AFTER A GRUELING DAY OF SAILING AND SNACKING ON CANAPÉS. The Yacht Club is another riff on the Manhattan format. It seems like an aged rum would be more appropriate here, but this drink is all about the subtle interplay between the apricot and vermouth; the light rum is just there to tie it all together. The simplicity of the ingredients belies the depth of this combination, which unfolds with subtle hints of fruit and chocolate.

INGREDIENTS
2 oz [60 ml] light rum

1 oz [30 ml] sweet vermouth

¼ oz [7.5 ml] apricot liqueur

DIRECTIONS
To a mixing glass, add the rum, vermouth, apricot liqueur, and ice. Stir, strain into a chilled coupe glass, and serve.

APRICOT COOLER

BACK BEFORE THE MODERN CRAZE FOR LIGHTLY FLAVORED ALCOHOLIC SELTZERS, WHEN YOU WANTED A TALL, SPARKLING, REFRESHING COCKTAIL, YOU HAD TO MAKE IT YOURSELF. Frankly, we suggest that you still should. The Apricot Cooler is low ABV, irresistibly refreshing, and the perfect poolside cocktail. Leave the White Claws at the convenience store and mix yourself a crisp, 1930s-era cooler instead.

INGREDIENTS
2 oz [60 ml] apricot liqueur

½ oz [15 ml] fresh lemon juice

1 barspoon (⅙ oz [5 ml]) grenadine

5 oz [150 ml] soda water

DIRECTIONS
In a highball glass filled with ice, add the apricot liqueur, lemon juice, grenadine, and soda. Stir gently and serve.

PENDENNIS CLUB

DID YOU GROW UP WITH ANYONE WHO TRANSFERRED SCHOOLS, CHANGED THEIR STYLE, AND BECAME MORE POPULAR AS A RESULT? The Pendennis Club is kind of like that. Named after the Kentucky club where it originated, the first recipe for the Pendennis Club from 1908 was a simple gin and apricot martini. It more or less disappeared for an entire century before being resurrected in Ted Haigh's *Vintage Spirits and Forgotten Spirits*, where it reemerged as a sour and proceeded to become a cocktail bar standard. If you enjoyed the Pegu Club (page 76) from earlier in the book, you'll probably like this one too. The Pendennis Club is in the same neighborhood structurally, if not geographically.

INGREDIENTS

2 oz [60 ml] gin

1 oz [30 ml] apricot liqueur

¾ oz [22.5 ml] fresh lime juice

2 dashes Peychaud's bitters

Lime wheel, for garnish

DIRECTIONS

To a shaker, add the gin, apricot liqueur, lime juice, bitters, and ice. Shake and strain into a chilled coupe glass. Garnish with a lime wheel and serve.

A TO B

THERE'S AN UNHERALDED GENRE OF TWO-INGREDIENT COCKTAILS THAT CONSIST OF NOTHING MORE THAN A BASE SPIRIT AND A LIQUEUR. The most enduring of these is the Rusty Nail, which is just scotch mixed with the herbal liqueur Drambuie, but there are a handful of others that fit the profile, such as the Tipsy Coachman (page 142). We've found that apricot liqueur and cognac work marvelously well in combination too. With no bitters, syrups, or other modifiers, it's as simple as A to B (or apricot to brandy).

INGREDIENTS

1½ oz [60 ml] cognac

¾ oz [30 ml] apricot liqueur

Orange peel, for garnish

DIRECTIONS

To a mixing glass, add the cognac, apricot liqueur, and ice. Stir and strain into a rocks glass over ice or a single large cube. Garnish with an orange peel and serve.

ANGEL FACE

WE MENTIONED THAT *THE SAVOY COCKTAIL BOOK* FEATURED A TON OF COCKTAILS WITH APRICOT LIQUEUR. The Angel Face is one of the more unusual ones. It's a spirit-forward cocktail that's simple and easy to love. The combination of apple and apricot makes it perfect for early autumn when the leaves are changing but it's still a little warm outside. This is also another instance of apple brandy showing well as a partner to other base spirits; the original recipe calls specifically for Calvados, which is indeed an ideal choice.

INGREDIENTS

1 oz [30 ml] apricot liqueur

1 oz [30 ml] apple brandy

1 oz [30 ml] gin

DIRECTIONS

To a mixing glass, add the apricot liqueur, apple brandy, gin, and ice. Stir, strain into a chilled coupe glass, and serve.

PARADISE

ONE THING THAT EARLY BARTENDERS AGREED ON WAS THAT WHEN THEY THOUGHT OF PARADISE, THEY THOUGHT OF APRICOT LIQUEUR. "Paradise" cocktails featuring the ingredient were legion, though the recipes shared little else in common. Our favorite comes from the Waldorf-Astoria in New York, where their Paradise is essentially a light rum Old-Fashioned sweetened with apricot liqueur. In the latest update to *The Waldorf-Astoria Bar Book*, Frank Caiafa adds a few dashes of orange bitters and a lemon peel to the drink, an idea we thoroughly endorse.

INGREDIENTS

2 oz [60 ml] light rum

1 oz [30 ml] apricot liqueur

2 dashes orange bitters

Lemon peel, for garnish

DIRECTIONS

To a mixing glass, add the rum, apricot liqueur, bitters, and ice. Stir and strain into a rocks glass filled with ice or a single large cube. Garnish with a lemon peel and serve.

CHAPTER 20

SHERRY

"SHERRY, NILES?" FANS OF THE AMERICAN SITCOM *FRASIER* MAY REMEM-
BER THAT SHERRY WAS A PREFERRED WINE OF THE CRANE BROTHERS. In
the show, it was meant to signal their status as effete snobs. After all, who keeps
bottles of sherry at home and drinks them on the regular? Answer: you, by the end
of this chapter. Sherry never deserved its reputation as an elitist tipple exclusively
for highbrow intellectuals, and that image would have been completely foreign to
nineteenth-century barrooms where sherry flowed freely into all sorts of cocktails.
If you've yet to discover the joys of drinking sherry, we are happy to introduce you.

With sherry we take a break from hard spirits to revisit wines. As you'll recall from
the vermouth chapter (page 64), fortified wines use the addition of distilled spirits
to bring up their alcohol content. Sherry often shares this characteristic with
vermouth, though unlike vermouth, it's not aromatized: There are no botanicals
added to sherry. It derives its unique flavors instead from a complex and fasci-
nating production process. (It's also not always fortified with spirits, with some
sherries achieving their higher ABV entirely through fermentation.)

Entire books have been written about sherry and we can only scratch the surface
of it here. Its production is centered in the area surrounding the Spanish town of
Jerez in southwestern Spain, and in Europe only wines from this region can bear

the sherry name. Sherry production begins like any other wine, with pressed grape juice fermented into alcohol. It's in the next steps that things get interesting.

After fermentation, the wine is often fortified with a distilled grape spirit to raise its level of alcohol and then transferred to large casks known as sherry butts. The casks aren't filled quite to the top, leaving some headspace that exposes the wine to air. From here, depending on the style of sherry being produced, aging can take a few different paths, as we outline in Sherry 101.

We've been writing as if all of this happens in one cask, but even that is an over-simplification. One of the other things that makes sherry so unique is its solera aging system. Rather than emptying an entire cask for bottling, only a fraction of the wine in the oldest barrel in a solera is removed each year. That cask is then topped off with wine from the next oldest in the solera, and so on, moving along a chain of progressively younger barrels. As a result, it's impossible to pin a precise age on these sherries the way one would for a whiskey; instead, most age statements on sherries reflect the average age of sherries in the blend, which can reach thirty years or more.

We've also been discussing only dry sherries, which are the styles we'll be reaching for to make the cocktails in this book. There are also sweet varieties of sherry made in whole or in part from moscatel or Pedro Ximénez grapes. The latter, labeled PX, are intensely sweet with rich, complex notes of dried fruit and leather. "Cream sherries" blend these sweeter wines with drier styles, marrying the best of both worlds. These sweeter sherries are wonderful on their own and also in cocktail applications, but to keep things simple we'll be focused on cocktails made with dry sherry.

As with vermouth, you'll want to keep your sherry sealed tight and refrigerated once you open the bottle. Also like vermouth, you'll find that it adds brightness, lightness, and depth to cocktails, proving the worth of increasing your home bar arsenal with a variety of flavorful wines, not just distilled spirits.

SHERRY 101

THE EASY DEFINITION OF SHERRY IS THAT IT'S A TYPE OF WINE—TYPICALLY A FORTIFIED WINE—ORIGINATING IN SOUTHWESTERN SPAIN, PARTICULARLY FROM AROUND JEREZ. The definitions of specific styles of sherry, however, get a lot more complicated:

FINO AND MANZANILLA: These sherries are the lightest, palest styles. They are aged under a layer of yeast called *flor* that forms on the surface of the wine within the barrel, minimizing interaction with the air. These sherries are crisp, nutty, and bone dry.

AMONTILLADO: These sherries spend some of their aging period under flor and some without it. An additional style you may come across is *palo cortado*, which lacks a precise definition but blends sensory qualities of both oloroso and amontillado. In both cases, the sherry darkens and takes on complex, nutty flavors due to oxidation. (Like we said, it's complicated.)

OLOROSO: These sherries are aged without flor, which causes them to take on a pronounced nutty, oxidative flavor. They are fortified to a higher ABV and spend their entire aging period exposed to air.

Contrary to its reputation as a sweet after-dinner drink, most sherry is very dry. We suggest picking up an amontillado to keep on hand for cocktails, but exploration of other styles (including sweeter ones like cream and PX) is certainly rewarding. And since sherry is a wine, we'll repeat our admonition from the vermouth chapter . . .

REFRIGERATE YOUR BOTTLES ONCE YOU'VE OPENED THEM!

So, where to begin? With a real sherry from Spain, obviously, and in one of the dry styles. Fino and manzanilla styles certainly fit the bill, but they are also more fragile and go off more quickly once the bottle is opened. That's not a problem when you're enjoying them by the glass, but if you're just using small pours for cocktails, you may not go through a bottle fast enough. Amontillados and olorosos are hardier, so those are what we tend to keep around for cocktails. If you're picking up just one bottle, amontillado is probably your best bet: Sturdier than a fino or manzanilla but not quite as rich and dark as an oloroso, it's the perfect sweet spot for dry sherry. Just be sure to pick up a *dry* amontillado; most bottles you encounter will be dry, but if it has the descriptor "medium" on the label, it may tend toward the sweeter side.

BOTTLES WE REACH FOR

GONZÁLEZ BYASS VIÑA AB
Light in body and bright in flavor, this amontillado combines moderate oak influence with the nutty, oxidative character we crave in a good sherry. It works equally well in cocktails or paired on its own with cheese, nuts, and olives.

LA GARROCHA AMONTILLADO
Produced by Bodegas Grant, this sherry balances its approachable nuttiness with a bright and subtly sweet finish accented by hints of orange peel.

LUSTAU AMONTILLADO LOS ARCOS
Lustau is one of the most widely known sherry brands, and deservedly so. Their sherries are reliably good. The Los Arcos amontillado is supple and very nicely balanced with notes of hazelnut and leather.

BAMBOO

SECOND TO DRINKING SHERRY BY ITSELF, THERE'S ARGUABLY NO BETTER INTRODUC-TION TO IT THAN THE LATE-NINETEENTH-CENTURY COCKTAIL KNOWN AS THE BAM-BOO. The drink was a specialty of Louis Eppinger, a barman born in Germany who ended up practicing his craft in San Francisco, Portland, and eventually Yokohama, Japan. An equal-parts mix of sherry and dry vermouth, the Bamboo boasts the savory deliciousness of a well-made martini, but unlike the martini, it's not the kind of drink that's likely to send you tottering home. And the way the olive adds a touch of salt to complement the sherry and provides a little snack after the final sip? Yes, please.

INGREDIENTS

2 drops Angostura bitters

1½ oz [45 ml] dry sherry

1½ oz [45 ml] dry vermouth

2 dashes orange bitters

Olive, for garnish

Lemon peel, for garnish

DIRECTIONS

Gently tilt the Angostura bitters over the mixing glass to get a couple drops, not dashes, out of the bottle. Add the sherry, vermouth, orange bitters, and ice. Stir and strain into a chilled coupe glass. Garnish with the olive and lemon peel and serve.

VARIATIONS

If you flip through vintage cocktail books, you'll find a seemingly endless array of cocktails calling for some mix of sherry and vermouth accented with this or that. We could fill an entire chapter with them, but we feel like we'd lose a few readers if we tried. One we'll mention by name is the Adonis, which switches the dry vermouth for sweet, omits the Angostura bitters, and is garnished with an orange peel. It's a little richer than the Bamboo and almost as enjoyable. We recommend experimenting with the format, trying different sherries and vermouths with dashes of absinthe or whispers of herbal liqueurs. You might stumble onto a new favorite.

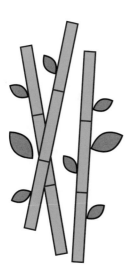

SHERRY COBBLER

NO, NOT A CHERRY COBBLER, ALTHOUGH WHEN THE SHERRY COBBLER APPEARS ON CONTEMPORARY MENUS, IT'S NOT FAR-FETCHED FOR PATRONS TO EXPECT THEY'RE GETTING A SLICE OF PIE RATHER THAN A COCKTAIL. That reflects the downward trajectory of the cobbler: Once among the most popular American beverages, a pinnacle of the drinking culture, the word now brings to mind baked goods or a person who does shoe repair. Let's do our part to restore the drink to its proper place!

The cobbler rose in popularity around the 1830s, possibly deriving its name from the little "cobbles" of ice that go into it. Crushed ice was one of the essential elements of the cobbler, the others being wine, fruit, and sugar. Alongside the julep, the cobbler helped usher in the popularity of ice in cocktails, and perhaps the use of drinking straws, as well. While many different types of cobblers are recounted in recipe books, it's the Sherry Cobbler that captured hearts and minds to become "without doubt the most popular beverage in the country, with ladies as well as with gentleman," as Harry Johnson wrote in his 1888 *Bartenders' Manual*.

To make one for yourself, you'll just need a fresh orange, a bottle of sherry, sugar, and crushed ice. The orange slices are shaken right along with the sherry and sugar, extracting their juices and flavor. Opinions differ as to whether the finished drink should be dumped from the shaker directly into the glass or strained out onto fresh crushed ice; we prefer the neatness of the latter. It's also worth taking the effort to get a little fancy with the garnishes on a cobbler. At the very least you should tuck a wheel of orange into the top of the glass, but if you really want to dress it up, you could add fresh berries, sprigs of mint, or other seasonal garnishes.

INGREDIENTS

4 oz [120 ml] sherry

Generous ¼ oz [7.5 ml] Rich Simple Syrup (page 33)

1 orange wheel

Orange wheel and seasonal herbs and fruit, for garnish

DIRECTIONS

To a shaker, add the sherry, syrup, orange wheel, and ice. Shake hard and strain into a rocks glass or metal julep cup filled with crushed ice. Garnish with an orange wheel and seasonal herbs and fruit as desired and serve.

FOGCUTTER

A CHAPTER ON DRY SPANISH SHERRY MAY NOT BE WHERE YOU EXPECT TO FIND AN ELABORATE TROPICAL DRINK, BUT FORTIFIED WINE PROVIDES THE ESSENTIAL FINISHING TOUCH TO THIS CLASSIC FROM TRADER VIC. There's a lot going on here with rum, gin, cognac, two citrus juices, and orgeat, yet it all comes together harmoniously and deliciously—almost too much so, given how much strong booze is lurking in this easy-drinking libation. The sherry comes in as just a float at the very end, providing beguilingly complex aromatics and an extra hint of nuttiness. A dark oloroso will stand out visually, but other dry styles will also do the trick.

INGREDIENTS

1½ oz [45 ml] light rum

½ oz [15 ml] gin

½ oz [15 ml] cognac

2 oz [60 ml] fresh orange juice

¾ oz [22.5 ml] fresh lemon juice

½ oz [15 ml] orgeat

½ oz [15 ml] sherry, for floating

Mint sprigs, for garnish

Cocktail cherries, pineapples, or orange twists, for garnish (optional)

DIRECTIONS

To a shaker, add the rum, gin, cognac, orange and lemon juices, orgeat, and ice. Shake and strain into a highball or rocks glass filled with ice. Float the sherry on top. Garnish with a bouquet of mint and any tropical garnishes desired, and serve.

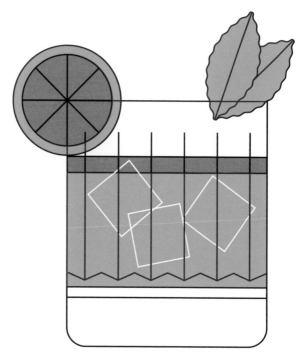

PARKEROO

DESCRIBED AS "A SORT OF BASTARD MARTINI" IN *THE STORK CLUB BAR BOOK*, THE PARKEROO IS ONE OF THE RARE EARLY SIGHTINGS OF TEQUILA IN THE VINTAGE COCKTAIL CANON. The name is silly but the construction is elegant: two parts sherry to one part tequila, accented with only a twist of lemon. There's no hiding inferior ingredients in this, so your enjoyment of the Parkeroo will be directly proportional to the quality of your sherry and tequila.

INGREDIENTS

2 oz [60 ml] sherry

1 oz [30 ml] tequila

Lemon peel, for garnish

DIRECTIONS

To a mixing glass, add the sherry, tequila, and ice. Stir and strain into a chilled coupe glass, garnish with a lemon peel, and serve.

LATIN TRIFECTA

INGREDIENTS FROM ITALY, SPAIN, AND MEXICO JOIN FORCES IN THE LATIN TRIFECTA. It's a drink from Jamie Boudreau, owner of Seattle's destination for rare and vintage spirits, the acclaimed cocktail bar Canon. This is the kind of straightforward cocktail that wrings amazing complexity out of a simple build, with the dry sherry perfectly balancing the bittersweet intensity of Cynar and the grassiness of blanco tequila. The flamed orange peel (page 26) provides the hint of smoke to take things over the top.

INGREDIENTS

1 oz [30 ml] tequila

1 oz [30 ml] Cynar

½ oz [15 ml] sherry

3 dashes orange bitters

Flamed orange peel, for garnish

DIRECTIONS

To a mixing glass, add the tequila, Cynar, sherry, bitters, and ice. Stir and strain into a chilled coupe glass. Garnish with flamed orange peel and serve.

DAYS LIKE THIS

ANDREW VOLK WAS TENDING BAR IN PORTLAND, OREGON, UNTIL HE DECIDED TO LEAVE US FOR THAT OTHER PORTLAND ALL THE WAY ACROSS THE COUNTRY IN MAINE. Unfortunately, we haven't had the chance to visit him at his new digs, The Hunt & Alpine Club, a Scandinavian restaurant and cocktail bar he opened with his wife, Briana, but we have enjoyed re-creating some of his cocktails from afar. Case in point, the Days Like This. It's a recognizably Manhattan-ish cocktail, but made with aged rum and definitely on the drier side. Try it out when you're in the mood for something spirit forward, bracing, and complex.

INGREDIENTS

2 oz [60 ml] aged rum

¾ oz [22.5 ml] sherry

¾ oz [22.5 ml] dry vermouth

2 dashes Angostura bitters

Orange peel, for garnish

DIRECTIONS

To a mixing glass, add the rum, sherry, vermouth, bitters, and ice. Stir and strain into a chilled coupe glass. Garnish with an orange peel and serve.

NEUTRAL GROUND

IN NEW ORLEANS, CANAL STREET FORMED THE BOUNDARY BETWEEN THE HISTOR- ICALLY AMERICAN PARTS OF THE CITY AND THE FRENCH AND SPANISH AREA NOW KNOWN AS THE FRENCH QUARTER. Local bartender Rhiannon Enlil named her Neutral Ground cocktail after the median of Canal Street, drawing on ingredients from all three countries for this Manhattan homage that debuted on the menu of Bar Tonique.

INGREDIENTS

2 oz [60 ml] rye

½ oz [15 ml] sherry

½ oz [15 ml] Benedictine

3 dashes orange bitters

Orange peel, for garnish

DIRECTIONS

To a mixing glass, add the rye, sherry, Benedictine, bitters, and ice. Stir and strain into a chilled coupe glass. Garnish with an orange peel and serve.

NOME

BACK IN THE CHAPTER ON CHARTREUSE IN THE DESCRIPTION OF THE PURITAN (PAGE 185), WE MENTIONED A COCKTAIL CALLED THE ALASKA. While the Alaska has its adherents, we feel it's a little too boozy for its own, and your own, good and prefer the Puritan's addition of vermouth. The Nome accomplishes the same thing with sherry. Nome, Alaska, is one of the northernmost towns in the United States, and the Nome cocktail may be the pinnacle of drinks in the Alaska format.

INGREDIENTS

2 oz [60 ml] gin

½ oz [15 ml] sherry

½ oz [15 ml] yellow Chartreuse

2 dashes orange bitters

Lemon peel, for garnish

DIRECTIONS

To a mixing glass, add the gin, sherry, Chartreuse, bitters, and ice. Stir and strain into a chilled coupe glass. Garnish with a lemon peel and serve.

SHERRY MOJITO

WE LOVE MOJITOS, AND WE LOVE SHERRY, SO WHY NOT A SHERRY MOJITO? THE IDEA ISN'T THAT FAR-FETCHED. The Sherry Cobbler (page 250) proves that sherry and citrus on crushed ice is a winning combination. There's also a locally popular Andalusian drink called a Rebujito, which combines sherry and sparkling lemonade. This draws on the same basic idea, bringing fresh mint into play. It's an ideal cocktail for backyards in the summer, fun and refreshing without a ton of booze.

INGREDIENTS

6 to 8 mint leaves

½ oz [15 ml] Rich Simple Syrup (page 33)

2 oz [60 ml] sherry

¾ oz [22.5 ml] fresh lemon juice

Crushed ice

3 oz [90 ml] soda water

Mint sprig, for garnish

DIRECTIONS

In the bottom of a tall glass, gently muddle the mint leaves with the simple syrup, lightly pressing the leaves to extract their flavor. Add the sherry and lemon juice, rinsing the muddler with them as you pour. Fill with crushed ice, top with soda, and stir to combine. Garnish with fresh mint and serve.

CHAPTER 21

ELDERFLOWER
LIQUEUR

WE'VE INTRODUCED A LOT OF DIFFERENT FLAVORS ON OUR SPIRITUOUS
JOURNEY—TART, BITTER, SWEET, HERBAL, WOODY, ETC.—BUT ONE FLAVOR
WE HAVEN'T TOUCHED ON MUCH IS FLORAL. It's high time we change that. Floral
notes can play a wonderfully appealing role in cocktails. They soften assertive
ingredients, pair exceptionally well with citrus and sparkling wine, and contribute
to drinks that seem tailor-made for spring and summer weather.

Floral liqueurs have been making their way into cocktails for well over a century,
typically in spirits flavored with violet flowers. The floral liqueur category changed
dramatically in 2007 with the introduction of St-Germain, a French liqueur made
with flowers from the elderberry bush. The brand was a smash success, and sud-
denly elderflower liqueur was everywhere. It was such a craze in the cocktail world
that some even began referring to it as "bartender's ketchup," alluding to mixologists' tendency to put it into everything.

We suspect that nickname was driven by a touch of envy, because St-Germain's
success is honestly well deserved. It's a transformative ingredient that appeared on

the market when there wasn't really anything else like it and opened up delicious possibilities for mixing. (Savvy marketing helped too, with a distinctly elegant bottle, recipe postcards featuring risqué vintage photographs, and romantic tales of French farmers hauling baskets of elderflowers down from the mountain slopes on their bicycles.)

Today there are many more options on the market, including other elderflower liqueurs, elderflower syrups, and liqueurs flavored with a wide range of flowers and botanical ingredients. Any of these could potentially perform well in the cocktails that follow, although we happily reach for St-Germain; it's well balanced, it's readily available, and it's the spirit we used to test these recipes. If you select a different bottle, you may need to make some minor adjustments to account for varying levels of sweetness and intensity of flavor.

Regardless of which one you choose, we think you'll find elderflower to be an unexpectedly versatile ingredient. It's right at home in light sparkling cocktails but also provides a sweet and soft counterpoint to boisterous spirits like Campari and Cynar. Put the petal to the metal and take these floral cocktails for a spin.

IF YOU LIKE ELDERFLOWER LIQUEUR, TRY...

CRÈME DE VIOLETTE

Made with an infusion of violet flowers, crème de violette has a strong floral flavor that is essential in a handful of classic cocktails, most notably the Aviation and the Attention. Sometimes referred to as violette liqueur, we've enjoyed the bottlings from Combier, Rothman and Winter, Tempus Fugit, and Giffard.

CREME YVETTE

Whereas crème de violette is intensely floral, this proprietary liqueur balances violet with a blend of four different berries, taking the spirit in a fruitier direction.

ITALICUS

This Italian rosolio offers a slightly more bittersweet and citrusy profile than elderflower liqueurs thanks to contributions from bergamot and gentian, although it can play a similar role in cocktails.

QUEEN BEE

NEIL KOPPLIN WAS THE FIRST PERSON IN PORTLAND TO HIRE JACOB AS A BAR-
TENDER, A PORTENTOUS DECISION THAT LED INDIRECTLY TO THE EXISTENCE OF THE
BOOK IN YOUR HANDS RIGHT NOW. (Please direct all complaints to Neil.) The bar was
called the Carlyle, and it did a brisk happy hour service with employees from nearby offices
who would reliably stream in for after-work cocktails. The bestseller by far was Neil's
Queen Bee. Originally garnished with fresh cranberries, it's equally good with a twist of
lemon peel. Mix up some of these the next time you're hosting a backyard soirée or have a
thirsty crowd of office workers arriving at precisely 5:01 pm.

INGREDIENTS

¾ oz [22.5 ml] vodka

¾ oz [22.5 ml] elderflower liqueur

¾ oz [22.5 ml] fresh lemon juice

¼ oz [7.5 ml] Honey Syrup (page 33)

1 oz [30 ml] sparkling wine

Lemon peel or cranberries, for garnish

DIRECTIONS

To a shaker, add the vodka, elderflower liqueur, lemon juice, syrup, and ice. Shake and strain into a chilled coupe glass. Top with the sparkling wine, garnish with a lemon peel or cranberries, and serve.

ELDERFLOWER SPRITZ

EVERY ONCE IN A WHILE, A SUCCESSFUL COCKTAIL COMES FROM A SPIRITS BRAND
RATHER THAN A BARTENDER. The Elderflower Spritz is a noteworthy example. The
St-Germain Cocktail, as it was known, is a floral riff on the spritz formula, combining
liqueur, sparkling wine, and soda. It's simple but also very hard to resist.

INGREDIENTS

1½ oz [45 ml] elderflower liqueur

2 oz [60 ml] sparkling wine

2 oz soda water

Lemon wheel, for garnish

DIRECTIONS

In a tall glass filled with ice, add the elderflower liqueur, sparkling wine, and soda. Stir gently to combine. Garnish with the lemon wheel and serve.

ALTO CUCINA

THE ALTO CUCINA ISN'T WIDELY KNOWN, BUT IT HAS ALL THE MAKINGS OF A POTEN-TIAL MODERN CLASSIC. Created by bartender Stephen Shellenberger, it deftly uses elderflower liqueur to tame the assertiveness of scotch and Cynar, balancing the bitterness of the latter with a subtle floral sweetness. It's an unexpected combination of ingredients that works incredibly well. More than that, it's the kind of drink that you can have fun with by swapping out various components with similar ingredients, in much the same way that the Negroni (page 129) and Last Word (page 181) have spawned numerous variations. Try keeping the proportions intact but experimenting with different base spirits, fortified wines, amari, and floral liqueurs. You'll find that the format is amenable to all kinds of riffs.

INGREDIENTS

1 oz [30 ml] scotch

1 oz [30 ml] dry vermouth

½ oz [15 ml] elderflower liqueur

½ oz [15 ml] Cynar

Orange peel, for garnish

DIRECTIONS

In a mixing glass, add the scotch, vermouth, elderflower liqueur, Cynar, and ice. Stir and strain into a chilled coupe glass. Garnish with an orange peel and serve.

ELDERFLOWER DAIQUIRI

ELDERFLOWER LIQUEUR LENDS ITSELF PRACTICALLY AUTOMATICALLY TO A TASTY DAIQUIRI. Its flavor is sweet but not overpowering, which is just what you want in a light, three-ingredient cocktail. It plays subtly as a replacement for sugar, rounding out the cocktail with a floral finish.

INGREDIENTS

2 oz [60 ml] light rum

¾ oz [22.5 ml] elderflower liqueur

1 oz [30 ml] fresh lime juice

DIRECTIONS

To a shaker, add the rum, elderflower liqueur, lime juice, and ice. Shake, strain into a chilled coupe glass, and serve.

HAT TIP

THE MODERN COCKTAIL RENAISSANCE WAS DRIVEN NOT JUST BY BARS AND BAR-TENDERS, BUT ALSO BY THE INTERNET. In the early days of the revival, an enthusiastic community of cocktail bloggers helped rediscover old drinks, spread the word about new bars and ingredients, and experiment with innovative recipes. Part of the fun was trying other writers' recipes and adapting them for your own tastes and whatever you happened to have on hand in your own bar. With that adventurous spirit in mind, this is our remix of the Bitter Elder, a cocktail posted in the comments section of the *Cocktail Chronicles* weblog by an anonymous reader. We've tweaked it just a bit, cutting back the Campari and adding simple syrup, to bring it into an extremely approachable balance.

INGREDIENTS

1½ oz [45 ml] gin

¾ oz [22.5 ml] elderflower liqueur

¼ oz [7.5 ml] Campari

½ oz [15 ml] fresh lemon juice

1 barspoon (⅙ oz [5 ml]) Rich Simple Syrup (page 33)

DIRECTIONS

To a shaker, add the gin, elderflower liqueur, Campari, lemon juice, syrup, and ice. Shake, strain into a chilled coupe glass, and serve.

LE TOUR

THIS DRINK STARTED OUT AS OUR ATTEMPT AT MAKING A SLIGHTLY FLORAL COGNAC MANHATTAN. Then before we knew it, it had morphed into a multilayered, spirit-forward cocktail comprised entirely of French ingredients. With cognac, dry vermouth, elderflower liqueur, and Chartreuse, you could say this is a virtual tour de France.

INGREDIENTS

1½ oz [45 ml] cognac

¾ oz [22.5 ml] dry vermouth

½ oz [15 ml] elderflower liqueur

1 barspoon (⅙ oz [5 ml]) green Chartreuse

DIRECTIONS

To a mixing glass, add the cognac, vermouth, elderflower liqueur, Chartreuse, and ice. Stir, strain into a chilled coupe glass, and serve.

SOUTHERN POINT

THIS DELIGHTFUL EQUAL-PARTS COCKTAIL COMES TO US FROM NEW YORK BAR-TENDER ERYN REECE, who created it with St-Germain, Cointreau, and bonded applejack. The absinthe rinse is a great touch, offering up inviting notes of anise on the aroma.

INGREDIENTS

Absinthe, for rinse

¾ oz [22.5 ml] apple brandy

¾ oz [22.5 ml] elderflower liqueur

¾ oz [22.5 ml] orange liqueur

¾ oz [22.5 ml] fresh lemon juice

DIRECTIONS

Coat a chilled coupe glass with a little absinthe, discarding the excess (or mist the glass with a few spritzes of absinthe from an atomizer). To a shaker, add the apple brandy, elderflower liqueur, orange liqueur, lemon juice, and ice. Shake, strain into the prepared coupe glass, and serve.

OLIVETTE

THE OLIVETTE IS ANOTHER SURPRISINGLY GOOD COCKTAIL DEVELOPED BY ST-GERMAIN, THIS ONE ORIGINATING WITH FORMER GLOBAL BRAND AMBASSADOR CAMILLE VIDAL. As professional bartenders, we tend to approach branded cocktails with skepticism, but this one won us over. It's simply a fifty-fifty martini softened with elderflower liqueur. It's elegant and easy, and the subtle touch of brine from the olive keeps it just on the right side of sweet.

INGREDIENTS

1 oz [30 ml] gin

1 oz [30 ml] dry vermouth

½ oz [15 ml] elderflower liqueur

Olive, for garnish

DIRECTIONS

To a mixing glass, add the gin, vermouth, elderflower liqueur, and ice. Stir and strain into a chilled coupe. Garnish with an olive and serve.

LITTLE HONEY

One of the advantages of expanding your home bar with a variety of liqueurs and other accenting bottles is that it enables you to revisit the classics and make them in a new way. Take the Whiskey Sour (page 47) from our very first chapter, for example. That drink called for bourbon, lemon juice, sugar, and egg white. Here we revise that formula by making elderflower liqueur the primary sweetener, adding a dry and slightly herbal note with vermouth, and bringing in a little depth with honey.

INGREDIENTS

1½ oz [45 ml] bourbon

¾ oz [22.5 ml] elderflower liqueur

½ oz [15 ml] dry vermouth

½ oz [15 ml] fresh lemon juice

¼ oz [7.5 ml] Honey Syrup

1 egg white

Orange peel, for garnish

DIRECTIONS

To a shaker without ice, add the bourbon, elderflower liqueur, vermouth, lemon juice, syrup, and egg white. Dry shake to aerate the egg white. Add ice and shake again, then strain into a rocks glass filled with ice. Garnish with an orange peel and serve.

CHAPTER 22

MEZCAL

MEZCAL HAS ENJOYED THE KIND OF BOOM IN POPULARITY THAT OTHER LESSER-KNOWN SPIRITS ONLY DREAM ABOUT. Over the past decade, it has made the leap from niche spirit familiar outside of Mexico to only serious aficionados, to a bottle you'll find in cocktail bars all around the world. This is due to expanded availability of high-quality mezcal, which has in turn created new converts and increased the demand for mezcal even further.

While these quality mezcals have been greeted with enthusiasm, a firm grasp of just exactly what mezcal is seems to have found less thorough distribution. If you've tried mezcal before, there's a good chance that you were introduced to it as a sort of "smoky tequila." While this description isn't quite right, it is a useful jumping-off point.

A GOOD WAY TO BEGIN LEARNING ABOUT MEZCAL IS BY COMPARISON TO ITS MORE FAMILIAR MEXICAN PEER. SO, A QUICK REFRESHER ON TEQUILA:

- IT'S MADE FROM EXCLUSIVELY ONE TYPE OF AGAVE, TEQUILINA WEBER, AKA BLUE AGAVE.
- IT'S PRODUCED ONLY IN THE MEXICAN STATE OF JALISCO AND PARTS OF FOUR OTHER STATES.
- IT'S OFTEN MADE IN HIGHLY CAPITALIZED DISTILLERIES WITH MODERN, EFFICIENT EQUIPMENT.

NOW LET'S LOOK AT MEZCAL:

- IT CAN BE MADE FROM ANY TYPE OF AGAVE.
- IT CAN BE PRODUCED IN TEN DIFFERENT MEXICAN STATES.
- IT'S OFTEN PRODUCED IN SMALL, OPEN-AIR DISTILLERIES, UTILIZING TRADITIONAL, CENTURIES-OLD TECHNIQUES.

This bird's-eye view shows that in comparison to tequila, mezcal is made from a wider variety of agaves, across a larger geographical area, and with more hands-on production. If you remember all that, you're well on your way to understanding the spirit. Let's go into each of those points a little further.

While there are more than two hundred different types of agave, only about thirty of them have what it takes to be fermented and distilled into mezcal. Just as the varietal of grape affects the taste of a wine, the type of agave affects the taste of mezcal. In this regard, buying mezcal is a lot like picking out a bottle of wine. You'll want to know what agave it's made from, and it's worth spending some time in a good mezcal bar sampling different varieties. That said, it's advisable to start with one called Espadín (*agave angustifolia*). Espadín is easy to cultivate, matures relatively quickly (seven to ten years), and is the most inexpensive to produce. It's perfect for when you need a bottle that you can sip neat or mix in cocktails.

Also as with wine, you'll want to know where your mezcal comes from. Mexico is an incredibly diverse country, and the states that produce mezcal have unique climates, agaves, and traditions of distillation. The largest exporter of mezcal is the state of Oaxaca in southwest Mexico, and a bottle of Oaxacan Espadín mezcal is a great way to get started.

The combination of hard work and skilled technique that goes into making mezcal is stunning and worthy of a book of its own. We'll focus on one essential aspect: the roasting of the agave. If you remember from the tequila chapter (page 83), agave plants contain complex starches that transform into fermentable sugars when they are cooked. The tequila industry most commonly uses steam ovens or giant pressure cookers to accomplish this, but mezcal producers typically still rely on older, more rustic methods. Often that might mean something as simple as digging a hole in the ground, lighting a fire, and roasting the agaves in an earthen pit. This is where the smoky character of many mezcals comes from.

That's the way mezcal has been made for more than four hundred years, and for many producers very little has changed. If it ain't broke, why fix it? It takes three to seven days just to cook the agave when making mezcal, and that's just one element of an extremely labor-intensive process in which making one batch can take anywhere between ten days to a month. The term *artisanal* is such an accurate description of the process that it's a legally recognized type of mezcal. (An even more labor intensive style of mezcal production is called "ancestral.")

As you mix your way through the drinks in this chapter, you'll find that mezcal works wonderfully in split-base cocktails in which it's paired with another spirit. Tequila is the obvious pairing, but it's often even better with gin or cognac. Speaking of gin, mezcal's flavor is similarly complex. It can be simultaneously earthy, herbaceous, citric, and fruity, and this makes it a good candidate to replace gin in classic cocktails. We've provided a few options, but feel free to try mezcal in some of your favorite gin drinks.

Although mezcal has been around for centuries, it was, aside from a few low-quality exports, mostly absent from the era of vintage cocktail creation in the United States. As a result, mezcal drinks are either riffs on the classics or completely new inventions from contemporary bartenders. This chapter explores both aspects, starting with the former and moving on to the latter.

Lastly, it's never a bad idea to sit down with a sip of mezcal. Like bourbon, cognac, and scotch, this is another spirit that's worthy of appreciation straight from the bottle. That's the way it's often enjoyed in Mexico too. Four hundred years of tradition can't be wrong.

MEZCAL 101

MEZCAL WAS ONCE THE WORD USED TO DESCRIBE ANY AGAVE DISTILLATE MADE IN MEXICO, BUT ITS LEGAL DEFINITION NOW REFERS EXCLUSIVELY TO CERTI- FIED PRODUCERS IN NINE MEXICAN STATES. Roughly thirty different agaves can be used to produce mezcal, although because of Mexico's vast cultural and environmental diversity, the exact number of agave varieties has not been pinned down. We recommend you start with Espadín and then never stop exploring.

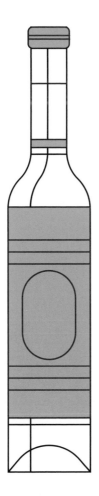

Agave used for mezcal is typically cooked in underground ovens with live fire, which gives the spirit its smoky character. While this smoke flavor can be wonderfully appealing, keep in mind that agaves can take from as few as six years to as long as two to three decades to mature. Look for mezcals that find balance between the smoke from the roast and the complex flavor of agave.

Though not common, mezcal is sometimes aged in barrels. Similar to tequila, if it is aged 2 months to a year it's called reposado, 1 to 3 years is anejo, and 3 or more years is extra anejo. Unlike with tequila, the terms *blanco* and *joven* are interchangeable and both imply that the spirit is unaged. It can be fun to try oak-aged mezcal, but it is by no means an essential part of learning about the spirit. Mezcals labeled "madurado en vidrio" were aged in glass, usually underground, for at least a year. This is more traditional than aging in barrels, and it softens and rounds out the flavors present in the distillate, rather than adding extra flavor from oak.

As a final note, not all mezcal producers choose to buy into the official regulatory system and therefore label their products as "destilado de agave" or something similar. Some of the best "mezcals" we ever had were labeled as such. If you find some on the shelf in a bar or liquor store, you're probably in a pretty cool place. Befriend the staff.

WHEN BUYING MEZCAL, CHOOSE BOTTLES WITH THE WORDS *ARTISANAL* **OR** *ANCESTRAL* **ON THE LABEL, PREFERABLY DISTILLED FROM ESPADÍN AGAVE, AND PRODUCED IN OAXACA.** These are legally regulated terms that guarantee a higher standard of production. Mezcal is a truly handmade product that takes an enormous amount of skill and hard work to produce, so be wary of the cheapest bottles on the shelf—that likely signals a corner cut somewhere in the production process and a low-quality, boring spirit. You may also come across more expensive mezcals made from rarer types of agave; these are rewarding to explore on their own but probably not what you'll be reaching for to mix a cocktail.

BOTTLES WE REACH FOR

VAGO ESPADÍN

Bottled at a strength more typical of artisanal mezcal, Vago's Espadín releases are made in small batches by a few different mezcaleros. The flavors will vary with each producer and batch—something very common with traditional mezcal—but we have yet to find one we don't love.

BANHEZ ENSAMBLE

A blend of mostly Espadín and some agave barril, Banhez does a great job of capturing just enough smoke and earthiness to make its presence known in drinks without taking over. We also love that it operates as a co-op owned by the farmers and producers.

UNIÓN UNO

Another Espadín-based blend, this time with a hint of herbaceous agave cirrial, Unión Uno is on the lighter side, both from a smoke standpoint as well as alcohol level. At 40 percent ABV, it's great when you want a mezcal cocktail with a bit more subtlety.

SOMBRA

Made from 100 percent agave Espadín, Sombra is big and bold, bottled at a lively 45 percent ABV. We reach for it when mixing with a smaller measurement of mezcal or when paired with bold flavors. It's great in a mezcal Last Word (page 268).

ALIPÚS SANTA ANA DEL RIO

While the entire Alipús line showcases how terroir affects the flavors of Espadín and is very worth exploring, if you have to start with just one bottle, this is a great option. Bright, vegetal, and with deep minerality, this Espadín from the tiny town of Santa Ana del Rio pushes the agave to the fore with just a hint of smoke.

MEZCAL MARGARITA

EVEN THOUGH THEY'RE BOTH DISTILLED FROM AGAVE, SWAPPING MEZCAL FOR TEQUILA IN A COCKTAIL DOESN'T ALWAYS GO AS SMOOTHLY AS ONE MIGHT EXPECT. Fortunately, though, the Margarita (page 87) is one drink that has no issues embracing mezcal as a base spirit. Mezcal tends to bring a little more smoke and earthiness to the drink than you'll find in a traditional Margarita. If you're new to mezcal, this is an excellent first cocktail to try with it. You can also ease into things by blending the two spirits, perhaps using 1 oz [30 ml] each of mezcal and tequila instead of fully committing to one or the other, and enjoying the best of both worlds.

INGREDIENTS
Lime wedge

Salt, for garnish

2 oz [60 ml] mezcal

¾ oz [22.5 ml] orange liqueur

¾ oz [22.5 ml] fresh lime juice

DIRECTIONS

Using the cut side of a lime wedge, wet half the exterior edge of a chilled rocks glass and then dip it into a shallow dish filled with salt so that the salt sticks to the rim. To a shaker, add the mezcal, orange liqueur, lime juice, and ice. Shake, strain into the prepared glass, and serve.

VARIATIONS

As with the classic margarita, those desiring a little extra sweetness can add a barspoon (⅙ oz [5 ml]) of Rich Simple Syrup (page 33) or agave nectar.

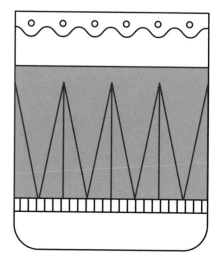

MEZCAL LAST WORD

IT WAS ONLY A MATTER OF TIME BEFORE ONE OF THE MOST RIFFED-ON COCKTAILS IN THE MODERN MIXOLOGY MOVEMENT GOT THE MEZCAL TREATMENT. While this variation has gone by several names, it's the kind of drink that comes up frequently enough that we just call what it is: a Last Word (page 181) made with mezcal in place of gin. We mentioned in the introduction to this chapter that mezcal and gin can switch roles surprisingly well, and this is a shining example of how the herbaceousness and earthiness of mezcal can be a wonderful stand-in for the botanicals of gin.

INGREDIENTS
¾ oz [22.5 ml] mezcal
¾ oz [22.5 ml] maraschino liqueur
¾ oz [22.5 ml] green Chartreuse
¾ oz [22.5 ml] fresh lime juice

DIRECTIONS
To a shaker, add the mezcal, maraschino liqueur, Chartreuse, lime juice, and ice. Shake, strain into a chilled coupe glass, and serve.

MEZCAL NEGRONI

CONTINUING OUR STRING OF CLASSIC COCKTAILS ADAPTED FOR MEZCAL, NEGRONI LOVERS HAVE TO TRY IT IN THEIR FAVORITE DRINK. This is another variation you'll often find at cocktail bars, if not on the actual menu, then at least in the hands of some patron ordering it by name. That patron knows what they're talking about. Mezcal and the Negroni took off in popularity around the same time in the United States, so the combination was inevitable. Fortunately, it's also delicious. The robust smokiness of mezcal makes an excellent stand-in for gin and proves once again the endless versatility of the Negroni.

INGREDIENTS
1 oz [30 ml] mezcal
1 oz [30 ml] sweet vermouth
1 oz [30 ml] Campari
Orange peel, for garnish

DIRECTIONS
To a mixing glass, add the mezcal, vermouth, Campari, and ice. Stir and strain into a rocks glass filled with ice or a single large cube. Garnish with an orange peel and serve.

MAXIMILIAN AFFAIR

IN THE HISTORY OF MEXICO, THE "MAXIMILIAN AFFAIR" REFERS TO WHEN THE FRENCH EMPEROR NAPOLEON III INSTALLED MAXIMILIAN OF HABSBURG, THE ARCHDUKE OF AUSTRIA, AS THE EMPEROR OF MEXICO IN 1862. As one might imagine, this went over rather poorly among Mexicans, and within a few years the French had made a hasty departure and Maximillian faced a firing squad. Boston bartender Misty Kalkofen's Maximilian Affair cocktail combines elements of France and Mexico far more harmoniously. The smokiness of mezcal plays up delightfully against the sweet floral notes of elderflower liqueur.

INGREDIENTS
1 oz [30 ml] mezcal
1 oz [30 ml] elderflower liqueur
½ oz [15 ml] sweet vermouth
½ oz [15 ml] fresh lemon juice

DIRECTIONS
To a shaker, add the mezcal, elderflower liqueur, vermouth, lemon juice, and ice. Shake, strain into a chilled coupe glass, and serve.

MAGUEY SOUR

THIS CLEVER MEZCAL SOUR RIFF FROM SAN FRANCISCO BARTENDER JACQUES BEZUIDENHOUT ACHIEVES ITS REMARKABLE COMPLEXITY BY SPLITTING THE SWEET ELEMENTS OF THE DRINK BETWEEN BENEDICTINE AND ORGEAT. What really ties the drink together are the garnishes, so don't skip them; the orange and nutmeg are perfect anchoring flavors and contribute an enticing, welcoming aroma.

INGREDIENTS
2 oz [60 ml] mezcal
½ oz [15 ml] Benedictine
¾ oz [22.5 ml] fresh lemon juice
½ oz [15 ml] orgeat
1 egg white
Orange peel, for garnish
Freshly grated nutmeg, for garnish

DIRECTIONS
To a shaker without ice, add the mezcal, Benedictine, lemon juice, orgeat, and egg white. Dry shake to aerate the egg white. Add ice and shake again, then strain into a rocks glass filled with ice. Garnish with orange peel and grated nutmeg and serve.

EL CAMINO

IF WHILE SIPPING THE MONTE CARLO (PAGE 158) FEATURED IN THE RYE CHAPTER YOU THOUGHT TO YOURSELF, *THIS IS GOOD, BUT I WISH IT HAD SOME MEZCAL IN IT,* THEN THIS IS THE COCKTAIL FOR YOU! Originating at the Chestnut Club in Santa Monica, this combo of smoke, spice, and sweet is delicious as it slowly dilutes on a big cube of ice, and it stands as proof that ever-versatile Benedictine is as equally at home in a stirred mezcal cocktail as it is in a sour.

INGREDIENTS
1 oz [30 ml] mezcal
1 oz [30 ml] rye
½ oz [15 ml] Benedictine
4 dashes Peychaud's bitters
Orange peel, for garnish

DIRECTIONS
To a mixing glass, add the mezcal, rye, Benedictine, bitters, and ice. Stir and strain into a rocks glass filled with ice or a single large cube. Garnish with an orange peel and serve.

PORT OF SPAIN

CALIFORNIA BARTENDER DOMINIC ALLING GREW UP IN TRINIDAD, HOME OF ANGOSTURA BITTERS, AND IT WAS THE MEMORY OF HIS MOTHER GIVING HIM SHOTS OF ANGOSTURA WHENEVER HE HAD A STOMACHACHE THAT INSPIRED THIS DRINK. Named after the capital city of Trinidad and Tobago, the Port of Spain is a mezcal take on the Trinidad Sour (page 165). It's a perfect example of how mezcal creates space in a cocktail for other big, bold flavors, enabling a recipe that calls for sizeable pours of orgeat and Angostura bitters to still end up beautifully balanced.

INGREDIENTS
1½ oz [45 ml] mezcal
1 oz [30 ml] orgeat
¾ oz [22.5 ml] fresh lime juice
½ oz [15 ml] Angostura bitters

DIRECTIONS
To a shaker, add the mezcal, orgeat, lime juice, bitters, and ice. Shake, strain into a chilled coupe glass, and serve.

1910

THIS MODERN MEZCAL MANHATTAN FROM BARTENDER EZRA STAR IS JUST ABOUT PERFECT. The drink is a bit like the moment when the peak of one large wave combines with the trough of another and you get a temporary placid sea in the midst of a storm. There are formidable flavors here that could overwhelm one another, but they're so precisely nestled together that the end result is both perfectly balanced and surprisingly approachable.

INGREDIENTS

1 oz [30 ml] sweet vermouth

¾ oz [22.5 ml] mezcal

¾ oz [22.5 ml] cognac

½ oz [15 ml] maraschino liqueur

2 dashes Peychaud's bitters

Orange peel, for garnish

DIRECTIONS

To a mixing glass, add the vermouth, mezcal, cognac, maraschino liqueur, bitters, and ice. Stir and strain into a chilled coupe glass. Garnish with an orange peel and serve.

DOLLY ZOOM

THE DOLLY ZOOM IS A DRINK WE CREATED TO PAIR THE EXPANSIVE FLAVORS OF MEZ-CAL WITH THE LINGERING SWEETNESS OF APRICOT LIQUEUR. It's a nod to the similar smoke and fruit combination that works so well in the world of barbecue. The bold ingredients are given some breathing room with dry vermouth and just a touch of herbal complexity is added by the Chartreuse. We found that stirring with a lemon twist, as opposed to expressing it over the finished drink, adds the right hint of citrus brightness.

INGREDIENTS

1¼ oz [37.5 ml] mezcal

¾ oz [22.5 ml] apricot liqueur

¾ oz [22.5 ml] dry vermouth

1 barspoon (⅙ oz [5 ml]) yellow Chartreuse

Lemon peel

DIRECTIONS

To a mixing glass, add the mezcal, apricot liqueur, vermouth, Chartreuse, a strip of lemon peel, and ice. Stir, strain into a rocks glass filled with ice or a single large cube, and serve.

CONOR'S FAVORITE

WHEN JOURNALIST AND COCKTAIL CONNOISSEUR PETER SUDERMAN VISITED THE
TASTING KITCHEN IN VENICE, CALIFORNIA, AND ASKED FOR SOMETHING "STIRRED,
BOOZY, AND WEIRD"—THIS DRINK WAS THE RESULT. He liked it so much that he asked
for the recipe and it became one of his favorites to mix at home. If the marriage of smoke
and earthy bitterness appeals to you, it may become one of yours too.

INGREDIENTS

1 oz [30 ml] mezcal

1 oz [30 ml] Cynar

2 dashes orange bitters

Orange peel, for garnish

DIRECTIONS

*To a mixing glass, add the mezcal, Cynar,
orange bitters, and ice. Stir and strain into
a rocks glass filled with ice or a large cube.
Garnish with an orange peel and serve.*

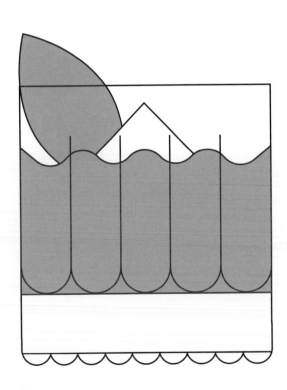

CHAPTER 23

CACHAÇA

IF THE WORD *CACHAÇA* (PRONOUNCED "KA-SHA-SA") IS NEW TO YOU, THEN YOU'VE BEEN MISSING OUT ON ONE OF THE WORLD'S BIGGEST SPIRIT CATEGORIES. More than a billion bottles of cachaça are sold every year, produced by an estimated forty thousand distilleries (a few of which are even legal). That's bigger than gin, cognac, tequila, and many other more familiar spirits. So, why don't you see cachaça in every bar and on every cocktail menu? Mainly because the vast majority of those bottles are never exported outside Brazil. It's the only country in the world that can make cachaça, and while the United States and Europe are learning to appreciate its role in cocktails, consumption abroad is still a drop in the bucket compared to Brazil's mighty thirst for its national spirit.

What is cachaça? Like rum, it's a spirit distilled from sugar cane. You could say that it's a type of rum, although many Brazilians would beg to differ. Unlike the rums we encountered earlier in the book, which are typically produced from molasses, cachaça must be made from fresh sugar cane juice. As soon as you pop open a bottle, you'll recognize that this makes a dramatic difference: In a good cachaça, you'll pick up tropical fruit aromas, spice notes, and a distinct grassiness. Whereas light rum provides a relatively neutral slate for mixing, cachaça is unmistakably present. You'll pick up its aroma and characteristic funk in any cocktail you mix with it.

273

This puts cachaça alongside what we might more broadly describe as the "funky rums." Other examples include the rhum agricole style from Martinique and other islands in the French Caribbean, which is also distilled from sugar cane juice; Jamaican pot still rum, which derives its wildly aromatic character from its unique fermentation process; and Batavia arrack, a rustic spirit distilled from molasses in Indonesia. We love them all, and in a longer book we'd have a hard time resisting the temptation to devote a chapter to each of them. We choose to focus on cachaça for its particular versatility as a main ingredient in cocktails, and in one cocktail in particular: the Caipirinha.

The Caipirinha is the quintessential Brazilian cocktail, the drink most responsible for putting cachaça on the map outside of Brazil, and deservedly the very first cocktail we'll visit in this chapter. But just as tequila has potential far beyond the confines of the margarita, cachaça is eminently mixable in all kinds of other drinks. By the end of this chapter, we hope you'll have a new and unexpected go-to spirit for creative cocktails.

When buying cachaça, it's vital to pick out a good one. Only a handful of brands make it to the United States, and there's a wide gulf between the ones that empha-size quality and the ones that make mass-produced, industrial cachaça. The latter tend to be distilled in such a way that they either lose the distinctive character that makes cachaça so appealing or they are simply too rough and harsh to deserve space in your glass. A quality cachaça will be distilled from fresh sugar cane juice, land gently on the palate, and be redolent with tropical aromas.

Among quality cachaças, there's also the question of whether to buy an unaged expression or one that has been aged in barrels. We suggest starting with the former, especially for its role in the classic Caipirinha. That said, barrel-aged cachaça is an exciting world of its own. If you enjoy the cocktails in this chapter, we highly recommend eventually expanding your bar with an aged cachaça to sip neat or enjoy in stirred, spirit-forward cocktails.

NOVO FOGO SILVER

Grassy notes of fresh sugar cane and tropical aromas of banana emerge from this cachaça as soon as one pops the cork. Made from organic sugar cane in copper pot stills near the coast of Brazil in Parana, it stands out in cocktails while still being an excellent team player.

LEBLON

One of the brands that introduced artisanal cachaça to the United States, Leblon makes a very good spirit in Minais Gerais that is aged for a short time in brandy barrels. It's restrained up front but finishes with fruity notes of banana.

AVUÀ PRATA

This pot-distilled cachaça delivers tropical and grassy notes along with a hint of lime peel, and at 42 percent ABV it offers a little extra strength for mixing.

RHUM AGRICOLE

With production centered in the French Caribbean, particularly Martinique, rhum agricole is set apart from most other rums by its fermentation of fresh sugar cane juice instead of molasses.

JAMAICAN POT STILL RUM

This molasses-based rum derives its funk from its unique fermentation process and flavorful, high-ester distillation. This characteristic can be relatively subdued and approachable, as in rums from Appleton, or completely in your face, as in rums like the 114-proof Smith and Cross.

BATAVIA ARRACK

Indonesian arracks are produced through a complex process involving molasses, rice, and fermentation starter. The resulting spirit offers intense hogo, which makes it work wonderfully as an accent in cocktails or as a foundation for punch.

CAIPIRINHA

THE USES OF CACHAÇA WITHIN BRAZIL ARE WONDERFULLY DIVERSE, BUT AT AN INTERNATIONAL LEVEL THE SPIRIT IS PRACTICALLY SYNONYMOUS WITH THE CAIP-IRINHA. Try one and you'll instantly see why. The quintessential beach drink, it's hard to pronounce but easy to like. Like the Daiquiri (page 98), it's a simple combination of lime, sugar, and a sugar cane spirit. The method of preparation, however, is completely different. The Caipirinha is made by muddling fresh lime and sugar, extracting the juice of the lime and dissolving the sugar directly into it. It's then all shaken with cachaça and ice and poured straight into the glass with no straining, fruit, and pulp all mixed together. It's much more rustic than the standard daiquiri, as befits a drink whose name translates roughly to "little country person."

We've provided the recipe for the classic Caipirinha, but it's one of those drinks that's wide open to interpretation. You can add all sorts of fresh fruits to the Caipirinha and yield excellent results; try picking up fresh berries in the summer and muddling those right in with the lime and sugar, for example. Oh, and as for how to say it: "Kai-pee-reen-ya." See, it's not so hard.

INGREDIENTS
1 tablespoon [15 g] sugar
½ lime, cut into quarters
2 oz [60 ml] cachaça

DIRECTIONS
In the bottom of a shaker, muddle the sugar and lime, pressing to extract the lime juice. (If your lime isn't yielding much juice, feel free to add more of it.) Add the cachaça, rinsing the muddler with it as you pour. Add enough ice to fill your glass. Shake, dump the contents directly into a rocks glass without straining, and serve.

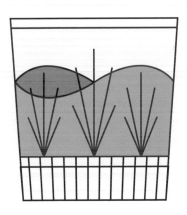

RABO DE GALO

TRANSLATED LITERALLY, THE RABO DE GALO IS THE "TAIL OF THE COCK," A.K.A. THE "COCKTAIL." And the drink does indeed fit a classic cocktail format, following the well-trod path laid down by the Manhattan, martini, and countless other drinks that mix a base spirit with vermouth. In much of Brazil, the Rabo de Galo would be served with only cachaça and sweet vermouth; in São Paulo, we've heard, they tend to replace the latter with Cynar. We say, "Why not both?" This version, using all three ingredients, is one that has justifiably caught on in global cocktail bars. Given the Rabo de Galo's similarity to a Manhattan (page 68), you might guess correctly that this is an excellent drink in which to use a barrel-aged cachaça. That said, there's enough richness in the vermouth and Cynar to get by quite well with a quality unaged expression.

INGREDIENTS

2 oz [60 ml] cachaça

½ oz [15 ml] sweet vermouth

½ oz [15 ml] Cynar

Orange peel, for garnish

DIRECTIONS

To a mixing glass, add the cachaça, vermouth, Cynar, and ice. Stir and strain into a chilled coupe glass. Garnish with an orange peel and serve.

BRAZILIAN NEGRONI

IF YOU THOUGHT THE NEGRONI VARIATIONS WERE GOING TO STOP WITH MEZCAL, THEN THINK AGAIN! Cachaça is another spirit we love to swap in to the classic formula. Whereas gin brings a botanical edge, and mezcal an earthy smokiness, cachaça layers its tropical aromas and bright grassy flavors into the drink. It's a very summery take on the Negroni (page 129). We adjust the proportions a bit from the classic equal-parts formula to emphasize the cachaça, which allows the relatively subtle flavors of fresh sugar cane to shine through.

INGREDIENTS
1¼ oz [37.5 ml] cachaça
¾ oz [22.5 ml] sweet vermouth
¾ oz [22.5 ml] Campari
Orange peel, for garnish

DIRECTIONS
To a mixing glass, add the cachaça, vermouth, Campari, and ice. Stir and strain into a rocks glass filled with ice or a single large cube. Garnish with an orange peel and serve.

HEATHER

ACCORDING TO SEATTLE BARTENDER, SPIRITS WRITER, AND ILLUSTRATOR ANDREW BOHRER, this cocktail was a spur-of-the moment improvisation that came about one night when a woman strode into his bar and asked him to make her a drink. She loved his concoction so much that she ecstatically demanded he name it after her. Hence, "Heather." Light, citrusy, and a little bit floral, it's actually rather aptly named. Heather, wherever you are, thanks for inspiring this one.

INGREDIENTS
¾ oz [22.5 ml] cachaça
¾ oz [22.5 ml] dry vermouth
¾ oz [22.5 ml] elderflower liqueur
¾ oz [22.5 ml] fresh lime juice
Lime peel, for garnish

DIRECTIONS
To a shaker, add the cachaça, vermouth, elderflower liqueur, lime juice, and ice. Shake and strain into a chilled coupe glass. Garnish with a lime peel and serve.

TRANSATLANTIC

OUR FRIEND TOM LINSTEDT HAS A DEEP LOVE FOR FUNKY RUMS AND A DEFT HAND FOR USING THEM IN COCKTAILS. His Transatlantic originally called for a blend of spirits, but we've adapted it to work with 100 percent cachaça. The nuttiness of sherry pairs very nicely with the tropical banana notes of cachaça, and the mint and nutmeg garnishes layer on even more aromatics. Served over crushed ice, this is the kind of cocktail you can sip and savor for a long time.

INGREDIENTS

2 oz [60 ml] cachaça

¾ oz [22.5 ml] fresh lemon juice

½ oz [15 ml] dry sherry

¼ oz [7.5 ml] Rich Demerara Syrup (page 33)

1 dash orange bitters

Crushed ice

Mint, for garnish

Freshly grated nutmeg, for garnish

DIRECTIONS

To a shaker, add the cachaça, lemon juice, sherry, syrup, bitters, and ice. Shake and strain into a rocks glass filled with crushed ice. Garnish with mint and freshly grated nutmeg and serve.

PEY-LÉ

THIS DRINK CAME ABOUT FROM EXPERIMENTING WITH CACHAÇA, HONEY, CITRUS, AND AMARO. We knew there was something to this combination, but the versions we tried all seemed to fall just a little bit short of the deliciously tart and bitter cocktail we envisioned. Finally, we tried replacing the amaro with an extravagant pour of pure Peychaud's bitters. Eureka! A flourishy bicycle kick to the senses.

INGREDIENTS

1½ oz [45 ml] cachaça

1 oz [30 ml] Honey Syrup (page 33)

¾ oz [22.5 ml] fresh lemon juice

½ oz [15 ml] grapefruit juice

½ oz [15 ml] Peychaud's bitters

DIRECTIONS

To a shaker, add the cachaça, syrup, lemon juice, grapefruit juice, bitters, and ice. Shake, strain into a chilled coupe glass, and serve.

C.R.E.A.M.

IF YOU START GETTING INTO TIKI CULTURE, ONE OF THE THINGS YOU'LL DISCOVER IS THAT MANY OF THE CLASSIC TROPICAL COCKTAILS RELY ON BLENDS OF MULTIPLE RUMS. It's not a technique you see often with other spirits—you rarely find cocktails calling for two bourbons or two gins, for example—but with rum it makes sense. The characters of various rums can be so wildly different that blending them makes a drink much more complex. We use that idea here to combine the tropical funkiness of cachaça with the sweet vanilla notes of a typical aged rum. The combination of lime and cream is also unusual, which is why we call this C.R.E.A.M (Cachaça Rules Everything Around Me).

INGREDIENTS

1 oz [30 ml] cachaça

¾ oz [22.5 ml] aged rum

¾ oz [22.5 ml] orgeat

½ oz [15 ml] cream

1 barspoon (⅙ oz [5 ml]) absinthe

½ oz [15 ml] fresh lime juice

Freshly grated cinnamon, for garnish

DIRECTIONS

To a shaker, add (in this order) cachaça, rum, orgeat, cream, absinthe, lime juice, and ice. Shake and strain into a chilled coupe glass. Garnish with freshly grated cinnamon and serve.

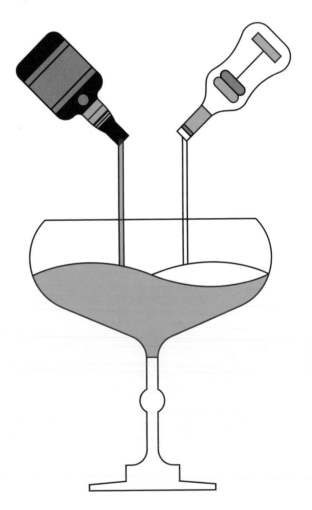

CHAPTER 24

FERNET

YOU'RE IN FOR A TREAT IN THIS CHAPTER. And by a "treat," we mean an intense tasting experience that may have you questioning whether to trust anything we say ever again. Fernet is the third and final amaro we call for in this book. It's the most assertive by far and, we'll be honest, not the easiest to like. Watching the expression on people's faces when they take their first sip of fernet is among the reliable joys of bartending. For some, that first sip is also their last. For others, there's something beguiling about fernet that keeps them coming back for more.

We speak of fernet as a category of amaro, but it's indelibly associated with one brand in particular: the famous Fernet-Branca. While there are other brands of fernet on the market, and many of them are quite good, we recommend that you start with this one. It's the most famous, the most widely available, and the one against which other fernets are measured.

The official history of Fernet-Branca dates back to 1845, when Bernardino Branca began selling his elixir in Milan. The precise origins of both the recipe and the name are murky. Some theorize that Bernadino was aided by a long-lived Swede named Dr. Fernet, although there are no records of his existence beyond early advertisements for the brand. Another possibility is that the name is derived from the French name *Fernet*, with the Italians having changed the pronunciation to "fer-net" with a hard *t*. We'll likely never know the full story.

What we do know is that Fernet-Branca is made from twenty-seven botanicals that are macerated in alcohol or distilled, with the whole mixture marrying for a year in barrels before bottling. The exact recipe is a secret closely held by the Branca family, but known botanicals include aloe, rhubarb, gentian, cinchona, bitter orange, saffron, and myrrh. The resulting spirit is powerfully aromatic and flavorful, with a bitter edge and a distinctly mentholated note. It's strikingly medicinal and, like many such elixirs, was marketed for its healing properties. Its usefulness in treating cholera was, as far as we know, never substantiated, but it is a fine remedy for an upset stomach or a hangover that requires some hair of the dog.

Its importance in the bar world is one reason we chose to include fernet in the book. Another is that we believe every good home bar should have at least one bottle that's a little weird and intimidating, the kind of thing you might offer your guests to drink on a dare.

Consider this our dare chapter, an opportunity to take a chance on an ingredient you may have to wrestle with a bit. It'll be fun. We promise.

IF YOU LIKE FERNET, TRY...

BRANCAMENTA
Created in the mid-1960s and reportedly inspired by Italian singer Maria Callas's preference for mint in her fernet, Brancamenta is a mintier and somewhat more approachable altnerative to the standard Fernet-Branca. Though rarely called for in classic cocktails, you can find a place for Brancamenta in variations on the daiquiri or mint julep, or simply pour it into hot chocolate.

BRAULIO
Made so far north in Italy that it has a Swiss cross on the bottle, Braulio is fernet gone to ski school. It's alpine, minty, and herbal, but not quite as wild and unruly as fernet.

AMARO SIBILLA
Although its flavor profile is completely different from that of fernet, we appreciate this amaro's ability to offer a similar level of challenge to the palate. Intensely bitter and barky, its flavors unfold on repeated sips to reveal its sweeter, fruitier notes.

FERNET AND GINGER

FERNET CAN BE DIFFICULT TO DRINK ON ITS OWN, BUT IT BECOMES FAR MORE APPROACHABLE IN BUBBLY TWO-INGREDIENT COCKTAILS. Fernet and cola, also known as the Fernandito or Fernet con Coca, is the most consumed fernet cocktail in the world thanks to its popularity in Argentina. You'll also find fernet mixed with club soda or tonic water. One of our favorite such combinations is fernet and ginger beer. The latter takes the edge off the fernet, allowing its herbaceous qualities and pronounced menthol note to complement the spice of ginger. It's great when you're in the mood for an easy, refreshing cocktail but still want to taste something complex.

INGREDIENTS

1 oz [30 ml] fernet

About 4 oz [120 ml] ginger beer

Lime wedge

DIRECTIONS

In a rocks or highball glass filled with ice, add the fernet and ginger beer. Squeeze the lime wedge into the drink and drop it in. Stir gently to combine and serve.

HANKY PANKY

LET'S EASE INTO THE SPIRIT-FORWARD SIDE OF FERNET COCKTAILS WITH A SIMPLE STIRRED DRINK THAT USES JUST A TINY BIT OF THE ELIXIR. The Hanky Panky is the enduring creation of Ada Coleman, the first woman to hold the role of head bartender at the acclaimed American Bar at the Savoy Hotel in London, where she was promoted to the position in 1903. Fernet essentially plays the role of bitters here, accenting the familiar combination of gin and vermouth with its unique spice notes.

INGREDIENTS

1½ oz [45 ml] gin

1½ oz [45 ml] sweet vermouth

1 barspoon (⅙ oz [5 ml]) fernet

Orange peel, for garnish

DIRECTIONS

To a mixing glass, add the gin, vermouth, fernet, and ice. Stir and strain into a chilled coupe glass. Garnish with an orange peel and serve.

NEWARK

FERNET PLAYS A SIMILAR ROLE IN THIS COCKTAIL AS IT DOES IN THE HANKY PANKY (PAGE 284), ALTHOUGH THE DRINK IS ACTUALLY MODELED AFTER A CLASSIC MANHAT-TAN VARIATION KNOWN AS THE BROOKLYN. Jim Meehan and John Deragon of New York City's pathbreaking bar PDT joke that by the time they came up with this one, there were so many cocktails already named after New York neighborhoods that they had to extend their search into New Jersey. It's a fitting choice, given that New Jersey is also home to the Laird's apple brandy that they used at the bar. The Newark is an autumnal drink in the Manhattan family, perfect for a crisp fall evening.

INGREDIENTS

1 oz [30 ml] apple brandy

1 oz [30 ml] sweet vermouth

½ oz [15 ml] fernet

½ oz [15 ml] maraschino liqueur

DIRECTIONS

To a mixing glass, add the apple brandy, vermouth, fernet, maraschino liqueur, and ice. Stir, strain into a chilled coupe glass, and serve.

TORONTO

ONE PROBABLY WOULDN'T ASSOCIATE FERNET WITH TORONTO, CANADA, IF NOT FOR THIS COCKTAIL, WHICH WAS REPORTEDLY QUITE POPULAR THERE IN THE EARLY TWENTIETH CENTURY. Early recipes called for a punishingly strong mix of equal parts whiskey and fernet, and if that's your idea of a well-balanced cocktail, then more power to you. Modern takes on the drink tend to steer it more in the direction of an Old-Fashioned (page 45), with the whiskey taking center stage and the fernet just there to add a little bite and complexity. That makes its role here similar to that of the previous two drinks, except that now there's no vermouth to smooth things out. Thus, striking the right proportions of ingredients is extremely important. A poorly made Toronto is no fun at all, but when it's made right, it sings.

(As you might guess from the geography of the name, the "rye" called for in early recipes was likely Canadian whisky. Feel free to make it that way if you have it, but the spice of American rye works nicely here too.)

INGREDIENTS

2 oz [60 ml] rye

¼ oz [7.5 ml] fernet

1 barspoon (⅙ oz [5 ml]) Rich Demerara Syrup (page 33)

2 dashes Angostura bitters

Orange peel, for garnish

DIRECTIONS

To a mixing glass, add the rye, fernet, syrup, bitters, and ice. Stir and strain into a rocks glass filled with ice or a single large cube. Garnish with an orange peel and serve.

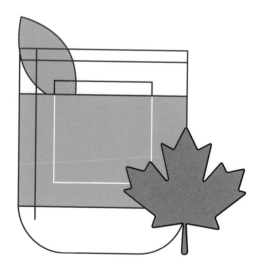

CORNERSTONE

ALL CACHAÇA IS MADE IN BRAZIL, BUT THE NOVO FOGO BRAND HAS A SPECIAL CONNECTION TO THE PACIFIC NORTHWEST THANKS TO OUR LONG-TIME FRIEND AND FOUNDER OF THE COMPANY, DRAGOS AXINTE. In the early days of introducing his cachaça to craft bartenders, and despite having no bartending experience himself, he audaciously set about creating a few cocktails that he took into Seattle's finest cocktail bars to mix up for their staffs. Not only that, but he started with a recipe that included fernet, because that's what the bartenders took as shots after work. This plan could have gone disastrously wrong. Miraculously, it worked. The Cornerstone, as this drink came to be called, is beautifully balanced, with the fruitiness of the grenadine and the tropical notes of cachaça soothing the strident flavors of fernet. Dragos's original recipe called for his barrel-aged cachaça, but we find that a fragrant silver expression works wonderfully too.

INGREDIENTS

1½ oz [45 ml] cachaça

½ oz [15 ml] grenadine

¼ oz [7.5 ml] fernet

2 dashes orange bitters

Orange peel, for garnish

DIRECTIONS

To a mixing glass, add the cachaça, grenadine, fernet, bitters, and ice. Stir and strain into a chilled coupe glass. Garnish with an orange peel and serve.

HUNGER PROVOKER

THIS STRAIGHTFORWARD COMBINATION OF FERNET AND SWEET VERMOUTH COULD GO BY ANY NUMBER OF NAMES, but we're partial to the "Hunger Provoker" from an obscure 1903 volume called *The Bachelor Book.* As cocktail names go, you can't beat it for accuracy. This is a great aperitivo, perfect for when you want something low-proof and stimulating before a big meal.

INGREDIENTS
1½ oz [45 ml] sweet vermouth
¾ oz [22.5 ml] fernet
Slice of orange, for garnish

DIRECTIONS
In a rocks glass filled with ice, add the vermouth and fernet. Stir gently to combine. Garnish with a slice of orange and serve.

APPETIZER À L'ITALIENNE

IN A SIMILAR VEIN TO THE HUNGER PROVOKER, the Appetizer à l'Italienne is a brilliant cocktail from William "The Only William" Schmidt's 1892 book *The Flowing Bowl.* It takes the vermouth and fernet combination and adds even more richness with absinthe and sugar. It's deep, dark, and complex but still low enough in proof to enjoy early in the evening.

INGREDIENTS
2 oz [60 ml] sweet vermouth
1 oz [30 ml] fernet
¼ oz [7.5 ml] absinthe
Scant ¼ oz [7.5 ml] Rich Simple Syrup (page 33)

DIRECTIONS
To a mixing glass, add the vermouth, fernet, absinthe, syrup, and ice. Stir, strain into a chilled coupe glass, and serve.

TELLING PHOEBE

WHEN WE ASKED OUR FRIEND CHANTAL TSENG, a prolific bartender in Washington, DC, if she had any fernet cocktails for our book, she responded with an astounding twenty-one recipes; her deep repertoire comes from years of hosting literary cocktail nights. This one, which marries fernet with scotch and Benedictine, was in homage to R. O. Kwon's *The Incendiaries*. Chantal makes this with a peated blend, so if you've acquired a bottle of smoky scotch, this would be a fun cocktail to try it in. We find it's also very agreeable with a good unpeated bottle of the sort recommended in our scotch chapter (see page 228).

INGREDIENTS
1½ oz [45 ml] scotch

¾ oz [22.5 ml] sweet vermouth

½ oz [15 ml] fernet

½ oz [15 ml] Benedictine

Cocktail cherries, for garnish

DIRECTIONS
To a mixing glass, add the scotch, vermouth, fernet, Benedictine, and ice. Stir and strain into a chilled coupe glass. Garnish with cherries and serve.

SMOKE AND BITTERS

WE OPENED THIS CHAPTER WITH A COUPLE VERY APPROACHABLE FERNET DRINKS, and we're closing it with one that pushes the boundaries of assertive, spirit-forward cocktails. With smoky mezcal and a double-amaro wallop of Cynar and fernet, it's easy to imagine this drink going off the rails. And yet, as strong as these elements are, they all come into balance. It's an impressive feat of mixology from Trey Hughes of the Hunt & Alpine Club in Portland, Maine, and the second contribution to our book from that venerable bar.

INGREDIENTS
1 oz [30 ml] tequila

1 oz [30 ml] Cynar

½ oz [15 ml] fernet

½ oz [15 ml] mezcal

Grapefruit peel, for garnish

DIRECTIONS
To a mixing glass, add the tequila, Cynar, fernet, mezcal, and ice. Stir and strain into a chilled coupe glass. Garnish with a grapefruit peel and serve.

CHAPTER 25

CRÈME DE CACAO

THIS IS OUR FINAL CHAPTER, SO WHY NOT END ON A SWEET NOTE? We've encountered a few nightcaps and dessert drinks in the book already, but now we'll embrace them in all their glory thanks to the addition of one last bottle to your bar: crème de cacao. As the name implies, this is a liqueur flavored with chocolate. The word *crème* indicates that it's a particularly sweet liqueur, dosed with enough sugar to take on an almost syrupy consistency. It plays heavily in cocktails, bringing intense flavor and a rich mouthfeel.

Cacao liqueurs likely date back to seventeenth-century France, and they were intended for enjoyment on their own more than as a cocktail ingredient. They're not often consumed this way today, although enjoying a small pour of a high-quality crème de cacao is something we'll admit to on occasion. Crème de cacao is typically associated with sweet and creamy drinks, in which it naturally excels. We include variations on that theme here, albeit some that take it in unexpected directions. Yet chocolate mixes in some less obvious ways too. It's often encountered with citrus and gin. It can lend depth to stirred cocktails made with aged spirits like whiskey, brandy, and rum. And chocolate and Chartreuse? One of the best pairings ever!

It's important to distinguish crème de cacao from chocolate liqueur and chocolate cream liqueur. Crème de cacao is not made with cream, and it gets its flavor from cacao rather than from finished chocolate. When buying crème de cacao, there are two main considerations to keep in mind. The first is to make sure you get a good one. There's a massive difference between bottom-shelf crème de cacao liqueurs and the somewhat costlier high-quality bottles. The latter aren't too expensive and they're absolutely worth the money, especially when you consider that you'll rarely be using them more than an ounce at a time. The cocktails in this chapter will often be the sort you sip as a nightcap, so make sure you mix them with quality ingredients worthy of going into your final drink of an evening.

The second consideration is whether to get a white or a dark crème de cacao. The difference is primarily aesthetic; it matters less in a creamy cocktail, but using dark liqueur in a cocktail made with light spirits will make the drink look muddy. For that reason, we suggest starting out with a white crème de cacao, although both varieties certainly have their place. Whichever bottle you end up with, think of this chapter as the well-earned dessert course to our lengthy cocktail tasting menu.

BOTTLES WE REACH FOR

GIFFARD CRÈME DE CACAO (WHITE)

This is pretty much everything we look for in a crème de cacao. Silky on the palate with creamy notes of distilled cacao and a chocolatey finish, it works in everything from stirred, spirit-forward cocktails like our Chocolate Martini (page 295) to cream-based drinks like the Brandy Alexander (page 291).

TEMPUS FUGIT CRÈME DE CACAO

We never thought we'd want to sip crème de cacao on its own, but this is so velvety and complex that we can't resist a little nip now and then. It supplements its first distillation of cacao with an additional maceration of cacao and vanilla, and it's very sweet, so a little goes a long way. Our only note of caution is that its brown color will tint clear cocktails; if you don't mind that, by all means, pick up a bottle.

BRANDY ALEXANDER

"BRANDY ALEXANDER ALWAYS GETS ME INTO TROUBLE," LESLIE FEIST SANG ON HER 2007 ALBUM *THE REMINDER.* Alexanders are the ultimate guilty pleasure drink. The original recipe called for gin, crème de cacao, and cream—a combination that honestly tastes much better than it sounds—but it's the brandy version that captured imaginations and became the standard-bearer for sophisticated, creamy dessert cocktails. As Feist noted, it's a drink that "goes down easy" and has a way of sneaking up on you, but we highly recommend giving it a try.

INGREDIENTS

1 oz [30 ml] crème de cacao

1 oz [30 ml] cognac

1 oz [30 ml] cream

DIRECTIONS

To a shaker, add the crème de cacao, cognac, cream, and ice. Shake, strain into a chilled coupe glass, and serve.

VARIATION

If you want to make the original Alexander, simply substitute gin for cognac.

ACE OF CLUBS

THE DAIQUIRI (PAGE 98) IS A VERSATILE COCKTAIL, BUT A DAIQUIRI WITH CHOCOLATE? Don't knock it until you've tried it. This unexpected combination appeared in the April 1939 issue of *Esquire* magazine, hailing from the Ace of Clubs lounge in Bermuda. Contemporary versions of the drink tend to tone down the crème de cacao, but we take it full bore. This is another one of those instances where the modern fear of making a drink that's "too sweet" robs the original of what made it special. Yes, this is a lot of crème de cacao. But you know what? Crème de cacao is delicious. Embrace it.

INGREDIENTS

2 oz [60 ml] aged rum

1 oz [30 ml] crème de cacao

¾ oz [22.5 ml] fresh lime juice

DIRECTIONS

To a shaker, add the rum, crème de cacao, lime juice, and ice. Shake, strain into a chilled coupe glass, and serve.

RACQUET CLUB

WE TEND TO ASSOCIATE CRÈME DE CACAO WITH SWEET DRINKS, BUT IT DOESN'T HAVE TO BE USED THAT WAY. Take the Racquet Club, for example. It's an 1890s riff on the dry martini that adds just a barspoon (⅙ oz [5 ml]) of crème de cacao to the mix. Sweet? Definitely not. The liqueur instead contributes just a little extra heft and a very pleasant hint of chocolate.

INGREDIENTS

2 oz [60 ml] gin

1 oz [30 ml] dry vermouth

1 barspoon (⅙ oz [5 ml]) crème de cacao

2 dashes orange bitters

Lemon peel, for garnish

DIRECTIONS

To a mixing glass, add the gin, vermouth, crème de cacao, bitters, and ice. Stir and strain into a chilled coupe glass. Garnish with a lemon peel and serve.

MARIA DOLORES

NAMED AFTER THE DAUGHTER OF THE FOUNDER OF THE LEGENDARY BOADAS BAR IN BARCELONA, THE MARIA DOLORES IS A SUPERB NIGHTCAP. Maria herself ran the bar for many years, keeping the craft of cocktails alive during the low period of mixology in the late twentieth century. With only three ingredients in equal parts, her namesake cocktail deserves far wider recognition: it's rich, decadent, compact, and superbly easy to make.

INGREDIENTS

¾ oz [22.5 ml] crème de cacao

¾ oz [22.5 ml] cognac

¾ oz [22.5 ml] orange liqueur

Cocktail cherry, for garnish

DIRECTIONS

To a mixing glass, add the crème de cacao, cognac, orange liqueur, and ice. Stir and strain into a chilled coupe glass. Garnish with a cherry and serve.

TWO BIRDS

AS WE WERE CONSIDERING WHAT COCKTAILS TO INCLUDE IN THIS FINAL CHAPTER, ONE OF OUR GOALS WAS TO PROVIDE ANOTHER USE FOR YOUR BOTTLE OF SCOTCH. We also wanted to make sure we featured the combination of Chartreuse and chocolate, one of the all-time great pairings in the world of spirits. What if we could kill two birds with one stone? That's how we stumbled upon this rich, complex, and slightly herbaceous take on the Rob Roy (page 231) that we recommend adding to your repertoire of spirituous nightcaps.

INGREDIENTS

1½ oz [45 ml] scotch

1 oz [30 ml] sweet vermouth

¼ oz [7.5 ml] crème de cacao

¼ oz [7.5 ml] green Chartreuse

1 dash Angostura bitters

1 dash orange bitters

Orange peel, for garnish

DIRECTIONS

To a mixing glass, add the scotch, vermouth, crème de cacao, Chartreuse, both bitters, and ice. Stir and strain into a chilled coupe glass. Garnish with an orange peel and serve.

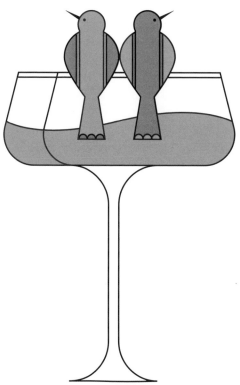

MEZCAL-EXANDER

IS THE ALEXANDER A CLASSIC COCKTAIL? It doesn't have the stature of a Martini (page 70) or Manhattan (page 68), and no one has devoted an entire week to celebrating it like they have the Negroni (page 129). (Can you imagine how out of shape we'd get if there was an Alexander Week? Please, no one do this.) Yet if two measures of a classic are staying power and providing inspiration for numerous variations, then the Alexander is definitely in the running. As proven by the Brandy Alexander (page 291), changing out the base spirit of this cocktail can produce great results. One notable example is the Mezcal-exander, which swaps the gin for mezcal. The drink delivers potent aromas of smoke and chocolate, an utterly seducing combination.

INGREDIENTS

1½ oz [45 ml] mezcal

1 oz [30 ml] crème de cacao

¾ oz [22.5 ml] cream

Freshly grated nutmeg, for garnish

DIRECTIONS

To a shaker, add the mezcal, crème de cacao, cream, and ice. Shake and strain into a chilled coupe glass. Garnish with freshly grated nutmeg and serve.

CAMPARI ALEXANDER

HOW FAR CAN WE PUSH THE BOUNDARIES OF THE ALEXANDER? At the influential bar Anvil in Houston, Texas, one of their cocktail menus featured this variation on the drink that swaps bitter Campari for the base spirit. Mixed with cream and crème de cacao, it comes out looking like a soft, pink, fluffy bunny, but its flavor punches like Evander Holyfield. It's a really fun combination. At Anvil they originally served this with dehydrated Campari crystals as a garnish, which you too can attempt if you're feeling ambitious. We keep things simple and make it as in the recipe below.

INGREDIENTS

1 oz [30 ml] Campari

1 oz [30 ml] crème de cacao

1 oz [30 ml] cream

DIRECTIONS

To a shaker, add the Campari, crème da cacao, cream, and ice. Shake, strain into a chilled coupe glass, and serve.

CHOCOLATE MARTINI

THIS IS A CHOCOLATE MARTINI, BUT IT'S NOT *THAT* KIND OF CHOCOLATE MARTINI. You know the kind we mean: super sweet, with bottom-shelf vodka, lots of cream, and cheap chocolate liqueur. This is our idea of what a Chocolate Martini *should* be. It's spirit forward, complex, balanced, and multilayered. It relies on vodka for the base, but it's accented with deep notes of cacao, cherry, smoke, and citrus. You won't find anything like this on the menu at a chain restaurant, but if you've followed along with us this far, you have everything you need to make it in your home bar.

INGREDIENTS

1¼ oz [37.5 ml] vodka

¾ oz [22.5 ml] dry vermouth

½ oz [15 ml] crème de cacao

¼ oz [7.5 ml] mezcal

1 barspoon maraschino liqueur

1 strip lemon peel

DIRECTIONS

In a mixing glass, combine the vodka, vermouth, crème da cacao, mezcal, maraschino liqueur, lemon peel, and ice. Stir, strain into a chilled coupe glass, and serve.

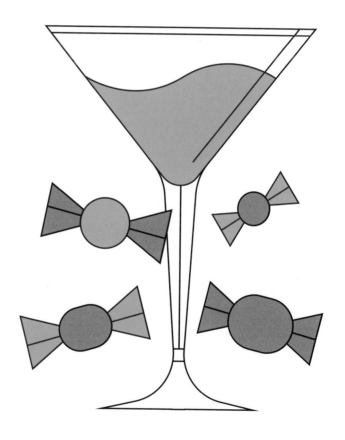

CONTINUING THE JOURNEY

CONGRATULATIONS! IF YOU'VE MADE IT THIS FAR, YOU ARE NOW IN POSSESSION OF A SERIOUSLY WELL-STOCKED HOME BAR AND THE KNOWLEDGE TO PUT IT TO GOOD USE. You have the ingredients and experience to make a nearly endless range of cocktails, from time-tested classics to combinations improvised on the fly. We've reached the end of this particular book, but we hope that for you this is the beginning of a lifelong appreciation for spirits and cocktails.

The question before you now is, "What next?" Now that you've mastered the basics, there are many different avenues of further exploration you may want to venture down. We barely touched on tropical cocktails, for instance. If you enjoyed the few we included in this book, perhaps you should stock up on rums and syrups and get into that. Do you love to cook? Then perhaps you should branch out into culinary approaches to mixology, bringing in fresh produce and making homemade ingredients. We limited our stock of bitters to just three bottles, but there are tons more out there that are worthy of dashing into your cocktails.

Another option is to dive deep into a particular spirit, learning as much as you can about it and building up your collection at home. Then take a vacation to visit distilleries where it's made. Love scotch? Visit Scotland! Want to know more about mezcal? Go to Oaxaca! Make spirits education part of your next unique trip. There are many amazing liquors we didn't have space to include here, such as aquavit, pisco, grappa, sotol ... you get the point. The world of spirits is vast and you can spend a lifetime finding new things to try.

Before you set off though, we thought it wise to leave you with a few lessons we learned over the years to help guide your next steps.

1. TASTE WIDELY

When you taste a challenging new brand or spirit, resist the urge to assign negative value judgments to it and instead just try to describe it. Everything you sample adds to your knowledge and your personal library of tastes. Sometimes it takes a while to come around on something, so revisit them over time. And on the positive side, try to develop a multitude of favorites. You don't have to have just one favorite whiskey, for example. You could have a favorite whiskey for sipping after dinner, a favorite for mixing Manhattans, and a favorite for when you're at a dive bar. You contain multitudes.

2. PERFECTION IS A MOVING TARGET

"Perfect" is a malleable concept, and it depends on the setting. We can think of a long list of foods that are better than hot dogs, but when we're in the stands at a baseball game, nothing beats a ballpark dog. Perfection is a moving target. Move with it. In addition to changing contexts, be aware that your palate will evolve too as you get older and more experienced. Revisit spirits and cocktails you loved or loathed in the past. You might be surprised to find your opinions changing. When they do, embrace it. You have new favorites now! That's a good thing.

3. PLAY THE CLASSICS

When you get really into cocktails, it's tempting to get drawn into every exciting new thing or to make up complicated cocktails. When you have a well-stocked bar and an eagerness to create new drinks, it can be hard to resist adding in multiple ingredients to make a creation really pop. Sometimes it works; some drinks really do need nine ingredients. More often than not, however, you end up with a drink that tastes vaguely of "cocktail" but specifically of nothing. Revisiting the classics drives home their straightforward brilliance and acts as a reminder that you can often do more with less.

4. DRINKING IS MORE FUN THAN HOARDING

The beauty of distilled spirits is that, unlike wine or beer, you don't have to finish a bottle right away when you open it. It's fun to have a few spirits in your collection that you save for special occasions and slowly savor. But—and we say this as recovering booze hoarders ourselves—there are diminishing returns to amassing a large collection of dusty, half-consumed bottles. Invite friends and family over. Drink your good stuff. Enjoy it, recycle the empty bottle, and move on.

5. DON'T DRINK TOO MUCH

We sincerely want you to have a lifelong, healthy relationship with alcohol. Our hope is that in your old age, you'll still have the adventurous approach to learning about spirits and cocktails that you have now, and that your family, friends, and doctor will approve of your hobby. If you want to get there, you can't go too hard now. So, don't. There's always an occasion to drink if you go looking for one, but it's important to be willing, able, and happy to not drink too. The booze in your house isn't going anywhere. There's always tomorrow to try a new cocktail, so don't rush it.

AS WE REACH THE END . . .

We hope that you've had as much fun reading and mixing the recipes in this book
as we had writing it. Now venture onward and enjoy!

RESOURCES

Your home bartending experience will be more enjoyable with the right tools and glassware. Here are a few of our favorite places to procure our gear.

BAR KEEPER
614 North Hoover Street
Los Angeles, CA 90004
(323) 669-1675
www.barkeepersilverlake.com

THE BOSTON SHAKER
69 Holland Street
Somerville, MA 02144
(617) 718-2999
www.thebostonshaker.com

BULL IN CHINA
2304 NW Savier Street
Portland, OR 97210
(503) 893-5172
www.bullinchinapdx.com

ONLINE RETAILERS

Cocktail Kingdom
www.cocktailkingdom.com

Piña Barware
www.pinabarware.com

BOOKS

There is a vast landscape of books that you may find of interest as you continue your exploration of cocktails. Here are a few of our favorites.

Liquid Intelligence by Dave Arnold

Smuggler's Cove by Martin Cate and Rebecca Cate

Vintage Spirits and Forgotten Cocktails by Ted Haigh

Death & Co by David Kaplan, Nick Fauchald, and Alex Day

Meehan's Bartender Manual by Jim Meehan

The Bar Book by Jeffrey Morgenthaler

Imbibe! by David Wondrich

ACKNOWLEDGMENTS

When we started planning this book in late 2019, we envisioned a fun year of hosting cocktail parties with friends as we tested all the recipes. For obvious reasons, writing this in 2020 was a very different experience. We and the few people in our "bubbles" tested hundreds of recipes, which isn't the hardest job in the world, but we're grateful for the help nonetheless. Elizabeth Eisenstein and Karen Locke pulled particularly heavy duty. Our virtual "League of Extraordinary Cocktail Tasters" also provided valuable feedback: thanks to Paul and Michelle Willenberg, Nico Galoppo, Martin Hulth, Thomas Samson, Courtney Knapp, Brandon Johnsen, Derek Pettie, and Matthew Brown for tasting through rival recipes.

Certain chapters also benefited from expert advice from friends in the industry, especially Tim Master, Jacob Briars, Dan Searing, Dragos Axinte, Jake Parrott, Chantal Tseng, Matt Robold, Clayton Szczech, and, of course, Goldie for supervising the creation of her name-sake punch. Our book is far more complete thanks to the contributions of cocktails from bartenders credited throughout the book. Thank you all!

Dialing in our recipes required a flood of booze, so thank you as well to everyone who provided us with samples to work with: Jeremey Barkley, Stephan Berg, Eric Seed, Dane Belber, Jon Lewis, Kaj Hackinen, Douglas Derrick, Ari Shapiro, Joslyn Tinkle, Curtis Day, Christi Crosby, Dana Bruneau, Cameron Holck, Dominic Ailing, Alec Kennedy, Stephanie Anger, Jordan Sanchez, and anyone else we've forgotten.

This is a book about cocktails, but the writing of it was fueled by coffee. Thanks as always to Saint Simon in Portland, OR, for the cozy atmosphere in which to spend hours camped out writing and editing.

A book like this is a massive team effort to produce. Our hard-working agent Jud Laghi refined our proposal and brought it to Chronicle. Cristina Garces, Deanne Katz, and Dena Rayess all helped define the scope and improve the text through editing (hopefully aided by the new cocktails discovered along the way). Lizzie Vaughan guided the vision for the design. Tera Killip, Steve Kim, Jessica Ling, and Gabby Vanacore helped usher it to the finish line. And lastly, we are thrilled and delighted by the illustrations from Woody Harrington, who brought our text to life in a stylish and whimsical way.

INDEX

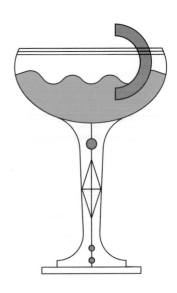